"For an avowed introvert, Adam McHugh lets it all hang out in *Blood from a Stone*, a very personal, soul-searching tale about a dying career, difficult divorce, and ultimately, inspiring rebirth thanks to Santa Barbara County wine country. Along the way, McHugh educates the reader in an engaging, accessible manner about the great sagas of wine, both those from Old World antiquity and more recent stories from the Santa Ynez Valley. This book should entertain wine neophytes and experts alike, or just about anyone who's pulling for the underdog."

**Matt Kettmann,** author of *Vines & Vision* and contributing editor, *Wine Enthusiast*

"Read, savor, and listen for the low hum of deep faith in this personal story of a man who writes with a keen awareness of grief and a self-deprecating honesty. You'll leave with a renewed longing for food and meaning, cheese and history, and wine you can't pronounce."

**Emily P. Freeman,** author of *The Next Right Thing*

"Adam McHugh is one of the most effortlessly funny writers I know. In his new work, *Blood from a Stone*, Adam combines his wit with a tender vulnerability to tell a story as poignant as it is funny."

**Susan Cain,** author of *Quiet* and *Bittersweet*

"A sparkling delight, laced with deep and earthy emotion but ultimately finished with notes of hope and love. In *Blood from a Stone*, Adam McHugh gives us a cultural history of wine alongside his own history, letting us taste the cycles of grief, darkness, and joy that mark every life. With good humor ar  won depth, he coaxes us toward the attentiveness that great wine, ar            can foster— and the result is nothing short of wonderful."

**Alissa Wilkinson,** author of *Salty: Lessons on F*
*Revolutionary Women*

"Adam McHugh is a gifted story                    wonderful tour guide through the rich history o            ook toward salvation and purpose from the depths of hu            despair. As creatures with feelings, we can all relate by persona            ce to his emotional love story. Anyone with an interest in wine, history, and culture will find his writing entertaining and provocative. Thank you, Adam, for baring your soul to remind us we are all pilgrims on the labyrinthine trail toward eternal and internal peace, love, and harmony; and thank you for bringing us back to the importance of humility, compassion, and sympathy in our daily living."

**Richard Sanford,** winegrower, Sta. Rita Hills, California

"What a treat to read a wine book about something other than 'tasting notes.' Who cares whether you find that a wine smells like cherries or berries or Ethiopian coffee beans? How boring! Adam McHugh is after a more interesting game. History, religion, and his passion for one of his God's greatest gifts, for example. Page by page his wine pilgrimage, as he calls it, grows more interesting, humorous, and soulful."

**Kermit Lynch,** wine importer and author of *Adventures on the Wine Route*

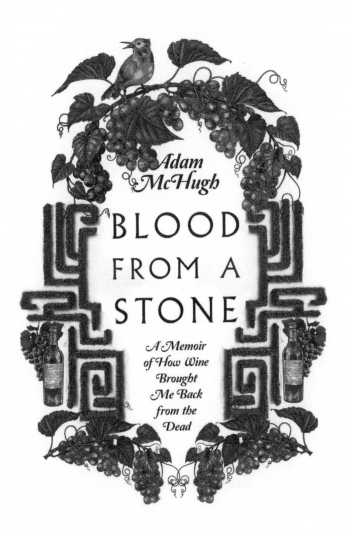

Adam McHugh

# BLOOD FROM A STONE

*A Memoir of How Wine Brought Me Back from the Dead*

An imprint of InterVarsity Press
Downers Grove, Illinois

**InterVarsity Press**
P.O. Box 1400  |  Downers Grove, IL 60515-1426
ivpress.com  |  email@ivpress.com

InterVarsity Press® is the publishing division of InterVarsity Christian Fellowship/USA®. For more information, visit intervarsity.org.

While all stories in this book are true, some names and identifying information may have been changed to protect the privacy of individuals.

Maps of wine regions by Kevin Gleason, used with permission.

The publisher cannot verify the accuracy or functionality of website URLs used in this book beyond the date of publication.

Cover design and image composite: David Fassett
Interior design: Daniel van Loon

ISBN 978-1-5140-0088-5 (print)  |  ISBN 978-1-5140-0089-2 (digital)

Printed in the United States of America ♾

**Library of Congress Cataloging-in-Publication Data**
A catalog record for this book is available from the Library of Congress.

29   28   27   26   25   24   23   22      |      12   11   10   9   8   7   6   5   4   3   2   1

**FOR MY PARENTS,**

*who taught me to love wine and books*

# CONTENTS

*One*

# WINE HAPPENS

This is the story of how wine brought me back from the dead.

If I want to be more provocative, I could say a hearty portion of this story is how my life and work as a minister drove me to wine. Tales about drink and religion usually go the other way. Ordinarily in these stories a renowned Saturday-night lush wakes up to become a Sunday-morning teetotaler. I'm all for that when the alternatives are addiction and self-annihilation, but otherwise I think freshly discovered faith should be rewarded with a generous pour of something good. The path will get rough, trust me. Wine will help.

I was ordained as a Presbyterian, but I grew up a Lutheran. I was an only child—a fact that always prompts people to say, "That explains *so much*." My parents and I were a mildly churchgoing family, though most of the prayers offered in our household went up on Saturdays during University of Washington football games. Our minister back then would talk from the pulpit about the scotch he drank the night before. I don't remember his name, but I do remember he told me that my nerdish high school persona would one day translate into popularity with girls. So he was both a drinker *and* a liar. I underwent the two-year confirmation process in that Lutheran church to become a full-fledged member, though my dad made sure to stress that my studies were the priority.

Surprising to us all, during my senior year of high school, I found myself sitting in a Southern Baptist church. And not only on Sunday mornings. Often, I was there on Sunday nights as well, when I should have been studying. Southern Baptists have a lot of time for church because they are not out drinking on weekends. I spent so much of my time there for the same reason any seventeen-year-old boy avidly attends church. Her name was Hannah—she had a biblical name and legs that inspired much Bible study. She was the captain of the dance team at our high school, with long, fiery hair and the almost transparent alabaster skin tone only truly revealed in Pacific Northwest gloom. That relationship was heartache, but those abstemious Republicans at that church taught me a more spirited experience of religion than I had known before. Ironic, because they tried to persuade me that the cup of the Last Supper was nonalcoholic.

The truth is the ancient world knew no such thing as unfermented grape juice, at least not with a shelf life longer than Nana's afternoon nap. Grape juice doesn't happen for long without refrigeration and airtight seals. I suppose our ancestors could have boiled freshly squeezed juice to preserve it, but then they would be spreading it on Fertile Crescent rolls, not drinking it, and even then ambient yeasts would slowly make it into a happy brunch or sour vinegar. Grape juice as we know it wasn't invented until the 1860s, by a Methodist minister named Thomas Bramwell Welch, who was shocked to discover that all these wild grapes, without adult supervision, were turning into wine. He was determined to take the alcohol out of Communion wine and put a swift end to the wild Sunday sunrise parties raging in churches across the land. The advent of grape juice was an opening salvo in the war for national prohibition, bathtub gin, and organized crime. Reverend Welch employed the new tools available to his era: pasteurization—precisely heating a liquid to kill bacteria and alcohol-producing yeast, and refrigeration—cooling the juice to the point that airborne yeasts couldn't reactivate fermentation. Welch cooked up a few batches of what he called "unfermented wine," and Welch's grape juice was born. Church got just a little bit more boring.

❦

When I tell religious types that I used to work in ministry and now I work in wine, I get one of three reactions. If I am talking to a Southern Baptist or a Pentecostal, I get squinty eyes and sharp intakes of breath, pamphlets for healing prayer groups, signs of the cross while slowly backing away. I once put out on the internet that I keep a wine journal, and an evangelical type responded, "Is that like an alcoholic's diary?" But, if I tell the same thing to a Catholic or an Episcopalian, they exclaim, "Oh, that totally follows! Let me buy you a drink!" If I am talking to a Presbyterian or a Lutheran, I am awarded a lecture about craft beer. At one of my first wine jobs, we used to call these types "beerdos," which works on two levels because they have beards and are weird about beer.

Yet it was their equally eccentric hero, Martin Luther, who said, "Beer is made by men, wine by God," and before lab-manufactured grape juice, eight thousand years of religious tradition around the world declared that wine was a gift of the gods. Wine was not invented or conceived of by humans. *Wine was discovered.* It is not unlike the first time a guy hit two rocks together in frustration, sent up a spark, smoked out everyone in the cave, and slept outside alone that night.

All it takes to create wine are wild grapevines, sunlight to ripen sugars, and some peripatetic yeasts. There was probably a woman, a gatherer of wild grapes, who filled her basket to the brim and left it for a while. The grapes at the bottom were crushed by the weight, and they surrendered their juice to the yeasts wandering by and pausing on the grape skins, which then completed their proper vocation, transforming the sugars in the juice into alcohol and carbon dioxide. Wine, you see, wanted to be found.

When our sober ancestor returned to her basket after some time, the juice was bubbling and alive and strangely warm. Something had changed. It was a sticky and tantalizing blend of sweet and sour. It smelled different, it tasted different, and it felt different. When she tasted it, something changed in her. Her head felt a little lighter, her face a little warmer, her body a little freer. It was the ancient world's first mellow buzz.

Wine in its rawest form isn't made. *Wine happens.* Here is a little playful trickery, an intoxicating accident, a miracle tripped over. An elixir that can make a laborious life just a little bit easier. It would take a long while to figure out how to make and store good wine and how to recreate the miracle consistently. But over time the mystics, poets, and philosophers would come to celebrate wine for its ability to open the mind and free the body, to reveal the secrets of the heart, and to banish fear and worry. As the Roman poet Horace encouraged his friends, "Smooth out with wine the worries of a wrinkled brow." Is it any wonder that wine became the centerpiece of religious tables and a core symbol of heaven's love for earth that continues to this day? The ancient lyrics exult that "wine gladdens the human heart" and "cheers both gods and mortals."

At the time these wine revelations were first taking hold of me, I was leading a life that needed a tall glass of gladdening. I lived thirty miles or so east of Los Angeles, that sunny megalopolis I had once heckled from my misty northwestern perch of Seattle, and I was driving the 210 to the 605 to the 10 to nursing homes and strange neighborhoods at all hours of the day and night. I was a hospice chaplain.

If you are unfamiliar, hospice is end-of-life care, a service for the terminally ill, for when the doctor throws up his hands and says, "There is nothing more I can do." And I was a chaplain, a minister working outside church walls, who showed up at death's door to listen or pray or sit quietly at grieving bedsides. For a while I worked daytime shifts, and the sunshine illuminating my drives between nursing homes and shining in the windows of living rooms converted into dying rooms kept my spirits lighter. But then I was moved to the on-call night shift, when my work schedule became midnight to eight in the morning.

I was a hospice chaplain, working the graveyard shift. I was the Grim Reaper's wingman.

When a patient was dealing with an emotional or spiritual issue after hours, I was summoned. I would get a call at three in the morning that a patient was threatening suicide, which wakes you up considerably faster than coffee, believe me. I would keep him on the phone as long as I could, urgently empathizing, asking questions about the specificity of his plan, with a second phone nearby if I needed to call 911.

Those were the extreme situations, but most of my work was what we called "death visits." A patient on our service would die in the night, and Telecare would alert me to go help the family cope with their loss. Each night I slept, or tried to sleep, with a beeper next to my ear. Yes, a bona fide circa-1991 beeper. For the record, when you take a beeper to the City of Industry in the middle of the night, people will assume you are a drug dealer.

After that dreadful piece of retro-tech would scream me awake, making my heart beat out of my neck, I would gather myself and don a button-down shirt with rolled-up sleeves and khaki pants, the outfit of choice for the casual, off-hours hospice chaplain. Then I would drive my black 2003 Honda CRV through the starless LA night, battling my grogginess with saccharine pop music, to the patient's house to witness the death. I would walk in the door and everyone would clear a path. "Shhhh, the minister is here," they would say. Sometimes the family would want me to sound official, to make a "pronouncement," so I would put two fingers on the patient's neck for a few seconds and then summon my best primetime doctor impression to say, "Time of death: 4:40 a.m., January 23." Then I would close the patient's eyes. I would call the funeral home, flush the Morphine and Ativan and other meds down the toilet, and then, if they wanted, sit with the family until the men in suits and white gloves appeared with a gurney, usually ninety minutes later. Then I would never see that family again.

Those were hard nights. In the years I did that job, they never got easier. I played a meaningful role, and the families I passed in the nights were usually grateful for my prayers, yet I felt there was a certain futility to it all. Secretly, I wondered if I was doomed to wander the earth in the dark watches of the night like Jacob Marley, observing human misery, unable to do much of anything about it.

In my off hours, I was the only person I knew who could drain the life out of the most jovial cocktail party by simply mentioning what I did for a living. Here would be an unsuspecting accountant just trying to make a little small talk, reaching for a piece of smoked gouda, asking innocuously, "So, Adam, what do you do for work?"

"Uhhh, well, I'm a chaplain and grief counselor in, um, hospice," I would stammer. The record would scratch, the room would freeze, and a Southern lady in the corner would faint. They would look at me like I just said, "I am a hit man, and *you* are my next target." It turns out that the only public topic more distasteful than religion is death.

In my work, I suffered regularly from what is officially called "compassion fatigue," and what unofficially feels like walking in ten feet of water. Everything is slow, exhausting, and a little blurry. I felt trapped in my best intentions to do good, flailing in a world that was slowly drowning me. Strangers always said, upon finding out I worked in hospice, "Oh, that takes a really special person." I knew I wasn't that special. At the same time, I did truly want to help people, to find genuine connection, to offer a teaspoon of comfort to these families on one of the worst nights of their lives. I was taking my shoes off to stand on holy ground night after night, sometimes holding hands with patients when they took their final breath. But then I would look down after a while and see that my naked feet were dirty and calloused and stained with blood. It was getting harder to walk. Sometimes I feared that my patients were not the only ones who were dying.

I gained a good twenty pounds during my hospice nights, a comfort-food layer of defense against the darkness. I would circle the Del Taco drive-thru or plant at the Claremont Village Grill counter regularly after death visits, less out of hunger and more out of late-night solidarity, just to encounter my brothers and sisters of the moonlight, anyone who was awake in those lonely hours while the world slept tight. My schedule and work were further straining a marriage that was slowly falling apart. I would stagger home at nine in the morning after an all-night bender of death visits, curl into the fetal position on my olive-green couch, and fitfully sleep through episodes of *Rick Steves' Europe* until dinnertime, not wanting to talk to anyone, dreaming of being anywhere else in the world other than here.

⌦≈≈≈≈⌫

While almost everywhere sounded better than my place of captivity, I was dreaming of a promised land, where the wine flows, the mountains climb out of the sea, and to my knowledge at the time, no one dies. A hundred and fifty miles north of my couch, the Santa Ynez Valley stretched like an accordion from the 101 Freeway west toward the bracing Pacific and east toward Los Padres National Forest. It is a fairytale world where pinot noir and cabernet sauvignon are practically neighbors, with only syrah in between. In the heart of Santa Barbara County, Santa Ynez is the first great wine region you come to when accelerating north out of LA, which I did often and with increasing speed after I first discovered it.

On the western outskirts of the Santa Ynez Valley is a coastal fogbound town called Lompoc, which was founded in 1874, in a tantalizing irony, as a temperance colony. If you bought land in Lompoc back then, you signed a contract that declared, "No vinous, malt, spirituous, or other intoxicating liquors shall ever be manufactured or sold upon any portion of the ranchos purchased by this corporation." The founding fathers of Lompoc kept the spirits at bay for twenty-five years, after which all its parched residents up and partied like it was 1899. Now Lompoc is home to some of the best pinot noir and chardonnay vineyards in the world.

Follow Route 246 east from Lompoc, and the average temperature climbs about a degree for every mile you travel away from the Pacific Ocean. Forty-five minutes later, you arrive at the eastern flank of Santa Ynez, to a sunbaked land called Happy Canyon, so named because during Prohibition this was where the moonshine was run. "I'm takin' a trip up Happy Canyon," you'd say in Santa Barbara in the Roaring '20s when you were on the hunt for bootlegged hooch. The name stuck, and the canyon is still a happy one, as now kingly Arabian horses run free and thirsty visitors find the most prized sauvignon blanc vineyards on the California Central Coast and some upstart cabernet. In France, pinot noir and cabernet sauvignon have to be planted an entire country apart in order to find the right climates for their flourishing. In the Santa Ynez Valley, pinot and cab are planted twenty-five miles apart.

As I struggled through my hospice nights, I couldn't stop thinking about Santa Ynez—this strange and beautiful valley stretched between a dry town and a wet canyon, a cool maritime climate

giving way to its hot inland neighbor, that felt like my elusive promised land but somehow also like a timeline, etched in dirt and written in skies, of my life and spiritual wanderings. Somehow in that
valley those fiery, teetotaling Southern Baptists who gave me faith
are squared off in perpetual conversation with the Episcopalians
who pour me the sacrament these days—and keep buying
me drinks.

Some time ago, I left hospice and moved to the Santa Ynez Valley.
Now I work in wine. This has been far from a straight trip up Happy
Canyon, believe me. Recently, a nosy woman on a wine tour I led
peppered me with personal questions all afternoon, and at the end
of the day she concluded, "Adam, your story is exhausting!" Tell me
about it. This is the corkscrewing tale of how I got to Santa Ynez,
eventually, and the questions that came up along the way. You and I
are going to take a long wine tour together on our way there, and we
will make plenty of stops for a glass and some local wine history. As
you will see, I reached into the old, old story of wine in order to find
my new story, which begins, as so many wine love stories do, in the
French countryside.

Most stories about religion and drink are stories of recovery. I'm
not sure if mine isn't a story about recovery, too.

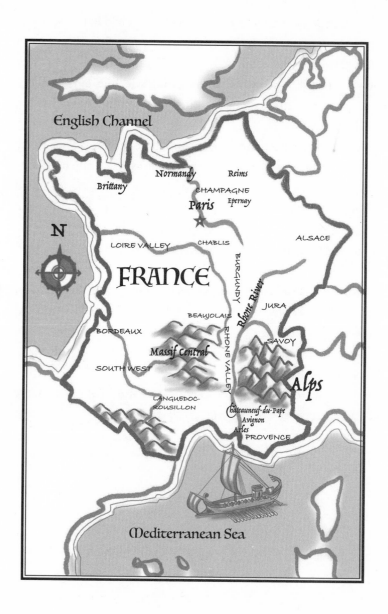

## Two

# THE WAY OF VAN GOGH

I became much more devoted to wine when I started working in hospice. This provoked a little concern among some in my family, since we admittedly have had a few wooden legs in our family tree, but I was spending more time reading about wine than drinking it. I kept issues of *Wine Spectator* in my car, and I would read them over lunch and in between patient appointments. Let's be honest though: sometimes knowing I had a half bottle of Chablis at home was enough to get me through a day of watching people die. It was better than bobbing for olives in a bucket of martinis.

I had enjoyed wine for years before that, thanks to the generous cellar in my family's basement in Seattle, mostly back then a collection of Napa Cab, which I first started to partake of during breaks in college. My parents uncorked a '73 Heitz Martha's Vineyard on the day I was born, and that probably sealed my fate as a future wine devotee. Like most men, however, I didn't think too much about wine until I started dating. Then I discovered that women were more impressed when you could order a bottle off the wine list, even if it was a fifteen-dollar Columbia Crest Merlot, rather than a metal pail of Coronas or a Cool Breeze smoothie.

After a few years of hospice work, I had hoarded enough vacation days for a summer wine adventure to France. Leading up to it, just the thought of two weeks away from hospice made me feel drunk with anticipation. Then, at eight in the morning on the first day of May, my boss called me into the conference room, where I was greeted by Human Resources and a purple folder containing instructions on how to apply for unemployment and extend my medical benefits. It was a very cordial layoff. But I didn't let that stop me from skipping my beeper across the conference table, saying, "Take the damn thing!" and drinking a healthy amount of Stag's Leap Cab that night.

A severe recession was ravaging the economy like a virus through a vineyard, though I noticed I was the only chaplain laid off from our hospice, even though others had been hired after me. My boss later explained that he chose me because I had recently signed a contract to write a book about listening, a skill that had been central to the job I just lost, so, he said, "You were in a better financial place than the others." It astounds me how the myth that writers make money continues to be so powerful. I consider it a ruse at least equal to the notion that pulling your friend's finger when he asks is a good idea.

Now that I was no longer leading the swanky lifestyle of a hospice chaplain, my wife and I thought about canceling our trip to France, but there had already been enough disappointment and tension between us that year. We would largely be spending money we didn't have, but for some reason I knew I *had* to go. I had never been to Europe. I had never been anywhere outside the United States except for a couple of highly controlled excursions off a cruise ship and a high school band trip to Victoria. A fortnight in France lay ahead, with one week in Paris and a second in Provence in the south. And a tootle on the train from Paris to Champagne.

Some people are born to wander, while others develop a taste for travel on a summer vacation or a semester abroad. My openness to international travel developed along with my palate. Wine lovers like to say that a wine is a trip in a bottle. By that measure I had traveled the globe without leaving my dinner table. I loved wine's ability to transport me, to enable me to taste a place and dine with people thousands of miles away. At the same time, the more I drank wines from countries I had never been to, the more I wanted to see them for myself. I found myself poring over old maps of France and Italy and Germany, when admittedly a few years before it would have taken me a couple of tries to point out France on a map of Europe.

I became enamored not only with tasting the wines of the world but with the history of wine and the people who have made it for over eight thousand years. All my history-nerd receptors were activated when I began to learn that the story of wine is nothing less than the story of Western civilization and of the Mediterranean cultures that shaped it. All the ancient societies I had studied in seminary textbooks were turning up again in my wine books, and this time I was paying far more attention. The earliest evidence of winemaking was discovered in a tiny Georgian village in the Caucasus Mountains near the Black Sea, dated to around 6000 BCE. From there and other nearby hills wine spread to all the peoples getting comfortable in the cradle of civilization. Wine would become the lubricant of empire. Over the centuries, the great empires, from Egypt to Greece to Rome, told the world of their power and culture with a steady flow of wine, and with it they toasted military victories, healed their sick, met and placated their gods, aroused fertility, and fueled philosophical debate. Some even ferried their dead to the shores of the afterlife on a river of wine.

I longed to stand on those holy and ancient soils, the hillsides where history and wine poured together. No drink inspires such pilgrim zeal for the places the raw materials are grown like wine. Yes, the Guinness brewery draws hearty crowds, and scotch devotees weep peaty tears on Highland moors, but those are where the draught and smoke water are made, not usually the source of the hops and barley. When it comes to beer and spirits, it is the *process* that makes the real difference. When it comes to wine, it is the *place*. The more I drank good wine, the more I found myself longing to hear the crunch of the ground between the vines that bear my favorite fruit. For me, the heart of wine culture beats in the stone villages of the French countryside. I knew I needed to drink at the source.

I am aware there is a segment of the population who discover their eyes involuntarily plunging back into their skulls the moment someone starts talking about wine. You may already know this, but the word *sommelier* is actually French for "professional wine douche." I am not entirely sure why oenophiles (wine lovers) are automatically relegated, by some sectors of society, to the realm of snobs and elitists and those who aspire to elitist snobbery. Perhaps it's because we use words like *sommelier* and *oenophile*.

I know from experience that wine as a pleasurable drink and dinner companion is one thing, but initiation into wine culture can be something else. For a business that specializes in supervising the graceful rotting of fruit, the wine industry takes itself terribly seriously. I have had moments of wondering if wine culture is the Hollywood of the beverage world—self-important and self-congratulatory, throwing itself parties and handing out awards when the rest of the world just needs a drink to get by.

This is nothing new: throughout the epochs of human history, wine has often been stored in the cellars of the few. Just like today, beer was the drink of the masses, though that narrative loses more credibility every time a guy in rural Pennsylvania orders an eleven-dollar IPA. Wine snobbery goes all the way back to ancient Egypt and Babylon, where because of climates too sweltering for growing quality wine grapes, wine had to be shipped in from mountainous regions of the Fertile Crescent, and steep transportation costs ensured wine's scarcity and expense. If you were in Babylon and wanted wine shipped from Armenia, for example, the trade route only went in one direction, with the flow of the river current. The vessel carrying the wine would be dismantled after it arrived in Babylon, so if you wanted wine from Armenia, you had to buy the whole damn boat.

Ancient wine was the beverage of kings and queens, who were entombed with quantities of wine sufficient for raging afterlife parties. One thirsty Pharaoh, Scorpion I, was buried with the equivalent of fifty-six hundred bottles of wine. Even the later Greeks, who championed democracy in both governing and drinking, doled out the good stuff to the higher classes, while the working classes drank a low-alcohol beverage called *lora*, made from leftover grape skins and water. It was a thin, bitter brew that would sometimes get contaminated by bacteria undeterred by the 3 percent alcohol solution. A good batch could be light and refreshing; a bad batch carried a perfume of eau de Aegean mouthwash. And later during the Middle Ages, the Catholic Church often withheld the sacramental cup from everyday drinkers, and the priests took the holy wine for themselves.

Still, most people don't know the long history of wine douchebaggery, and I struggle to fully understand why wine expertise provokes such ire in some people. I know a lot about baseball too, but when I talk about slugging percentage or the infield shift there aren't people in the room who look like they want to take the nearest bottle of Champagne and christen me like a ship. I suspect the problem is not wine itself but those few connoisseurs who want wine to be a rarified status symbol in order to prove something about themselves.

Every field will always have those people who want to turn their passion into social cachet, especially when the club membership dues are high.

I do think there is value in becoming more sophisticated in our tastes—and not just for the sake of ascending the snoot ladder. There was a time in my young life when I insisted on eating hot dogs for dinner when my parents ate steak. Now something feels off about going out for that special dinner and asking for spicy mustard and extra relish. But developing your palate to me is more about learning to pay attention, persistently seeking a fuller experience in a world of thin experiences. Perhaps the best antidote for boredom is attentiveness. If, instead of merely letting the pleasant effects of a wine passively wash over you, you get all your senses involved for a little while, then you can know not only *what* you like but *why* you like it. You can grow in your abilities to notice the subtle flavors and the small sensations that touch every inch of your palate. Tasting wine like this can inspire a surprising amount of joy, even teach us to listen better to life's whispers. Maybe tasting deeper can help us to live deeper.

I won't deny that wine is an intimidating subject, even for those of us who have studied it for years, but I maintain that wine should be far more scared of us than we are of it. For all the superiority and status wine inspires, let's remember it entered the world when someone stepped on a grape. I can only speak for myself when I say that not only has wine not closed me off from others or the world but it has opened me in so many ways. It has been through wine that I have embraced places and people and skies and dirt and even my own deepest desires in ways I never did before I started caring about crushed grapes.

That summer Paris was enchanting, magical, and perfect, and everything you have heard about it is true. I thought there was no way Paris could meet my soaring expectations, and it would be another mediocre Christmas morning after a sleepless night of anticipation. Imagine instead that you dreamed for months of a new baseball glove and bat, and you woke on Christmas morning to find you now own the Boston Red Sox and a lifetime supply of the flakiest croissants in all the land. That was Paris.

King Louis VII once remarked, rather ruefully, that "in France we have nothing but bread, wine, and joy." It's a hard life, Louie. I drank the best espresso of my life each morning looking across the Seine at Notre Dame. I shopped for books with Hemingway and Fitzgerald. I ate cake with Marie Antoinette. I took all kinds of opium at Montmartre with Picasso and Monet and Degas. I drank Bordeaux and Champagne with fromage and escargot and moules frites and boeuf bourguignon and bazooka-sized baguettes nine hours a day and didn't gain any weight. I ate raw beef and kept it down. Paris is a miracle. I have no idea when Parisians work because every café is full all afternoon and every bistro all night, and the streets bustle until two in the morning. Paris will make you question all the life and work choices you have ever made. Your life is a sham in Paris.

That about wraps up the City of Lights. My French romance really heated up a week later, beginning with the six-hundred-kilometer trip on the TGV south to Provence. Having lived in Southern California much of my adult life, I had grown accustomed to the rhythm of the 10 and 405 freeways, moving at the speed humans were designed to travel—an angry seven miles per hour. I was not prepared for the glories of European rail travel. The Metrolink in Los Angeles takes you through the underbelly of urban sprawl, stopping about every eight minutes to pick up more teenage hooligans and comic-book villains. The TGV was like a library hurtling south— quiet and clean, full of readers and whispers.

Heading south, the cityscape of Paris is quickly replaced by green hills capped with outcroppings of white rock, sprawling meadows,

and dense forests, broken up occasionally by weathered stone villages and men dressed like old-time sea captains mingling with herds
of cows and goats. It boasted a shade of green in mid-June that could
only be achieved by a historically wet March back in Los Angeles.
Aside from the bullet on rails whizzing by, it appeared to be a land
with little interest in modernity. I had to resist the urge to jump off
the train.

As we passed one particularly large woodland, I recalled that the
great forests in the center of France were once planted to build up the
French naval fleet. In the mid-1600s, the French finance minister
reported to King Louis XIV that the Dutch fleet outnumbered the
French navy thirty to one, with the Dutch boasting fifteen thousand
ships while the French set sail with a jaunty five hundred boats, most
of which were used for Riviera booze cruises. The Sun King felt ship
envy, and he ordered the planting of vast oak forests in the heart of
the country—including the Tronçais Forest, which our train must
have passed near on the journey south—to supply an armada he
hoped would rival the Dutch.

The reason I know this sweet piece of history is that now Tronçais,
among a select handful of French forests, supplies the timber for
French wine barrels. The French never became the looming sea
power the Sun King hoped for, but the trees he planted now make
the best and most expensive wine barrels in the world. A new French
oak barrel large enough to hold three hundred bottles of wine will set
you back as much as three thousand dollars. The secret to their barrels, because I know you are asking, is the character of the wood,
which is the result of the life in forests like Tronçais. Those white oaks
grow slowly in their misty, cool environment and they reach straight
up to the sky, clamoring for the sun shining above a crowded forest
floor. The slower a tree grows, the tighter together are the grains of
its wood, which makes for a less porous surface and less oxygen pen-
etrating its material. The timber of French oak is so straight, out of

the survival-motivated vertical instincts of the trees, that it is easily split with an axe, whereas American oak must usually be sawed. Younger American oak trees grow faster and less vertically, resulting in broader grains and more porous material.

The sum of it all is that wine stored in French barrels ages more gracefully, due to smaller amounts of oxygen seeping through the oak staves, and has subtle woody and spice flavors, whereas wine in American barrels ages faster, allowing more oxygen in, and has more prominent oak flavors. Bourbon is aged in American oak, and if you have ever had a young Bourbon straight out of a cask, you know it is like licking a drunk two-by-four.

This is what a wine geek thinks about while looking out the window of a French train. Only the French could manage to plant trees that are polished and well-bred. I think it is fascinating when wines reflect the broader culture in which they are raised. We will meet some exceptions to this in the Mediterranean heat, but French wines tend to be quiet and elegant, with somewhat hidden qualities that come out over time. They are not in a rush. They flirt and tease. Popular American wines, in turn, are often bold and outgoing, with higher alcohol percentages and more explosive flavors. They carry themselves like some of the other American tourists I encountered on the trip: loud and easy to pick out. Somehow, our oak barrels are more aggressive and eager to make their mark quickly. In America, even our trees are extroverted.

***

It had been up to me to decide which French wine region we would visit after Paris. I knew I wouldn't be content dabbling for a day or two in multiple regions, so I had to choose one. It was like ordering just a single course off the menu of a Michelin star restaurant. Every major wine region in France is iconic and unique, specializing in particular grapes and styles of wine and regional cuisine that is designed to meet the local wines at the table. Even though they are all of the same species—*vitis vinifera* ("wine-bearing vine")—individual varieties of wine grapes thrive in different climates. In the cool inland, Burgundy grows chardonnay and pinot noir; Bordeaux in the warm southwest farms cabernet sauvignon and merlot and sauvignon blanc, among a few others. Cab was my first love, but pinot is my ride home. When the state of California finally decrees that I can marry pinot noir, you will be getting your save-the-date.

In the end, I didn't choose the region to visit based only on wine. I chose where Vincent van Gogh used to paint. In the months leading up to the trip, I read everything I could find about Vincent. I developed a strange fascination with him, and he became a ghostly companion, an eccentric one-eared muse to me. I wanted to see horizons and lights and trees like he did, alive and talking to us. Like Vincent, I was beginning to find more life in landscapes and night skies than in religious buildings.

Back in the day, like every other college student in the Western Hemisphere, I had a print of *Starry Night* tacked to my dorm-room wall. But now there was something about impressionism, in this less sophomoric stage of my life, that was drawing me in again. While the vivid colors on nature scenes first enthrall your eye, there is something more existential in the way impressionist paintings are created. If you narrow your gaze to one small section of an impressionist painting, all you can see are wild splotches of color that appear to have no guiding purpose or shape. But when you stand back and take in the whole of the work, it all comes together. All those thick strokes of color combine, almost magically, to create a vibrant, incandescent scene that appears to the human eye to be alive and moving. On some subconscious level I needed that to be true about life, too.

The freshly unoccupied hours of unemployed life had brought some buried questions a little closer to the surface. I wondered that summer if my life had become a gallery of strange decisions, an unfinished hodgepodge of arbitrary, slapdash strokes. I was struggling to find any unity in it, much less conscious purpose or movement. I realized that for a long season of my life I had been making choices almost exclusively by whatever door happened to open to me, no matter whether I actually desired what was behind that door and without much thought for what pitfalls may lurk on the other side. What was I creating by merely walking wherever more ground appeared? I didn't know. I had no real allegiance to the career path I was on, no real commitment to where I lived or ties to the people I lived around.

How did I even end up as a hospice chaplain? I actually think I knew the answer to that question. Pain is what found me in hospice. I will have more to say about that later. For now I will say that pain is what drew me to Vincent.

A few details in the personal life of Vincent van Gogh have been thoroughly rehearsed. Yes, he presented his ear in a napkin to a lady of the Provençal nighttime, as you do when you're distraught. And he died of a festering revolver wound to the abdomen, which was assumed for decades to be the suicidal action of an unwell man, but in recent years that theory has come under scrutiny. No matter how unbalanced, who tries to take his life by shooting himself in the *stomach*? The prevailing theory goes that he aimed for his chest but missed, much like how sometimes I try to put my fork in my mouth but end up stabbing myself in the arm. Plus, at the time Vincent was painting in a flourish, producing almost a work a day, and he seemed to be in high spirits. Vincent's recent defenders have proposed the alternative theory that the local teenagers who harassed him out in the fields shot him, but Vincent, the sad, kindly man he was, covered for them by saying he shot himself. For reasons I didn't understand at the time, I deeply wanted this explanation to be correct. I became an ardent Van Gogh defender for a while, but I found "Did you know Vincent van Gogh didn't really kill himself?!" to be an awkward conversation starter with strangers.

There is much more to Vincent's life than those gory details. For example, you may not know that at one point he tried to marry his cousin. His uncle refused the engagement, not because it was super weird but because Vincent didn't make enough money. Try coming back from that. As his biographer Irving Stone, who wrote a novel based on careful readings of the artist's personal correspondence, portrays him, Vincent lived his life in the shadow of a great rejection, another spurned marriage proposal when he was young. Vincent proposed marriage with about the same frequency as most of us order a cappuccino. The first time around, he was a promising art salesman in London, his unguarded, squishy heart devoted to a young woman named Ursula. He couldn't wait any longer, and he let the paint spill one evening on his intention to marry her, in the garden outside her home. Ursula's response? "How extraordinary that you shouldn't know. I have been engaged for over a year." How extraordinary that you failed to ever mention a fiancé, *Ursula*. But Vincent, undeterred, leaned in to kiss her. Ursula pushed him away, and as she fled to the safety of her mother's house, she turned and yelled, "Red-headed fool!"

The marks made on Vincent's heart were permanent. He changed into a man who seemed to identify himself with pain, and here was where I began to relate to him. As Stone interpreted Vincent's letters to his brother Theo, "Pain did curious things to him. It made him sensitive to the pain of others. It made him intolerant of everything that was cheap and blatantly successful in the world about him. . . . The only pictures in which he could find reality and emotional depth were the ones in which the artists had expressed pain."

This could easily be the description of the inner life of a hospice chaplain. There is a perspective that comes from being with people at the end of life, a rejection of the trappings of success and happy disguises we wear to fool everyone and often even ourselves that we are invincible. When you start to see life through the lens of death that will one day mercilessly take us all, ordinary human behavior has a way of looking rather odd. The eccentric passions that humans devote themselves to, the inconveniences that cause such outrage, the relentless hours of work at the expense of intimacy, all of it starts to seem quite idiosyncratic and futile. Yet life outside of hospice goes on as it always has, people indulging all the strange instincts their genetics afford, and then there I am, standing behind soundproof glass, shouting, "Why don't you see what I see?! Don't you know this will all end?"

But another voice in my head says that the problem with viewing life with the end in mind is that it leaves you with nowhere to go. It has always been the peculiar glory of human beings that we live and work and have sex and play music and drain wine glasses while the sun is slowly setting on us all. Perhaps it is grace that most of us don't fade into hopelessness but keep trying to make meaning in a life that has an expiration date. As Vincent himself put it in a letter to his brother Theo, "However meaningless and vain, however dead life appears, the man of faith, of energy, of warmth . . . steps in and does something."

Even though I wasn't working in hospice at this point, it still had a way of shadowing me. Hospice had changed me into someone who empathized with pain wherever I went, even to search for it in its buried places. This was a dramatic shift for me, as I had lived so much of my life at arm's length, eagerly detached from the hidden lives of others. Now I seemed to have a sixth sense for the hurt of other people, and my outward presence must have opened, because now others were seeking me out to share their grief, when before they would have run far away. It was a dreadful softening of my heart. I was becoming more vulnerably human, more able to feel pain, and I was quietly grateful for that, but the heartbreak and loss that was rushing in threatened to crowd out my capacity for joy. Pain opened me, changed me, and sometimes pursued me like a hunter. Like Vincent, I began even to be attracted to situations and relationships scarred by pain.

You may not know that after his great heartbreak, Vincent became a missionary. Disenchanted with the shallow and profit-driven world of art dealers, he turned to the vocation of his father, a Dutch Reformed minister. He struggled, however, with traditional theological studies and instead found himself a few months later on a train to Brussels, as a missionary to a coal-mining community called the Borinage, or as he called it when he first saw it, "Black Egypt."

Vincent had a provisional appointment to this endangered, coal-streaked community, whose citizens spent more time underground than above, deep in the bowels of the earth. The lungs of the Borains were darkened with soot, their life expectancy shockingly low. Contracting black lung was not a matter of *if* in the Borinage but a matter of *when*. They were a forgotten people, served by a heartsick missionary, and unsurprising to those of us who are familiar with pain, Vincent found them attractive. He wanted the Borains to accept him, so he became one of them. He moved out of the rooms the relatively prosperous town baker had provided him and took up in a cold, damp hole with ramshackle furnishings. He stopped washing the coal streaks off his face. And the people loved him. They attended his services, they invited him into their homes, they even brought him down to the coal mine where they spent the majority of their lives.

Tragedy brought the collapse of Vincent's work in the Borinage. A section of the coal mine caved in, and fifty-seven miners, including children, died. A hush of despair came on the community. Faith in God was slowly abandoned. As Stone narrates it, the Dutch ministers from Vincent's missionary training program visited some time later and found him starved and sickly, his face and hair black with coal.

They reviled him, "What in the world have you done to yourself? . . . Have you no sense of decency, of decorum? Is this conduct befitting a Christian minister? Are you utterly mad, that you behave like this? Do you wish to disgrace our Church?" A chronicler of the local Protestant church wrote that Vincent had "lost his mind" and had "become a burden." They revoked his assignment to the Borains, and his time with the church was finished. It is not a surprise that years later, when Vincent painted *Starry Night*, the only building in the riverfront village that did not have lights in the windows was the church.

Vincent refused to leave the Borinage immediately and instead wandered through the town with paper and pencil, sketching the residents who would still welcome him into their homes. His sketches were rough and badly proportioned, but this was the beginning of his grand passion, revealed by pain, that would take him to Paris, where he first encountered the impressionists, and then to Arles, along the Rhone River in the south of France, where he hoped to start an artist's colony in the dazzling light of Provence.

The opportunity to walk the streets and docks and stand in the very spots where Vincent stood when he painted *Starry Night*, *Café Terrace at Night*, and *The Yellow House* was too much for me to resist. So instead of Bordeaux or Burgundy, I chose Provence. On the second morning of our visit to the south of France, we disembarked at the train station in Arles. It was pouring rain and I was sans umbrella. The dark clouds veiled the bright light of the Provençal horizons that fueled so much of Vincent's inspiration. The city of Arles has set up easels to mark where Vincent painted many of his most famous works. I walked the entire path of Van Gogh in the unrelenting rain. I knew I must. The way of the pilgrim requires suffering.

Afterwards we dripped our way into a café, and I ordered a croque monsieur and a carafe of red wine from the nearby village of Vacqueyras. Its aromas are locked in my sensory memories: black fruit, leather, and rubber bands. As it warmed me from the inside, I poured a little in another glass for Vincent. You magnificent, red-headed fool.

I didn't have the words for it yet, but I wanted to believe that Vincent didn't take his own life. I wanted to believe that he died as a martyr, not as a patient. I wanted to know that you can leave ministry and find happiness in a new passion. I wanted to believe I could keep the faith and find the light in a new place. I wanted to keep my soft heart, but I didn't want to keep chasing pain down the mineshaft. I wanted to believe the change wasn't gonna kill me.

There is one painting of Vincent's that is more special to me than all the others. It portrays the energy of autumn's grape harvest in flames of reds and mustards and violets. In the background, under the setting sun, approaches a solitary man walking along a road slicked by a recent rain, his shadow casting along the glistening cobblestones. I want to believe it is Vincent. The piece is called *The Red Vineyard at Arles*. It is the one painting that Vincent sold in his lifetime.

*Three*

# FEAST DAY

After he left the coal mines of the Borinage, Vincent moved hopefully to Paris, but the somber gray curtains and drizzle of the northern city dripped on his already melancholy disposition. He fled south, praying the breezy sunlight and the whir of Provençal color contained healing powers. I think that's why I followed him down there from Paris. I was in search of a healing place. And wine. I thought I would submit my life questions to a few bottles of Côtes du Rhône and listen for their answers. Turns out, they had been waiting for me. They had much to tell me about my future.

In geographical terms, Provence surrounds the mighty and ancient Rhone River in the south of France, extending down to the Riviera, the Mediterranean playground for the subset of the world's population that feels confident wearing white pants. In wine terms, Provence is at the heart of the Southern Rhone River Valley, as distinguished from the more rugged Northern Rhone region. In the north, the Rhone River originates in the Alps and hangs a sharp left at Lyon, slicing through narrow and inhospitably steep slopes, and the peppery syrah vines planted there cling to the angular granite hillsides as the alpine winds rush past. By the time you arrive in the Southern Rhone, the valley has fanned out and the landscapes have relaxed somewhat, much like its sun-drenched residents, with softer, tree-topped hills and vast fields of lavender caressing all your senses. The wine life of Provence is dominated by grenache, a plump red grape which luxuriates in the unrelenting Mediterranean sunshine that sends northern folk like myself scurrying to local shops in search of wide-brimmed hats.

<hr>

Avignon was our home base for our stay in Provence, chosen largely because the bullet train fired out of Paris emptied there, and I wasn't keen on renting a car and trying to decipher road signs in French. Learning foreign languages is decidedly not a gift of mine, as anyone unfortunate enough to sit at adjacent café tables learned when I attempted to order meals that week. I suspected that if I got behind the wheel of a French vehicle I would require the services of the American Embassy to extract me from the international crisis I created. I had already seen a tourist in Paris attempt to back up in a roundabout a few days before, and the hostility it incited was reminiscent of the atmosphere the day the Germans marched into town.

Avignon is encircled by a twenty-five-foot-high medieval wall that guards a palatial Gothic castle within. The city sits on the east bank of the Rhone, flanked by a famous stone bridge that French schoolchildren have been singing about since the 1500s. The bridge, le Pont d'Avignon, casts out about halfway into the river and stops right there. Someone with a questionable sense of humor might say it is "abridged." A chapel, devoted to Saint Nicholas, looks out from two levels at the bridge's edge, because, I'm guessing, the citizens of Avignon ask him every December for the other half. The original structure was built in the twelfth century, but the river surged in

1669 and wiped out the western half and its stately stone arches. The Avignon Visitors Center discourages you from walking the bridge at night.

Don't let its imposing medieval defenses fool you; housed within Avignon's walls is an easy welcome. Life here is enchantingly slow, even on its main streets. Meals are leisurely, languid days follow the long arc of the Mediterranean sun, and the walking pace is a stroll. On the first evening I ambled Avignon's most famous street, called Rue des Teinturiers—the Road of the Dyers. It wanders on a stone path under majestic sycamores and along a canal routed off the Rhone to power the surging textile industry of the nineteenth century. Now it is lined with outdoor cafés and shops, but four of the original waterwheels remain on the canal, quaint energy supplies of a once-burgeoning industrial age. It was a nostalgic time when your carbon footprint was so tiny and adorable that your parents bronzed it and displayed it on the mantle. Walking the cobblestones on an early summer evening, within the quiet created by the city walls, I was starting to breathe the longer, deeper breaths of a past era.

The history of Avignon is a delicious melodrama of religious intrigue and fourteenth-century French nationalism, but my personal history with Avignon seemed to turn around the meals I ate there. I think many people visit France for the food and wine and are pleasantly surprised to discover there are other things you can do while waiting for your next opportunity to eat. For the first couple days I brushed against the city squares largely while eating meals, walking off meals, or walking toward meals. The whole of Provence feels like one sprawling farmer's market, the garden to end all gardens, a moving sidewalk of spices and olives, crunchy-fresh vegetables and shirt-soaking tomatoes, sunflowers and lavender grown side by side, a blend of traditional Provençal ingredients and a spicy North African influence. This world was farm-to-table before anyone knew there was any other way to eat.

It was a long lunch in the courtyard of Avignon's grand palace that began to reawaken something in me that had been dormant for some time. On the list of my life's most memorable meals, this would have to take the crown. It was as much a personal quest as it was lunch. If this turns out to be my one and only trip to the south of France, I vowed to myself, then I will partake of as many Provençal culinary traditions as I can, in one meal. In Provence, if you are not sitting at lunch for three hours, you are just having a snack.

I started with pastis, a milky green aperitif and afternoon ritual here that I first read about in Peter Mayle's book *A Year in Provence*. If you are unfamiliar with pastis, imagine that someone made a scourge of black licorice vines and smacked you in the face with it repeatedly. The waiter explained to me that I was supposed to cut it with water to a ratio of one part pastis, five parts water. I tried it. It didn't help.

Fortunately, a carafe of rosé was not far behind, practically a staple of the Mediterranean diet, as at home on Provençal tables as ketchup at a burger joint. The south of France is known for two types of wine: muscular reds and spritely rosés. If pink-colored wine still triggers traumatic flashbacks from the 1980s of that uniquely American monstrosity, white zinfandel, take comfort. The rosés of the Côtes de Provence resemble nothing of the syrupy, cloying, neon-pink nightmare that your great aunt drinks over ice. Here rosés are lively, zesty, and dangerously easy, not unlike the particular class of ladies Vincent was acquainted with down here. They are red wines made like white wines that enjoy a mere dalliance with the grape skins before the juice is pressed out, and the result is a bone-dry, carnation-colored wine that alights on your palate like a swan on the river.

The house wines appear in a large carafe with a slash marking the fill line, and you are charged based on how far the wine drops from the line during lunch. Jokes that evaporation in the afternoon heat caused the drop will make you even more unpopular with your waiter. You will likely never find these wines in a bottle, because the man who made it from the grenache vines his *grand-père* planted in his backyard is often the same man who owns the café, who also bears a striking resemblance to the gentleman with the Inspector Clouseau mustache who brought it to your table. Winemaking here is more often family tradition than profitable enterprise. He will charge you about five euros per foot of rosé, and for the right food pairing he will suggest everything on the menu, and he is not wrong. But the perfect alchemy happens when you put rosé next to salad niçoise, which came next in my greedy march toward locavore nirvana.

I first discovered salad niçoise from a Julia Child recipe, and culinary wisdom says you should always follow Julia's instructions, especially if you can repeat them in her voice. My imitation sounds more like the Swedish Chef from *The Muppets*, and it only makes an appearance after eight inches of rosé. Julia followed Vincent's pilgrimage route from Paris to the south of France as well, and she even found her way to Santa Barbara, down the hill from the Santa Ynez Valley, in the last years of her life. There is a taco dive on Milpas Street that still bustles because Julia used to eat there. I bet she stood out.

Salad niçoise is all the goodness of Provençal gardens and seas piled high on one plate. Fingers of potatoes, green beans tossed with butter and herbs, tomatoes, hard-boiled eggs and crunchy lettuce are scattered with capers, those most adventurous of briny flower buds, and then topped with thinly sliced tuna and anchovies straight from the stalls of Les Halles, the town's central food market that Peter Mayle called "The Belly of Avignon." The salad is finished with its namesake niçoise olives from the nearby town of Nice and doused in olive oil whisked with Dijon mustard, garlic, lemon juice, and white wine vinegar, which is soaked up beautifully with the crispy pillows of bread teetering at the platter's edge. I declare to you today it is more than food. It is the Garden of Eden served up on a plate, an exultant celebration of life's bounty here, an offering of gratitude presented by a people that heaven and latitude have smiled on.

It remains a curiosity to me that the French serve a round of cheese after the main course. Who was the masochistic gastronome in Paris who first suggested, after a warming winter lunch of cheese soufflé floating in bechamel sauce, "You know what would help settle this lake of butter and cream I just downed at 1:30 on Tuesday afternoon? A wheel of brie!"? Anyway, in Provence the cheese is made from tangy goat's milk, and as hockey pucks of goat cheese and another basket of bread hurtled my way, with a lavender honey tarte still to follow, I took a few deep breaths, blinked away a sea-salt tear, and gave myself a pep talk. Listen, McHugh, this meal isn't about comfort—it's about victory! About honor! About avenging the deaths of your ancestors who perished in the potato famine! And I wondered if the reason the French sit at lunch for three hours is because they can't move.

<hr />

On this stretched out afternoon, there was something beginning to stir in me, and I don't mean the five pounds of salad I had just consumed. It felt somehow like my heart was resurfacing after years of being buried in my chest cavity. In these years of hospice work and now unemployment (a.k.a. writing), I wondered if I had been experiencing symptoms similar to what dying people undergo. People with a terminal diagnosis slowly detach from their lives, often losing interest in things they were once passionate about and retreating away emotionally from loved ones. For a while now it had felt like my system was shutting down. I had become a stranger to my own desires, undergoing a slow detachment from the things that once made me feel alive. It was as though the world turned cold with her gifts. The flavors of food had lost some of their intensity, the pierce of beauty some of its sting.

I had once burned with dangerous, impossible dreams, but now my loftiest goals seemed to turn around survival, on hanging on through the night. I had become aloof to friends and family, neglecting old friendships and keeping a safe distance from amicable newcomers. I answered my phone even less than usual. Long walks and long books, things that had brought me joy, now just felt long. It was a listlessness I had been unable, or even unwilling, to shake. Distance was how I kept my questions to myself.

The questions circled like buzzards. Through no real intention of my own, I had awoken to the pain of the world, and I knew I could never go back to sleep. Life questions usually scheduled for late middle age had shown up early, with arms empty. How do I live my life when so many are dying? How can I skip through a world where so many limp? How do I sleep peacefully when the lights from houses of grief across the street glare through my window? I started to feel like the chaplain had become the patient, as though I were sitting vigil at my own sick bed.

There was something in my belief system that was convinced that if I wasn't suffering, I wasn't doing something meaningful. If I wasn't pouring myself out on the altar of broken humanity, prepared to fling myself into the volcano as atonement for the world's agony, then I must lack faith. Now that I had opened enough to let in the pain of others, I felt I had lost the right to celebrate. Celebration seemed like denial, and denial is grief. In hospice, mourning a loss before it happens is called anticipatory grief. Celebration for me had become merely an act of anticipatory grief.

Yet, in this land of many courses, this place of such multicolored pleasures—its herb-scented hillsides aflame with mustards and magentas, its dishes and wines boasting such extravagant aromas and sultry textures—there was a spirit of celebration again beginning to bubble within me. My soul was coming alive through my senses. With each fragrant inhale I was becoming more wide-eyed. I asked

this place my question, *How can I possibly live when others are dying?*
It seemed to shout back at me, *How can you not?*

Maybe a life of faith doesn't mean overindulging at the table of the
world's pain. Perhaps celebration isn't a denial of life's struggle and
grief. What if it is a conscious letting go, an unclenching of our death
grip on control's false promises and a surrender to what is beautiful
and delicious? Should I mourn that the time will come when dessert
will end, my last coffee cup drained? Or should I tuck into each
course as hungrily as I can?

History tells us that some of the best parties happen just before
the shit goes down. The ancient Hebrews roasted the best lamb and
emptied every wine cup before they ran for their lives. As the sun was
dying and the season of light ending, the Celts spun choice meats on
the spits, drank the only fermented beverages of the year, and reveled
around the bonfire before winter's long darkness enveloped them.
Most of our beloved Christmas lighting rituals—Christmas trees,
Yule logs, twinkle lights—were all originally a way of proclaiming,
"We're gonna light this house on fire so the creeping dark can't get us."
It's coming for us all, but not tonight.

What I was coming around to is that to celebrate life's pleasures
and occasions has always been not only an act of gratitude but of
defiance, this night's epicurean triumph over the forces of darkness.
Future loss and uncertainty make today's dishes that much richer,
tonight's wine all the more decadent. We can get as cerebral and
sophisticated about wine as we choose, but on some level wine will
always be an antidote to grief and a defense against worry. "These are
not solemn alcoholic dosages," said Robert Capon. "They are cheerful minor lubrications of the frequently sandy gears of life."

❧

The reason why wine has survived eight thousand years of planetary
history is not because it carries aromas of mulberry and forest floor.

It's because wine for our ancestors was a way of making a hard, short life just a little easier. There is good reason to believe many of our ancient friends were drinking wine that by modern standards was worthy of the spit bucket. The Greeks used to add sea water to their wines; the Romans blended in just a little bit, I kid you not, of lead, because it was a natural sweetener. It's problematic when poison makes your wine more appetizing. But wine has transcended time and culture because it relieved pain and care for a night, it was the most potent antiseptic the ancient world knew, and it inoculated suspect drinking water when mixed. It eased social strife, inflamed the sexy passions, enhanced religious ritual, powered economies and commerce, and stirred the classic after-dinner conversations.

The Greeks would clear the dinner plates, move the tables, and offer the first unmixed cup to the powerful Dionysus, "the Good Deity," god of wine and high times. Both the Greeks and Romans cut their wine with water to a ratio of three or four parts water to one part wine. The epic poet Homer suggested a twenty-to-one ratio of water to wine. Another name for a beverage composed of twenty parts water and one part wine is *water*. But Dionysus got the pure stuff. Then that night's host would blend the wine and water in a vase-like bowl called a krater, and the next toast would be offered up to Zeus, chief of the Olympians and father of Dionysus, the giver of rainwater that diluted the wine, so the drinkers could keep their wits, and the wind that mixed it all up. This was the Greek *symposium*, which the Romans adopted as a *convivium*, both of which basically mean "let's drink together—woooo!" but became the settings for many of the great conversations about democracy, philosophy, and ethics. They would go around the room waxing eloquent and toasting in turn. Sometime later in the evening guests would toss the dregs of their wine at targets while naming the person they pined for, a game called kottabos. Even later, things would get *real* weird.

My afternoon-long lunch in the Avignon courtyard had become a symposium in my own mind, with each internal voice getting its chance to raise its glass and make its case. I locked grief and joy in the same room, hoping they would come to an understanding instead of just flinging wine at each other. It felt like a wedding attended by two families who hate each other, a wondrous occasion of side-eyed mingling. But I knew they must learn to coexist. Neither one of them was going anywhere. Each must be allowed to speak, and each must learn how to listen to the other.

Something was changing inside me, but it was hazy. I could feel my soul opening a crack, but I could also tell that something else was closing. The recurring question of whether I needed to leave the ministry in order to find lasting joy was close to the surface. The image I couldn't shake was that I was wearing a nametag with "Reverend McHugh" scrawled on it, but during my rainy pilgrimage to Vincent's easels in Arles the ink had started to run.

❧

That big question was amplified by the magnificent building providing the shade for this lunch symposium. I was sitting in the presence of the largest Gothic castle ever built. Twin turrets pierce the skies above the main entrance, which opens into a maze of stone archways and echoing corridors lined with sculptures and colorful tapestries. Eventually you find yourself in a vast banquet hall, with a ceiling that once soared with frescoes of stars twinkling on a midnight-blue backdrop, designed to mirror the evening sky outside. No, this isn't the great wizarding hall of Hogwarts, this is Tinel Hall, in Avignon's Palace of the Popes. The palace is an enduring symbol of one of the strangest eras in church history.

My Protestantism is starting to show here, but it was breaking news to me that in the fourteenth century this was the most powerful building in all of Christendom. I must have been sick, or bored, the morning they taught this in Church History 202. Somehow, I entirely missed that seven hundred years ago the pope downsized from his posh digs in Rome to a sensible, twelve-towered castle in Avignon, and he and his successors stayed there for seventy years.

In what may be the funniest line ever penned in a church history book, which, trust me, does not face stiff competition, Williston Walker wrote, "In 1309, after four years of wandering about southern France, Clement V took up residence at Avignon on the river Rhone." I have so many questions. Was the pope backpacking across Europe? Exactly how much vacation time does the pope get? Who was in charge of the mass back in Rome this whole time? Did he carry his own gear when hiking? You'd think the enormous hat would have discouraged him from walking too far.

From what I can gather, the true sovereign of the church back then was not a pope but a king. Philip IV was king of France, nicknamed the Iron King, and the popes during the Avignon papacy, all French by the way, danced to his tune, even after he died. There was a new nationalism ascending among European countries, when loyalty to your king and people was slowly taking precedence over loyalty to pope and church. When the Italian pope Benedict XI died in 1304, King Philip leaned on the mostly French cardinals to elect the arch-bishop of Bordeaux, Bertrand de Got, as the new pope. He assumed the name Clement V, which narrowly beat out his second choice, Bert the Dawdler, and packed his robe and staff collection for his new holy bachelor pad in Avignon, where the papal seat would remain uncontested until 1377.

Did this go over well in the rest of Europe? It did not. England was convinced the church was now hostage to France, and furthermore that future English kings should be able to marry six or seven times. One of the French popes tried to interfere in a German election, and with one voice all Germans cried *Nein!* They declared the pope didn't have authority to tell them to hike up their lederhosen. An

Italian poet called the Avignon papacy the "Babylonian captivity" of the church. Dante went further, assigning Pope Clement to the eighth circle of hell in his *Inferno*, both for relocating the papal throne to Avignon to appease the French king, and also for colluding with King Philip in wiping out the Templars, the order of warrior-monks formed to protect the pilgrimage routes to the Holy Land.

The next four decades were even more fractured. Beginning in 1378 there were actually dueling popes, one in Rome and one in Avignon, each hunting furiously in rival towers for Saint Peter's lost keys. This era was called the Great Schism, and it lasted for forty years, another bewildering historic wander of the people of God.

⚜

After the long journey from Rome to Avignon in the fourteenth century, the throng of Pope Clement's courtiers clearly needed a glass of wine, or a barrel. I may have tuned out during droning lectures about medieval papal succession in seminary, but I snapped back in when I learned just how thirsty the Palace of the Popes was for French wine. Our blessed journeyman Bertrand de Got, in fact, already owned an estate vineyard in Bordeaux, bequeathed to him when he was appointed archbishop in 1299. All I got when I was ordained was an unlaminated card for my wallet. After his elevation to the papacy his Bordeaux estate was renamed Château Pape Clément, which to this day remains a renowned producer of cabernet in the gravelly soils of Pessac-Léognan. The estate belonged to the church until the French Revolution, when French wine lost its religion, but today you can still drink the pope's namesake wine for a plucky 150 dollars.

Nowadays, the Vatican annually tops the list for highest per capita wine consumption in the world, at seventy bottles per year for each of its eight hundred or so citizens, so perhaps the passion for wine in fourteenth-century Avignon should not come as a surprise. Clement's court was particularly smitten with the wines of Burgundy, aging in cold cellars 250 miles north of Avignon. Religion was already inscribed on Burgundy's wines, as the guardians of those hallowed vineyards were Benedictine and Cistercian monks, each of which Saint Benedict had allowed a quarter liter of wine per day. Reportedly, one of the reasons why the Avignon popes resisted a move back to Italy was because they feared losing access to Burgundy's wines. I get that. I would pick up my entire life, change my name, and disappear forever if it meant I could drink more Burgundy. Does witness protection ever relocate people to Gevrey-Chambertin?

⁓⚜⁓

The displaced papacy may have been an awkward time for the European faithful, but if nothing else it helped create the exuberant Provençal wine and food culture that I had just devoured whole. While I decided I would never, ever eat again, I was still thirsty. The legendary vines a few miles north of town were summoning me. They had a secret to tell. But first we need to take a fizzy detour to Champagne.

*Four*

# THE TRAIN TO CHAMPAGNE

There are a few short rows of vines that perch outside the heights of the Palace of the Popes, on a hillside overlooking the abbreviated bridge of Avignon. They are a tribute to the role the Avignon papacy played in elevating the winegrowing importance of the region. Those vines were, by far, my favorite part of the self-guided palace tour. The chapel inside the palace was impressive, but after surveying approximately ninety-seven medieval churches in ten days, I was bored and a little traumatized. Surely, I can't be the only one who finds the artwork of medieval cathedrals to be transcendent and exalting and a wee bit creepy. Eyes follow you, from statues and altars and ceilings and windows, from all angles searching you, questioning you, finding you thoroughly inadequate.

On a psychological level I have to wonder how much time a person should spend contemplating the frescoes of the final judgment that seem to adorn every Gothic ceiling. That can't be healthy after a while. If I spend too much time looking at judgment paintings, I start seeing eerie, medieval hospice scenes, painted in the brush strokes of the apocalypse. I see hospice patients, suspended between life and death, surrounded by people who are coping in their own ways. You have the angels, who seem unaffected, spiritual, talking about how the dying person is going to a better place. You have the chief mourners, who grieve out loud at the bedside, making the angels feel quite uncomfortable. And you have the goblins, resentful and manipulative, who use this sad time as an opportunity to try and tear people apart. I had seen so often in my hospice work that grief is a strange thing, unique to each person, when all your best and worst coping mechanisms and roles in the family system surface. I never knew what I was going to experience when I stepped into a grieving house. What should be a time of togetherness could be a time of great divide.

The main lesson here is that hospice chaplains shouldn't spend a lot of time staring at medieval doom paintings. Or watching shows about zombies. I grew restless touring old French churches. After a while they started to feel to me like macabre museums, cavernous period-pieces of worship that left me feeling cold.

⚜

There was one exception, which shone through a piece of stained glass in the royal cathedral of Champagne. Before we left Paris for warmer climates, we took the train to Champagne. While I would propose that as an expression for every time you open a bottle of bubbles, in this case "taking the Champagne train" was literal. On a drizzly Thursday morning, we embarked from the Gare de l'Est in Paris for Reims, which along with Epernay forms the historic heart of the Champagne region. Champagne was a realm long before it was a wine.

The Champagne region resides ninety miles northeast of Paris in a climate that really has no right to grow grapes. The town of Reims— locals pronounce it "Rans" in a way that rhymes with "France," because French pronunciation isn't already mystifying enough—sits above the forty-ninth parallel, at the same latitude as balmy Vancouver, Canada. This is one of the northernmost grape-growing regions in the world. Winter days are short and white, and autumns and springs are wet and moody. For three summer months the Champenois savor the cool sunshine, when the three permitted varieties of the region—two red grapes, pinot noir and pinot meunier, and one white grape, chardonnay—just threaten to ripen. But the extreme northern climate and the struggle for sugars in Champagne helped give birth to the divine serendipity that is sparkling wine.

Like so many of the world's great wines, Champagne was an accident of history, a rescued misadventure of a wine cellar in a cold spell. Harvest time in the area, hastened by incoming autumn rains, would gather up slightly unripe, highly acidic fruit. When you fill a tank with tart juice in a chilly northern cellar, fermentation is a struggle. Yeasts need heat to swim through sugars and convert them to alcohol, and as early winter dawned the languid yeasts would go to sleep before their work was done. All of Champagne would hibernate. But then at last spring would come, and as the sun shyly peeked into the cellar, the yeasts would wake up, famished. With springtime vigor they would feast on the residual sugars in the freshly bottled wines. And the bottles deep in the caves of Champagne would start to literally explode.

What was happening? Our hungry yeasts, those magic microbes, those fomenters of fermentation, you see, are also catalysts of carbonation. Along with alcohol, another byproduct of fermentation is carbon dioxide. That same deep magic that incites dough to bubble and rise was trapped in glass, and it wouldn't be contained. The thin glass bottles of the 1600s, fired from wood furnaces rather than the later, hotter coal furnaces, couldn't handle the pressure, and at least half of them would burst.

The workers in those volatile cellars of seventeenth-century Champagne were Benedictine monks, who wore iron masks to protect them from the shards of glass flying around them like bullets. The most famous of these monks was Dom Perignon, cellarmaster at the Benedictine Abbey in Hautvillers, the cradle of Champagne, where he was experimenting with bubbles in underground caves two hundred years before Moët & Chandon immortalized him on a highbrow bottle of vintage Champagne. The effervescent legend persists that Dom Perignon was the first to create sparkling wine, instead of merely hoping for the happy accident of a precocious winter, crying out to his fellow monks at the moment of discovery, "Bros, come quickly, I am drinking the stars!" It's a good story. But it seems rather that one of his later fanboys, Dom Grossard, fabricated that little delight, along with the myth that Dom Perignon was blind, because Grossard didn't understand what a "blind tasting" was. Some of these monks of the Middle Ages were suspect. In reality, an Englishman named Christopher Merrett published a paper in 1662, six years before Dom Perignon worked his first harvest, noting how English wine importers had learned to add sugar or molasses to still wines to produce sparkle.

So Dom Perignon wasn't the bubble inventor of the seventeenth century, but there is evidence he may have been the bubble savior. At the time he assumed cellarmaster duties at his monastery north of Epernay, Champagne bottles were sealed with wooden plugs soaked in olive oil. The seal was inexact, and the best you could hope for was a refreshing spritz in the bottle. Many of the precious sparkles would have slipped past the seal and wafted into the atmosphere. The mist filling the town must have been delightfully fragrant. But the story goes that one afternoon two Spanish monks visited his abbey, carrying water bottles plugged with cork, extracted from the bark of cork trees. The wet cork expanded to fit the bottles and created an airtight seal. Dom tried it on his bottles of wine, and Champagne exploded.

With corks and stronger bottles, Dom and his brothers were able to experiment more with their bottled stars. Soon, they were adding a sugar and wine cocktail to dry wines and sealing them in their caves to ferment a second time, the yeasts in the mixture creating the fine bubbles and briochy flavors of Champagne that now taste to the world like a good party.

When we disembarked at the Reims platform that June morning, Champagne was wearing its characteristic cloak of low clouds and mist, a stark contrast from the electric blue skies that would greet us in Avignon a few days later. Looking out from the train, I was disappointed there were no views of Champagne's vines. I was eager to see the famed Champagne chalk, which sprinkles the dirt between the rows like a light dusting of snow. The southern end of the Champagne region is an extension of the Paris Basin, the mere mention of which compels white wine zealots onto their hands and knees to lick rocks.

The Paris Basin is a vast white seabed composed of the calcium-rich shells and skeletons of ancient crustaceans, mollusks, and mermaids. It dives off the White Cliffs of Dover in southern England down under the English Channel, surfacing on the Alabaster Coast of Normandy and forming a bedrock of limestone in northern France that is called Kimmeridgian soil. Kimmeridgian is the ballroom floor on which three of the world's raciest white wines dance—Chablis to the northeast, Sancerre in the upper Loire Valley, and Champagne. These are wines that are celebrated for their freshness—imagine the sensation of biting into a crunchy green apple—and "minerality," by which wine drinkers mean they taste like rocks. I have been known to enjoy some white rock in my chardonnay.

Given the central role Champagne's wines play in life's frothiest moments, a part of me took the train to Champagne anticipating a place that feels like a never-ending New Year's Eve. This little adventure fell right around my birthday, which I was slowly learning to celebrate with more gusto. Birthdays in my family were not usually big occasions, in part because none of us relished being the center of attention. Most years you would get pancakes in the morning and some gifts in the evening while everyone kept one eye on the Mariners game. When I ask my parents what time of day I was born, they say, "I don't know, right around happy hour, I think." My dad's birthday falls around Christmas, and it seems when he was younger it was overshadowed by the holiday season, so downplaying birthdays became the norm. Christmas is the extravaganza in our family, and your birthday is something we do, too. But I was relearning how to celebrate on this trip, not only to mark occasions but to celebrate my actual life in this body of mine. Champagne seemed like the perfect place to be alive again. I would toast the good day of my birth with a little farmer fizz.

But, as we got our bearings in Reims, instead of New Year's Eve or a blowout birthday, I felt I had stepped into Memorial Day. There is a surprising amount of sobriety in such a bubbly place. This is a part of France that has been torn apart by war, and I think there are old burdens that this region and its people bear. I have tried to describe it to others who haven't been there, but my words seem to fall flat, like Champagne the morning after.

It's as if the somber clouds and heavy air of Champagne's skies are due to more than northern exposure. Perhaps I am projecting, but it feels like they carry memories—memories of loss and grief and fear and war—cast up into the atmosphere by generations now gone but still borne today by her current citizens. There was a quiet reverence to the people I met in Reims, whether in the passionate Champagne tour guides or in the affable server at the pizza restaurant near the cathedral where we ate lunch, their speech marked by the pauses of someone who gets lost remembering a loved one. Through much of the day, especially as we descended into the caves beneath the city, I felt compelled to whisper.

On September 4, 1914, the German army advanced on Reims and occupied her royal cathedral, where twenty-five kings of France had been crowned with the crown of Charlemagne since the thirteenth century. The Germans turned the cathedral into a military hospital, laying down straw pallets on the church floors for injured soldiers. One week later, Allied forces turned back German forces at Epernay, and they abandoned Champagne, for the time being, just as grape harvest would normally begin. The Germans encamped in the hills northeast of Reims, their big guns facing the city, and in one of the most culturally devastating moments in French history, would open fire on the cathedral within days.

It had been an uncharacteristically hot summer. The fruit was ripe, and if harvest was delayed, the grapes would soon wither on the vines. The women and children of Champagne, wives and sons and daughters of *vignerons* now fighting in the Resistance, marched out to the vineyards and, amidst crossfire, harvested the fruit. In the coming years, wine critics would deem the 1914 vintage of Champagne one of the twentieth century's very finest vintages.

Thirty years later, as another world war threatened to annihilate Europe, Winston Churchill rallied his troops: "Remember gentlemen, it's not just France we are fighting for, it's Champagne!"

As we descended into the network of underground tunnels beneath the Taittinger Champagne house, I immediately regretted wearing a short-sleeved shirt. My fellow bubble miners were wearing puffy coats and winter hats, and I must have looked extremely American. I was an extremely cold American, for I had entered a vast limestone refrigerator. In the fourth century, the Romans quarried thousands of tons of the soft limestone underlying Reims for their imperial stonecraft, creating miles of white caves. It was Benedictine monks nine hundred years later who realized the subterranean limestone created the perfect temperature and humidity for a wine cellar. The Taittinger house now owns the caves that once belonged to the thirteenth-century Abbey of Saint-Nicaise. In these labyrinths of limestone under the city, there are millions of Champagne bottles lining the walls and filling every nook, the outsides caked with dust and cobwebs, the insides beading with the classiest of bubbles. If you are lucky enough to become a winemaker in Champagne, you get to be called *chef de cave*, the "chef of the cave."

As the day went on and I tunneled deeper into the history of Reims, I started to feel like this was all too much for one person to bear. It wasn't just the chill of the cellar causing my goosebumps. The millennia-long stories Champagne has to tell, from the Romans to Dom Perignon to the great kings of France to the wars to end all wars—frankly it was enough to make a college history major wet himself. And I haven't even mentioned Joan of Arc.

On the cave wall was a plaque honoring François Taittinger, whom I remembered from a book called *Wine & War* I had read in anticipation of this day. In the first weeks of the German occupation of World War II, something like two million bottles of Champagne were pilfered from the wine caves. To combat this, the French intentionally mislabeled bottles and built fake walls in their cellars in order to divert the Germans from the good stuff. That is what got François Taittinger in trouble.

Each major France wine region was assigned a German *weinfuhrer* who was supposed to expedite wine delivery across the border and to German forces throughout Europe. Otto Klaebisch, a German wine importer, was appointed *weinfuhrer* of Champagne. The sneaky French houses thought they could get away with sending inferior Champagne to the Germans, but unfortunately for them, Otto Klaebisch had a good palate. He summoned François Taittinger to his office. "How dare you send us fizzy ditch water!" he yelled.

Twenty-year-old François retorted, with the same spark of defiance I also saw in the current generation of Champenois that day, "Who cares? It's not as if it's going to be drunk by people who know anything about Champagne!"

François was thrown into jail. A few days later, his older brother arranged a meeting with Otto Klaebisch to plead for his release. The two drank Champagne together over the next couple of hours. Eventually, Otto got blotto and agreed to let François out.

Champagne became a den of French resistance during World War II. Freedom fighters figured out that the Germans would order large quantities of Champagne for the places they expected big military victories. At the end of 1941 the Germans placed a large order for Champagne bottles that would be specially packed and corked for surviving the conditions of a "very hot country." The French resistance notified British intelligence, who thanks to the Champagne underground knew that the Germans were about to start their North Africa offensive in Egypt.

Our tour guide, a diminutive, earnest, and somewhat bored silver-haired woman, walked us through the basics of Champagne making, with the guarded enthusiasm of someone who has given a speech ten thousand times. Every corner hosted A-frame racks with Champagne bottles stuck in neck-down, like medieval pillories for guilty wine bottles. The racks are used for a process called *riddling*, which involves painstakingly spinning and tilting each bottle downwards, over a period of weeks, so that all the yeasty sediment gathers in the neck of the bottle before it is disgorged. There are people who make an entire career of riddling bottles of Champagne in these cold caves. If you are the best of the best at your craft, after spending years riddling deep under the ground you attain the title "Master Riddler," until a tricksy hobbit comes along and steals your ring.

Our tour guide pointed out the names and years that had been scrawled into the walls, cave paintings of the early twentieth century. In World War I, as the Germans rained shells on Reims and her cathedral, the remaining residents took refuge underground. Fifteen hundred people lived and slept and went to school and attended church in these caves, sitting on cases of Champagne as makeshift pews. On the ceiling above I could see the smoke stains from the fires they burned during the winter. I was shivering in June, and I can't imagine how bitterly cold January in Champagne must be a hundred feet below the ground.

Victory in Champagne truly was a celebration hard won. Next time you open a bottle, know that, in two world wars, people dodged bullets in vineyards, watched their cultural treasures collapse, and lived in frigid basements of stone in order to ensure that pleasing *pop!* would still sound today. Those stars stored up in those bottles in the darkness helped keep hope alive. The greatest celebrations come from the hardest fights, don't you think?

In the spring of 1945, Supreme Allied Commander General Eisenhower relocated his headquarters from Versailles. On May 8, VE Day, the Germans gave their unconditional surrender at his new headquarters in Reims.

❧

As I approached the eight-hundred-year-old Reims Cathedral, another course on this Gothic church binge, I wondered if this one would be any different. There were still too many eyes watching me, from the over twenty-three hundred statues populating the cathedral, but some of them seemed a little happier. The angels at the entrance were actually smiling, like well-caffeinated church greeters. One of these cheerful angels is named "The Smile of Reims," made famous during World War I when the Germans wiped the smile right off her face—by decapitating her. Fortunately, her head was saved and re-attached after the war, and her trials did not alter her lovely smile.

There was a small crowd gathered at the stained-glass windows created by modern artist Marc Chagall, and the typical group of uplookers, occasionally bumping into each other, straining their necks to take in the vaulted arches reaching for the heavens. Then there were the few people seated in the nave or kneeling quietly at the altar, there to meditate or light a candle, while all the tourists looked at them like they were relics in a medieval church museum. Clearly this is no place for prayer, you guys.

I was on a mission, but I did take note of the plaque in the stone of the central aisle leading up to the altar, dedicated to the first king who was crowned here in Reims. Clovis was a fifth-century ruler of Frankish tribes skirmishing with other Germanic clans for control of formerly Roman Gaul. He was a pagan king, supposedly descended on his grandfather's side from a sea god, but he made a Constantinian sort of bargain: if God would help him defeat the powerful Alemanni tribe, he would become a Christian. The Alemanni king was killed in battle, and his troops surrendered. So in the year of our Lord 496, in a basilica on the location of the current Reims Cathedral, he was christened Clovis, King of the Franks, with his family at his side: his proud son, the Prince of Brats, and his loving wife, the Queenie of Weenie.

Notre-Dame de Reims is the cathedral of kings, hence Champagne is sometimes called the wine of kings. The town would swell from its population of fifty thousand to almost two hundred thousand during coronations, and I bet the price of wine inflated almost as much, especially when Charles VII was crowned. Joan of Arc, that pious, mystical, cropped-hair, badass knight that she was, stood by his side on July 18, 1429, shortly after spearheading the victory at Orléans and winning the Hundred Years War for France.

That was all quite thrilling, but I was on a hunt for the Champagne window. In the 1950s, commissioned by the great Champagne houses, Jacques Simon installed a series of stained-glass windows weaving the history of Champagne into his reflections on the Eucharist. I knew it adorned the south transept, but first I had to figure out what a transept was. It turns out that many Gothic churches were designed in the shape of a cross, and the transepts were the arms of the cross. So finally in the south arm, where Jesus' left hand would have been nailed, I found a piece of cathedral art that didn't creep me out.

The Champagne window is a trinity of colored glass, telling a three-thousand-year story in three panels reading from left to right. The modern labors of the Champagne wine industry are interwoven with an ancient story of exile and homecoming, death and new life. The churches of the many villages of Champagne wrap around the panels, with each village name written below its church.

So many of my heroes are gathered here. In the left panel you find Saint Vincent supervising the workers in the vineyard. It's a little mysterious how Saint Vincent became the patron saint of winemakers, but the cleverest theory is that in French pronunciation, the name Vincent sounds a lot like *vin-sang*, wine blood, or *vigne-sang*, the blood of the vine. The "blood of the vine" is another name for the sap that drips from the cuts after winter pruning and just before bud break. Saint Vincent's Feast Day falls on January 22 each year, historically the day European wineries have marked as the first day winter pruning is allowed.

In the center panel, Dom Perignon, who not only solved how to keep bubbles in Champagne bottles but taught a rigorous pruning and harvest regimen in the vineyards that elevated the quality of Champagne to new heights, keeps a watchful eye on the work in the cellar. In the right panel looms John the Baptist, patron saint to cellar workers after being thrown into the dungeon by King Herod, surrounded by monks riddling in underground caves and others stripping the bark off trees to make cork.

As your gaze moves upward, you realize the plot unfolding at the crests of the panels is what drives all the activity of the rest. In the top of the left panel, two Old Testament spies return from Canaan bearing a pole on their shoulders with a gigantic grape cluster hanging from the middle, the foretaste and symbol of the richness of the Promised Land. The place where those grapes grow would come to be called the Valley of the Grape Cluster. The Promised Land may have been a land of milk and honey, but no land is fully promising without the prospect of great wine. For the ancient Hebrews wine was a central symbol of God's blessing and inheritance, and of a community flourishing in the good life. For Christians, the pole and the suspended grape cluster became over time a symbol of Jesus hanging on the cross.

The story moves to the right, where in the middle panel, you see two angels holding a very similar looking pole, only they appear to be driving the grape cluster down into a wine press, with a third angel catching the wine in a chalice below. This theme in medieval church art is called the divine winepress, where Jesus is depicted as grapes crushed in a press, his sacrificial blood poured out as wine into a holy grail. The story doesn't end there. In the third panel stands Jesus and his mother Mary at the scene of his first miracle: the wedding of Cana, as told in the Gospel of John. There, when the wine runs out, Jesus turns water into wine, a sanguine symbol of purification and transformation, of life abundant, and of keeping the party going. To Messiah and Savior we add the title of winemaker. He creates the new vintage for a new feast, the foretaste of a world recreated, poured generously into every empty cup.

I have always appreciated that Jesus not only restocked the bar, but he brought the best wine to the party, just like I do when invited to a party, and then drink it myself. I have found myself reflecting on the Champagne window often since my chilly adventure there. What continues to strike me is how the artist ties together depictions of Champagne's villages with the Savior and the saints, the angels and the harvesters, all toiling together in the work of wine. Men and women present their work in the vineyards and cellars as sacrificial offerings performed in holy presence. I think of how the elements of the Eucharist invite human artistry and labor. We don't offer flour and grapes at the altar. We offer bread and wine. Wine is a gift of God but requires human participation and creativity, a most delightful collaboration between heaven and earth. So many ordinary people through the ages have peered through a glass of wine and seen the face of God. Here is a theology you can taste, a grace you can drink, a love that warms you from the inside.

When you consider leaving ministry there are people who wonder if you are giving up the faith. Sometimes I wondered that myself. Once you have flashed the unlaminated Reverend card it can be surprisingly hard to identify yourself in any other way. After wearing a robe behind a pulpit, donning civilian clothes and stepping off the stage can feel quite vulnerable, even ordinary. Can I find an expression of faith that doesn't involve standing up before others as a Holy Man? I'm not sure how well that look suited me anyway. But my pilgrimage to Champagne convinced me that the work of wine is equally the work of God. From age to age, wine has been one of the grandest expressions of God's love for us. Whatever path I chose, I wouldn't have to choose between faith and wine.

*Five*

# A SENSE OF PLACE

Debates about abstaining from wine in the church are so Protestant. The deeper I went into the winemaking villages of the French heartland, the more I saw that in the historically Catholic old-world there is no separation of church and wine estate. High crosses guard legendary vineyards. Chateaus are named after crumbling prayer chapels on their properties and the orders of monks who prayed in them for centuries. Wherever the Catholic Church goes, wine follows. It compelled a master sommelier I later took a class from, who had no affiliation with organized religion, to proclaim, "Thank God for the Catholic Church!"

There are aspects of Catholic spirituality that are not for me, but wine drinking as a spiritual practice is one I can definitely get behind. Truly, the moment Jesus of Nazareth took a cup of wine and said, "This is my blood," ensured theology's long association with wine and guaranteed that the cup, the vine, and the labor in the vineyard would all take on sacramental meaning, culminating in the taste of heaven's blood in a glass.

The one thing I remember from the political philosophy course I took in college, aside from my professor's habit of propping his leg up on the table in a way that resembled a flamingo, was that a noble land-owner in the Middle Ages would regularly send one of his sons to the monastery to join the clergy. Often another son would be sent to become a lawyer, so you needed a priest in the family to balance the scales of good and evil in the universe. This practice was a way of invoking divine favor for your fiefdom, but also a way of accessing the resources of the monasteries, which were both the premier educational centers of the medieval world and significant landholders in their own right.

I thought this was to be my role in life. I was the guy who was sent off to seminary to stir up some grace and mercy for the people, to ascend the winding staircase into the mind of God, to think the big thoughts from my perch with the bird's-eye view so that others on the ground didn't have to. They could go about their quotidian business while I dealt with eternity.

The problem with this analogy is that the brothers in the monastery a thousand years ago would say their prayers and copy their manuscripts and preach their homilies, but then they would go outside and move dirt and plant seeds and prune back vines. Medieval monks were farmers, and the monastic life involved not only spiritual hearts but dirty hands. If you wanted to be an initiate you had to submit to six services a day and a lot of calluses.

Bernard of Clairvaux considered the monastic labor in the vineyards to be training for heaven. He liked to speak of the human soul as a vineyard, which ought to be "planted in faith, its roots grounded in love, dug in with the hoe of discipline, fertilized with penitential tears, watered with the words of preachers, and so [the soul] abounds with the wine that inspires joy rather than debauchery. . . . This is the wine that gladdens man's heart, the wine that even the angels drink with gladness." He gently discouraged his brothers from drinking actual wine. Most ignored that suggestion.

After the fall of the Roman Empire, the church became the steward of Europe's grapevines, and the monks were the ones who tended them. Vineyards and the wine squeezed out of their fruit were a major economic engine for monasteries, as well as what filled the sacramental cup. The rockstar winemakers of the Middle Ages preferred singing the Psalms. In Burgundy, the Cistercian monks cultivated extensive acreage of the world's greatest pinot noir. The Clos du Vougeot was the jewel of their vineyard holdings: 125 acres of gifted land accumulated over two hundred years. It was an agreeable arrangement for all: nobles would bequeath land and vineyards to the monasteries in exchange for prayer and pinot. The monks would enclose the best vineyards with a low stone wall, called a *clos*. The Clos du Vougeot was a cloistered vineyard, a secret and contemplative garden of creation's most tantalizing gifts.

More and more on this trip, I was coming to believe that the places vines grow are hallowed ground, embedded with memories of men and women working the fields and cellars as an expression of their devotion. As I did, I felt I needed to redefine my role here. I was more than a boozy tourist on a French wine adventure. I was an accidental pilgrim. A wine pilgrim on an unintended spiritual journey. I had devoted so much time to invoking a world beyond. Now I was encountering people who spend their lives with their eyes to the ground. What if the best way to reach heaven is to plunge your hands into the dirt?

---

I woke up with a sore throat and a stuffy nose. This was our day for touring the Côtes du Rhône, the day I had been dreaming about since booking our plane tickets a year back. This was the raison d'être for the entire trip. And I had a cold. Your sense of smell is responsible for 85 percent of your sensory experience of wine. Depending on which scientists you talk to, the human olfactory system can detect anywhere between ten thousand and one trillion different aromas. Our sense of taste can detect exactly five things. If you can't smell, conversations about wine are brief.

Our tour guide was scheduled to pick us up from our Avignon hotel in an hour. I rushed to the nearest pharmacy on a hunt for a decongestant that would make a wild boar stop snorting. In the United States, pharmacies smell like a musty basement, with just a hint of death. In this Avignon pharmacy, even my laboring nose could detect fragrances of lavender, wrapped around a lively core of sunshine and hope. It was Sunday brunch served al fresco, where the napkins are dryer sheets. I desperately pointed at my nose to the clerk, who clearly had encountered crazy American wine tourists before, and she handed me a magic box. Never in my life have I encountered such a decongestant. You can be assured that the nasally pitch of some French speakers is, in fact, because they are judging you, not because they are stuffed up. Not only did this wondrous pill clear up my sinuses and remove my sore throat, but I kid you not, my symptoms never came back. If this wine thing doesn't work out for me, I am going to sell French cold medicine door to door. I still have a few of those pills stashed away, if you want to make me an offer.

Our tour guide, Antoine, was an English expat raised by a French mother, who told us a familiar story. A few years back, he and his wife relocated from the misty high-rises of London to the country life in the south of France. When I asked if he followed in Peter Mayle's footsteps, he scoffed loudly, which I took as confirmation. Peter wrote *A Year in Provence* after cashing out of London and moving with his wife to the Luberon, an hour or so east of Avignon. His tales of Provençal life were so popular in the United Kingdom, with their underground truffle negotiations and run-ins with quirky French yokels, all oozing with garlic and olive oil and hearty red wine, that eventually Peter fled across the ocean to Long Island, dodging all the English on holiday who would show up at his door uninvited, expecting lunch.

I am drawn to these kinds of stories. What wild blend of romance and daring is required to uproot yourself from what you know and transplant your life into new soil? I have always carried a certain restlessness, but that energy usually circles inside me and doesn't make its way to my feet. I found myself jealous of people like Antoine and Peter Mayle and afraid that I didn't have their courage or their tolerance for change. Security and predictability are surprisingly seductive forces. Inertia can be quite cozy. It's one thing when a person moves for a new job or relationship; they did it because they visited a new place and unwittingly stumbled upon home. I was getting very good at talking about leaving the world and life I knew. But would I go? And where?

❦

The hillsides—*côtes* means "slopes"—of the Southern Rhone toss and turn in irregular patterns, with gentle undulations on the valley floor overseen by melodramatic foothills crowned with forests of scrub oak. Posted above all of it are sentinels of jagged granite outcroppings that resemble sharp teeth or shark fins. The villages here are bunkered into the hillsides, constructed of stone weathered over centuries to varying shades of alabasters and ambers and salmons, with roofs of interlocking half cylinders of fired clay. Medieval village architecture strikes just the right balance between welcome and woe. It's a timeless design aesthetic that says friends may enter and drink freely; foes pay dearly at the door.

If you were a Roman legionnaire in the second century BCE, the most uncivilized element of the Barbarians to the north—properly known as the Gauls—was their shortage of good wine. Though the Gauls may have made a little wine and the wine world owes them a hearty thank you for inventing the oak barrel, the Gallic beverage of choice was *cervoise*, a brew made of fermented barley. To the Romans, they were beer-barians.

But wine was a daily necessity for homesick Roman soldiers. The Greeks were the first to plant vines in Provence, way back in the sixth century BCE in the southern port town of Marseille, but when the Romans conquered the known world, one of the flags they planted on their freshly annexed soil was a grapevine. I suspect that when Julius Caesar triumphed over Gaul in 52 BCE, his legions toasted him with lusty pours of precocious French wine.

The Romans moved out of the south of France a few centuries later, but like a bad roommate, they left all their old furniture. The name Provence comes from the Latin *nostra provincia*, "our province," and you can spend an entire vacation surveying the remarkably preserved ruins of the once-Roman province: gladiatorial arenas and amphitheaters, bridges, temples, aqueducts, and other marvels of arch and stone. But their greatest legacy in France may be the sticks they stuck into the ground. In my imagination the bloodthirsty garrison of armored soldiers was trailed by a skilled and sensitive gardener, whom they treated like the kicker on a football team. Let's call him Ampelos, after the Greek myth. The old story goes that Dionysus loved a boy named Ampelos, who was gored to death by a raging bull. In his grief, the wine god transformed Ampelos's body into the first grapevine. Wine has always been a means for coping with grief. Now *ampelos* is the Greek word for vine.

A quiver of vine cuttings strapped on his back, from his garden in Pompeii and perhaps some native vines he picked up along the way, our Roman gardener Ampelos kneeled down on newly conquered slopes, still dripping with Gallic blood, and planted a vine every few feet. He knew a gardening secret that would shape French vineyards for the next two thousand years. As they marched north, he planted vines on the south-facing slopes of the hills because he knew they would receive more sun exposure, and their fruit would be riper. He also knew that when you plant in the middle of the slopes, the chill evening air and fog slips down the hill to the valley, minimizing frost on the vines above. This would be particularly important when Ampelos's grandson started planting in northern climates like Burgundy a century later, where slopes facing southeast greet the morning sun, rousting their vines out of bed early.

A thousand years later, Burgundian monks concluded that Ampelos knew exactly what he was doing. The Benedictine and especially the Cistercian brothers may have been the original wine geeks. The Cistercians, taking their cue from Bernard of Clairvaux, placed a greater value on the humble training of manual labor, and on the science and spirituality of paying attention. They studied the minute details of the vineyards in their care and recorded their observations on the growth pattern of each vine and the character of the resulting wines from each plot with a ravenous zeal only found in celibate scientists.

The monks noticed that the vines on the valley floor, planted in fertile and damp soils, produced wines of less personality than the vines planted in the shallower and drier soils of the slopes above. The hillside vines ripened earlier and produced more luscious fruit. To demarcate all the differences they observed, they built paths and walls around individual vineyards, which were sometimes just a few acres in size, recognizing the uniqueness and personality of each section. They named each one like a patriarch naming a newborn child, to bless it and to shape its destiny.

It was a meticulous, even religious attentiveness that later gave birth to the "cru" system of Burgundy, which classifies vineyards, or "growths," with a four-tiered method that seems straight out of the feudal system that supported medieval monastic labors. At the top of the pyramid, in the position of the king in the feudal world, is grand cru. These are vineyards of the rarest and highest order, most of which are the swaths that Ampelos first planted—the middle of the hills that face the equator and the rising sun. Premier cru is just below, the nobles and priests in the feudal hierarchy. Premier cru vines usually sit on slopes in slightly less optimal positions than grand crus. Often, they are bands of vines just above the grand crus on the slopes and just below—the crusty bread of the pinot noir sandwich. Village-level vineyards come next as the pyramid broadens, holding the place of knights in the medieval world. Wines from vines planted on the valley floor around a village will feature the village name on the label. Finally, at the wide base of the pyramid are regional wines, which will simply bear the name Bourgogne on the label, made from fruit grown throughout the region as a whole. These are wines that correspond to the peasants in the feudal system—table wines for the tables of the common people.

The Cistercians didn't always know why such differences existed in the qualities of individual vineyard plots, but there seemed to be something about the struggle to survive which made for beauty, complexity, and richness. An ordinary vine will grow almost anywhere if it has the sunlight and water it needs. It will sprout foliage that will store up sugars in its fruit, and at the right time birds will swoop in to nab the sweet grapes and sow the seeds elsewhere. The life cycle of the vine will go on. But there are only a few special places where a grapevine will truly flourish and produce flavors so sultry that someone would change their life to be near it, and relentlessly prevent birds from playing the role nature gave them. The ideal conditions of those places involve abundance and growth, but not ease. There will be struggle. When vines have easy access to water and nutrients, they become complacent and produce too much foliage and thin, watery fruit. When they are deprived, their roots will reach deeper into the earth to get what they need, and they will produce less, but better, fruit.

"The vines need to suffer in order to produce grapes of character," people in the wine industry like to say, without knowing they are quoting Scripture. Not long after Ampelos planted on rocky, south-facing slopes, the apostle Paul wrote to the Romans, "We also boast in our sufferings, knowing that suffering produces endurance, and endurance produces character, and character produces hope" (Romans 5:3-4 NRSV).

Antoine picked us up inside the walls of Avignon that morning in a car that could be generously described as efficient. I was quickly learning that if your standard for wine tasting is Napa Valley, a wine tour in the French countryside may present some culture shock. Here in the southern Rhone we would not ascend the hillsides to the modern chateau in an aerial tram, or cross drawbridges over moats designed to protect sparkling wine castles from marauding beer-barians. In the rental car lineup, our wine touring vehicle would be listed in the "compact" category and would likely come with a trunk full of clowns. But we were off, pilgrims in pursuit of wine, beauty, and the wisdom of old places, poured into a crappy French car.

The air was heavy and humid, with the impending threat of rain. I was a little disappointed that the mistral, the infamous wind of Provence, was quiet. I was the only one. The mistral—"master" in French—is a merciless savage of a wind that builds rage in the Alps and then charges down the narrow river valley of the Northern Rhone, finally unleashing all its unprovoked fury on the mild-mannered citizenry of Provence, uprooting trees, lifting roofs off houses. It is enough, as Peter Mayle says, to "blow the ears off a donkey."

His mother's French heritage aside, Antoine was classically English, at least in accordance with my limited experience: tall and wry, educated, up with current events, more conversant in American politics than most Americans, always down for a stilted dinner party or will reading. He promised us an experience that would take us off the thoroughfares onto the back roads of the Côtes du Rhône. I wanted the secret knowledge, to dig up the treasures buried in the wine hinterland. I wanted to taste wines out of barrels that hid behind unmarked cellar doors with passwords that changed daily. I wanted to creep into dank caves to meet wine hermits that hadn't been seen in town in thirty years. I wanted to forage for the most agritouristic, natural, local-grower, minimal-intervention, ground-to-glass, wine-hipster shit we could find.

Turns out those experiences are the norm in this part of France. With few exceptions, there is little show here. We didn't visit glitzy tasting rooms with winery names splashed on t-shirts and branded into the cows outside. We weren't hostage to vanity projects or slick salesmanship. No one brandished their wine ratings or gold medals at us. Most of the wines were surprisingly inexpensive. We didn't meet celebrity winemakers because there aren't any.

We slinked into the back door of a barn and tasted wine among enormous cement tanks filled with grenache. I wasn't clear on whether Antoine actually knew the people who owned that winery, or if they knew we were there. We drove to a little hamlet and tasted at a wine cooperative that represented several small producers in the area. We lounged in a circle courtyard skirted by lavender bushes and olive trees, with a fountain dribbling at the center, drinking and eating cheese with the family who had owned the estate for seven generations, their children and dogs scampering around us.

This trip happened before I became a serious student of wine, but I am still bewildered that I didn't pay much attention to the names of the estates we visited. I only remember one: Domaine la Garrigue in the village of Vacqueyras. I remember the name because I asked Antoine what *garrigue* meant, and he explained it is the spicy underbrush of the Mediterranean hillsides. The exotic fragrances spread by the mistral are emitted by the briary rosemary, thyme, and juniper bushes growing wild. Together they make up the *herbes de Provence* that crust the meats and season the olive oils at every local table. But garrigue and herbes de Provence also regularly appear in descriptions of Rhone wines, and it is uncanny how the local wines seem able to absorb the aromas in the air. The oils of olives and lavender and sagebrush must massage the skins of the suggestible grapes ripening nearby.

Even though I desperately wish I recorded where we stopped that day, at the same time what captivated me about tasting wine in the French countryside is that no one I met seemed particularly concerned that I remember the name of their estate anyway. They were thoroughly nonchalant about whether I bought any of their wine, or even liked any of their wine. Though, of course, I did. Our day together became far less a rural shopping spree and more a glimpse into the domestic lives of farmers descended from farmers descended from farmers. They sat down to lunch with their families that afternoon and some Americans showed up. So they fetched a few more wine glasses.

In France, wineries don't have winemakers; they have *vignerons*—wine *growers*. I am always happy to be reminded that wine is farming, and that you can't make good wine unless you have good farming. Wine starts in the dirt. Behind the bottles on the wall of every uptown wine bar are a thousand farmers in dirty jeans pruning and disking and harvesting. It's a glorified farming no doubt, especially when your best crops can sell for a hundred dollars or more in the international marketplace, but it's farming nonetheless. I loved that in this part of the world, wineries are old barns and tasting rooms are well-loved living rooms in family farmhouses. We crossed paths that day with farming families who have had the dirt of their land under their fingernails for so many generations that it must be part of their DNA by now.

❦

My encounters with these French families on their land was another wistful reminder that a recurring theme in my own life is distance. Distance in all its metrics: social distance, geographical distance, emotional distance. It's not out of malice, just detachment. When I was young, my cousins Sam and Bill were my best friends, and we ate almost every Sunday dinner together at my aunt and uncle's little farm forty-five minutes away. We hunted for Easter eggs my Uncle Fred would hide in tailpipes or in branches ten feet above our heads that no kid could ever find. My dad would set the camera on a tripod in front of the Christmas tree and yell "Go!" when he started the timer. We would all race from down the hallway to our preassigned spots by the tree, falling all over each other and laughing ourselves out of breath.

My cousins moved away when I was a teenager. I haven't talked to them much since. I honestly don't know why. Sometimes I think I inherited detachment, like some people inherit freckles or a weak chin. Which I also inherited. Most members of my family tend to keep a safe distance from people, including each other. I live a thousand miles away from the closest of them. We prize self-sufficiency. We don't reveal much, and we don't ask much. Most of my relationships tend to drift away when I am looking somewhere else. If I finally look back, they are usually too far away. I don't keep up with any childhood friends and am always surprised when I learn that other people do. In college, I usually declined the invitation to go camping with my friends with some half-baked excuse. They would offer up the first toast over the campfire: "To McHugh, the man who wouldn't be here even if he could!"

I have often thought if someone were to write me into a story, they wouldn't cast me as the hero or the antagonist, and certainly not the romantic lead. I would be the narrator. Not just because I speak in the sonorous tones of an after-dark, jazz-station DJ. I am the narrator because I stand at a distance, and that is where the wide-angle view is. I may see more than those close to the center, but the price I pay for wallflower insight is the opportunity for wholehearted connection. Big ideas don't hug you back. That's why all the personality tests I took when I was younger seemed to say, in unison: go buy a big leather chair, a crockpot, a herd of books, and a pile of cats because you are gonna die alone, bro. You are love's casual bystander.

<hr/>

These families of French winegrowers we met that day seemed as deeply rooted in their soil as their vines. Granted, I only had a glimpse of one afternoon, but they seemed to me a profoundly grounded people, fitting of humans who work ground that has nurtured grapevines for two thousand years. There were memories stored up in their soil. There was a bond I could feel: a bond to their land, to their vines, to their family, to their ancestors. They were attached. They were living close.

I was drawn to them but disoriented. It's curious how something so terrestrial can seem so alien. It felt like stepping off the end of a moving walkway at the airport: the jolt you experience when you hit solid ground. The gathering table for generations of each family was a particular location on this earth. It is only one allotment of solid ground in a larger, interconnected place, but each plot of dirt has a unique story that tells of the drama of nature and humanity colliding in this very spot. This is *terroir*. Terroir is the story that each place tells. A wine born in that place is its scribe, trying to bottle the drama before it escapes.

The wine books will tell you that terroir is the total natural growing environment, the habitat, of a particular plot of vines. This encompasses the realities above—sunlight hours, temperature variation, weather patterns, wind intensity—and the realities below—soil, slope angle and orientation, elevation, water access and drainage, even the microbes teeming underground. And there is the human factor: the collective knowledge, memory, reverence, and hard labor of farmers working the land and passing on tradition. Terroir captures both the where of a place and the who. All of it works together to make a vine's home.

Terroir is not exactly a grape's happy place, for it may not bring ease or luxury. But it provides the nexus of relationships that make for a good home: the ancient alchemy of air, water, earth, and toil stirring up life and fruit, growth, struggle, and flourishing. As the diligently tended vines reach up, out, and down they find themselves more and more at home.

The true believers in terroir, spiritual descendants of the monks of Burgundy, say that wine from each little piece of land has a distinctive character that separates it from wine grown on every other little piece of land on the planet, including the adjacent plot. Just like children raised in different homes by different families, wines from different terroirs have unique traits and personalities. Grand crus and premier crus may be next-door neighbors, but their children turn out differently. Wine is the expression of a particular place, giving voice to the distinctive terroir in which it was raised. The more specific the place of origin, the more clarion the call of each wine will be. This is why a bottle of wine from a particular vineyard is more prized, and expensive, than a wine from a broad region, which will collect fruit from all over and have a more muffled voice. You can buy a bottle labeled Vin de Bourgogne for a song, but a bottle labeled La Tâche Grand Cru for Beethoven's piano.

Wine drinkers revel in wines that carry a "sense of place," by which they mean a wine that expresses the characteristics of a distinctive place, the liquid signature of a particular vineyard or region. In the southern Rhone, for example, a wine from the village of Gigondas has a unique profile that will differentiate it from a wine from Vacqueyras, a village just three miles away, even when the grape varieties are identical. A skilled and practiced taster is able to identify the villages in a blind tasting because places smell and taste different. Winemakers in this school believe their role is to display or reveal the uniqueness of each individual place rather than dressing it up or covering it over.

Allow me to clue you into a conversation that you probably didn't want to know about. If the internet has taught us nothing else, and it hasn't, it's that in every corner of the globe, or social media, there is an impassioned group of people who are fiercely debating a topic that no one else in the world gives a bag of monkeys about. In the wine industry that topic is terroir, and every day factions are gathering and clashing over it. Lob *terroir* into a table of wine geeks and it lands like a word grenade. Within moments the table will be overturned, and the geologists and the sommeliers will be challenging each other to duels at happy hour with weapons made of gunflint.

The debate pivots over whether you can actually taste the soil in a wine. Can the roots of a vine metabolize the minerals in the soil, absorb them into its growth cycle, and deposit those minerals into its fruit? Can I, for example, taste the chalk in a flute of Champagne, or the slate in a Riesling from Germany's Mosel Valley? The somms say, "I can taste the dirt"; the geologists say, "You're drunk, that's scientifically impossible." The sommeliers retort, "You're too sober, my palate is honed like a barbershop straight razor, and the science isn't that conclusive anyway."

That debate will rage like a delirium in a decanter until everyone blacks out. Personally, I am enchanted by the idea that a glass of wine is a portal to a place you may have never been, and that to imbibe is to participate in the life of a land and nearby village, and maybe even taste the local dirt. To love wine is to love place: the place where the grapes are grown, the place where the wine is made, and the place where you drink the wine, which includes who you drink it with.

One writer said that the experience of terroir in wine is the sense of "somewhereness." This wine in my glass comes from a particular somewhere, and that somewhere shapes what it is and my experience of it. It's so easy to buy a bottle with a pretty label and drink it on a Tuesday afternoon, never considering where it comes from, or who made it. But historically a bottle of wine has been the result of a collaboration between a community of people and the common ground they share. Terroir says we are here, not there, and where we are matters.

Spending a slow afternoon with French farmers and drinking the wine that flowed through their veins, I felt terroir as connection, about union with a land and a people. These were humans who had their own sense of place, and there, they had found home.

<hr />

The terroir conversation can get blustery, but I like to think of terroir as the story of home. Grapevines seem to have an easier time discovering home than I do. Sometimes my longing to find home feels antiquated, but also undeniable. Is my quest for home a matter of finding the right geographical location on this earth, the X marks the spot of my particular somewhere? Maybe, but it must be more than that. Home has to be more than a location or a roof suspended over a piece of dirt. Much of the experience of home may be below the surface. I think it describes a web of attachments that offers us identity, belonging, growth, and love. We may occupy a place, but place also shapes and changes us. To a significant degree, where you are, and who you are with, is who you are.

Is there a life out there where I could flourish and not just survive? Like grapevines, humans are survivors, and we can exist anywhere given a few basic needs. We will go on. We can adapt to almost anything, even adjust to spending most of our waking hours in the middle of the night. But my growing desire for a life of thriving, of abundance, was becoming impossible to ignore. I felt like a vine planted in the wrong place. Gardeners say that the right plant in the wrong place is a weed. Weeds will still grow and seed and keep on. But no one will say a weed has a sense of place. There is no grand cru for dandelion wine.

Surrounded by these people who had such a sense of place, I felt my own absence of place. Some sort of primal homesickness was awakening in me. I didn't want to keep my distance any longer. I wanted to come closer. I wanted to get my hands dirty.

*Six*

# BLOOD FROM A STONE

Remember the time you got so epically, spectacularly drunk that Michelangelo decided to immortalize it on the ceiling of the Sistine Chapel? Noah does. Or maybe he doesn't.

As the story goes, after the great floodwaters receded and he disembarked his ark, the seafaring Noah went three sheets to the wind and shed himself of the burden of all his clothes. In Noah's defense, he had just watched the entire earth and almost all its inhabitants swallowed up in a tsunami of wrath, and, worse, he had sheltered in place with his family for almost a year. Things were bound to get weird. Noah decided to settle into his tent for a good, early postdiluvian drunk, and later that night his sons found him, sloshy and pantless, with everything hanging out for the new world to see. He was only proving my long-held theory that the best restraint against drunkenness is not a moral code or a health warning, it's the stupid shit you say and do when you are drunk. In Noah's case, his bender landed him on a ceiling panel not far from *The Creation of Adam.* At least five million people visit it annually.

Drunk nights aside, the name Noah means "rest" or "comfort," and I have to think that some of the comfort he served renewed humanity came in the form of wine. The story tells us that the first thing this "man of the soil" did after setting foot on dry land again was plant grapevines. Noah was in the mountains of Ararat, in eastern Turkey, just south of the Caucasus Mountains where the earliest evidence of ancient winemaking has been discovered. In the first symbolic act of new creation, with the primeval waters of chaos held at bay and the seasonal rhythms back in step, Noah began the slow work of cultivating vines and making wine. This is true regenerative agriculture. Life had begun again, and wine was the promise of a better world. Wine was proof that heaven and earth were at peace.

The story of wine has always been a resurrection story. It still seems to me a miracle that humans can transform clusters of grapes on the short road to rot or raisin into a liquid that can endure, even improve, for years and years. If you farm tomatoes or asparagus or mushrooms, as delicious and perfect as they are, Mother Nature serves them up in just one form, and their life span is brief. If you farm grapes and let them ferment, you play host to a transformation. The flesh of the grape decays, but the soul of the wine lives on.

Because grapevines are perennial and deciduous plants, their life cycle became attached to ancient rituals of life, death, and rebirth. Cultivated vines are also hermaphroditic, meaning they have both male and female parts, and they don't need bees to pollinate, just a gentle breeze. In the springtime when their green shoots and flowers spontaneously erupted out of fields of dead sticks, it was nothing short of resurrection.

For the Egyptians, red wine was linked with the red floodwaters of the Nile that each spring would burst its banks—the river turning a rusty red by the sediment it carried—and bring rebirth and fertility to the land. Wine was a symbol of new life and of immortality. The ancient wine gods—whether Osiris of the Egyptians, Dionysus of the Greeks, or Bacchus of the Romans—all had origin stories involving resurrection, and over time they became not only gods of fertility and wine but also guardians of the afterlife.

Dionysus was the son of Olympic overlord Zeus and Semele, human princess of Thebes. On learning of their tryst, a jealously enraged Hera tricked Semele into looking on Zeus's true divine form, which killed her. But Zeus saved Dionysus from Semele's dying womb and sewed him into his thigh. Dionysus was the god who cheated death, hatched out of the thunder god's leg.

In Greek practice, wine became associated with the blood of Dionysus, just as for the Egyptians it was the blood of Osiris, their own god who came back to life. When the Greeks drank wine in their symposia and religious rituals, they believed they were drinking the god. Every second winter a rowdy and rapturous group of priestesses would take the pilgrim route to the shrine at the Oracle of Delphi, where they would engage in ecstatic ritual and dance, inspired by a few hearty pours of the god's blood and probably not a few magic shrooms. They would entreat Dionysus to rise again from the dead and usher in the resurrection of springtime renewal. The Romans held similarly spirited festivals called Bacchanalias. They danced for all the earth, together waiting for the wooly buds to emerge once again and the cycle of nature to be reborn, the annual triumph of life over death.

One of the earliest legends about the discovery of wine involves an ailing princess in the harem of Jamshid, ancient king of Persia. King Jamshid liked to snack on grapes, and his servants stored them in tightly sealed jars so he could eat them year round. But one of the jars of royal grapes had been marked poison, because upon unsealing it, the king's kitchen staff discovered the grapes had been broken and the juice spilled, filling the air with a strange, heady waft. Meanwhile, an unnamed member of his harem had lost favor with the king, and, seemingly as a result, suffered from terrible migraines. The exiled princess found the poisonous jar and, in her despair, drank it to end her life. She fell into a long sleep. When she awoke, her headache was cured! She told her story to King Jamshid, who received her back into his harem, and he ordered more grapes crushed to create more of this elixir. For the princess, the king, and their ancient courts, wine was medicine and it was magic, seemingly created by forces from beyond for healing, life, and joy.

My favorite theory about the birth of the Neolithic age, and we all have one, is that wine was one of the main reasons nomadic tribes decided to settle. They sampled the fruit and young wines of wild grapevines for a few intoxicating weeks each autumn, and that was enough to make a weary Mesolithic wanderer stop in his tracks and start cultivating grapevines. If this is true, and a few giddy paleontologists seem to think so, wine was the catalyst for the dawn of agriculture, and of civilization itself. From the earliest times, wine has gathered people together and made them feel at home. Wine creates a sense of place.

This brings us back to terroir, that elegant and elitist French understanding of place which, by the way, the French pronounce *tewah*, but most English speakers say *terwahr*; we will grant the French one fashionably unpronounced letter, but three silent *Rs* in a two-syllable word is just stupid. Have you ever wondered why French wines aren't labeled by varietal? Pinot noir, merlot, sauvignon blanc, syrah, or any other varietal are usually absent, and in most cases, are not allowed. The reason for this omission, contrary to popular belief, is not to befuddle Americans. It's because the French consider the place to be more descriptive of the wine than the grapes in the bottle. In Burgundy, even the producer takes a backseat to terroir. Burgundy bottles are labeled like a concert marquee, where the place of origin is the headliner in large letters and the producer is the opening act in smaller print below. The varietal doesn't even make the show. For French wines, the first question is not "What is in the wine?" but "Where is the wine from?" The varietals are important, in that they are the paints used to create the masterpiece, but the true artist is the place.

So when people ask me if there was one specific bottle that made me fall in love with wine, I say, no, it wasn't a particular wine. It was a particular place. That place is called Châteauneuf-du-Pape. It is the last terroir stop on this pilgrim trail before we head home.

Pope Clement V's international papal parade route may have ended in a stone fortress in Avignon designed to keep out Italians, but it was his successor, John XXII, who truly made himself at home in the south of France. Pope John was more interested in drinking local. During his reign he imported vintners from southwest France to expand vineyard plantings along the southern Rhone, and he also built a vacation home, really more of a staycation castle, about ten miles north of Avignon. Apparently in his day that was far enough to keep the scroungers and sycophants at bay. The pope inspired countless others throughout history to try and escape mooching family members by moving. The small village that grew up around his summer retreat came to bear the name Châteauneuf-du-Pape, which means "New Chateau of the Pope."

Pope John was also renowned for only eating white food—milk, egg whites, white fish, chicken, cheese—either because it was easier to detect poison in light colored food, as he had survived an assassination attempt early in his reign, or because the holy color of white could ward off black magic. When it comes to wine, however, the region ruled by the pope of white food became famous for dark, sultry, bewitching reds.

Châteauneuf-du-Pape is the crown jewel of the southern half of the Côtes du Rhône, some eight thousand acres of vines spread among five small towns, with Pope John's new digs lending its name to the region. These wines used to be called *vins de pape*, the pope's wines. They are some of the most celebrated in France. The name is a mouthful to say, and the wines are a mouthful to drink. They are some of the most broad-shouldered, full-bodied wines in France, a daring departure from typical French coyness, but not uncouth. An exotic blend of thirteen or so different grapes but mostly grenache, syrah, and mourvedre, they are suave monsters, wild and powerful but with a silky growl. I have heard CdP wines called the "primal scream" of French wines, but I think that's a bit harsh. They are more like someone cranked the French café music up to eleven.

I will grant that there is something old, even primal, about Châteauneuf-du-Pape wines, with their brambly dark berries and sun-dried spices, and their other signature, a leathery, meaty, sometimes animal aroma. There is a wild yeast that seems to proliferate in this easy Mediterranean climate called Brettanomyces, "Brett" for short, which carries an aroma reminiscent of a barn or horse stable. It is more pleasant than it sounds. If I were a local curmudgeon, guzzling pastis at my usual café in the long afternoons, I would tell the legend of a wild horse named Brett, heard but rarely seen, who works himself into a lather galloping through the vines and the brush of the spicy countryside. When the aroma he kicks onto the fruit is subtle, it is nostalgic and pleasing, and a perfect complement to smoked meat. When it is overly pungent, it will ruin your drinking experience. If Brett the sweaty wild horse crosses your path, he gives you a thrill, but you don't want Brett in your living room.

For me, all the goodness on this summer adventure that came before this was mere prelude to Châteauneuf. Our wine guide Antoine circled around it in the morning and early afternoon of our Rhône tour, and the anticipation was killing me. I had been smitten with the wines for years, with their florid, regal labels and bottles embossed with the papal tiara, Gothic letters, and the crisscrossed keys of Saint Peter, the unmistakable mark of authenticity for

Châteauneuf-du-Pape. The big-name chateaus of the Southern Rhone are all housed here—Beaucastel, Rayas, Vieux Télégraphe—though my favorite name in the region is Domaine de la Solitude, which has given me the perfect name for my house one day.

I knew the wines, but I didn't know the place. Châteauneuf-du-Pape is one of the most carefully guarded places in all of France. It was the first wine region in France to receive an official appellation, in 1936. The French appellation system protects places and what grows there. An AOC (*appellation d'origine contrôlée*) is essentially a patent for a place, an official seal for terroir. It's why you can't make Champagne in England or Roquefort cheese in Wisconsin. Roquefort was actually the first ever appellation, certified in 1411, and to this day there are only seven producers who are allowed to put Roquefort on their labels, and they must make their cheeses with raw sheep milk and age them in the caves of Roquefort-sur-Soulzon. Cheesemongers say that the grass the sheep graze on in Roquefort uniquely flavors their milk, so you won't find the same conditions anywhere else in the world. There are also appellations for honey, meat, butter, lavender, and lentils. Is it really important we protect lentils?

If you aim to put the name Châteauneuf-du-Pape on your wine, you have to follow the appellation laws to the letter, which dictate where and what you can plant, maximum harvest yields (three tons an acre, the lowest in France), irrigation practices (only for young saplings and in severe droughts), minimum alcohol percentage (which guarantees grape ripeness levels at harvest), and cellar aging time. Harvest must be carried out on the fall equinox by virgins wearing diadems of grape leaves, who hand pick the fruit at the exact moment the rising sun illuminates each cluster.

The French will stop at nothing to protect their wines, whether from others trading on their fame, or from alien invasion. In 1954, the *New York Times* reported that a railway worker in northern France named Marius Dewilde was out taking his dogs for a walk when he saw an aircraft, in the shape of a flying cigar, land near the train tracks. Two small figures, clad in what Dewilde described as deep-sea diver outfits, exited the craft and approached the gate to his garden. When he confronted them, the spaceship emitted a blinding green light, and before he could recover, their ship was gone.

This was the first of a flurry of reports across France over the following weeks about little men in *le cigare volant*, a flying cigar. The mayor of Châteauneuf-du-Pape put his foot down. He called his council together and quickly passed a decree:

> Article 1—The overflight, the landing and the takeoff of aircraft known as flying saucers or flying cigars, whatever their nationality is, are prohibited on the territory of the community.

> Article 2—Any aircraft, known as flying saucer or flying cigar, which should land on the territory of the community will be immediately held in custody.

If aliens ever were to visit Châteauneuf-du-Pape and return to their home planet to make wine, they would have to call it by another name, or almost surely the French would take interplanetary legal action.

In truth, under the chewy crust of all this bureaucracy is a belief that each appellation is a place to be protected, a process to be preserved, and farmers and a surrounding community to be upheld. An appellation circumscribes a place and recognizes its distinctiveness. There is something special and unique here that can't be wholly duplicated anywhere else. That is the value of naming something. A name sets a place apart. It honors the expression of life in this place that says something just a little different from all other places, and that should be vigilantly and lovingly guarded because it is sacred.

Antoine was taking his sweet time on the route to Châteauneuf, just to torture me. He dropped us off for a late lunch in the enchanted village of Gigondas, just as the sun first shone through that day. Above Gigondas, the spiked peaks menace like dragon teeth, and the village sits in the mouth below, gazing down on its vines and stony soils, a layer cake of medieval-storybook bliss. Our table in the dining room in Hôtel Les Florets gleamed with crystal and polished silver. With pilgrim gusto I ordered my first ever duck breast, which I had always avoided for its slippery texture, but it turns out that the oily duck fat worked perfectly with the chewy house red I was drinking. While you are rolling your eyes at that sentence, it will give me time to explain.

I never used to care about the rules for pairing food and wine. I subscribed to the popular theory that you should drink what you like and eat what you want. Then, some years ago, I invited friends over for dinner on a Saturday night, and I dished up some chicken piccata and served it with my favorite wine at the time, Australian Shiraz.

I might as well have thrown a toothbrushing party and served orange juice mouthwash. Or just punched my guests in the face. It was a horrifying crash of sour and bitter: prickly citric acid screeching into a bloodbath of prunes stewing over a wet wood campfire. No palates were spared. And the casualties included one of my favorite dishes and a pretty decent wine.

That's when I started to pay attention to wine and food pairings, and I learned there are features of wines that need to be balanced and managed. Now that your eyes are back in your sockets, let's return to Gigondas and duck fat. A "chewy" wine is one that has a lot of tannins, a chemical compound found in the skins of grapes and oak barrels. Red wines in the south of France are full of them. You experience tannins mostly as a drying sensation in your mouth, as they combine with the proteins in your saliva and impede its flow. I'm still not at peace with the idea that a liquid can dry your mouth out. But, if you eat some good fat, like, say, duck Provençal, with a tannic wine, the tannins combine with the fat rather than all your saliva, both softening the astringent texture of the wine and cleansing your palate of the oily texture of the fat. This is why the classic food and wine pairing is steak and cab. The mingling of fat and tannin enables you to drink more wine and eat more fat. Isn't that what we all want out of life?

The streets and squares of Gigondas are shaded by towering, protective plane trees, which were planted on no less than Napoleon's orders to provide cover for his troops marching through town. The trees in Provence are magnificent. After lunch, I peppered Antoine with tree questions from the backseat of his tiny car like a sugar-filled toddler.

"Why are they called plane trees?"

"Because their bark strips off in long, thin planes."

"What are all these pointy trees that look like asparagus tips?"

"Cypress. Often they are planted in threes around farmhouses for good luck."

"What are those trees that look like umbrellas?"

"Umbrella trees."

The Provençal even train their vines to look like small trees. Instead of vineyards that resemble long rows of crosses with arms extending out and shoots and vegetation raised skyward, here each vine stands alone as a small tree or bush. Their trunks grow thick and gnarly, and the branches spread out and drape with gravity. This is called the *gobelet* system, because each vine resembles a leafy goblet. It is ideal in a blistering climate because the branches shade the fruit from the sun and hot wind, and you can plant the vines farther apart so they don't compete for precious water. The grape trees here are kept low to the ground, huddled underneath the howling mistral.

Then, at last, I saw it. As the road curved and the trees parted, the crumbling castle of Châteauneuf-du-Pape, set on the highest hill, climbed over the tiled rooftops of the tiny village below. Now it is not much more than clay-colored walls with windows to nowhere and a collapsed parapet. Once this was the pope's new chateau and these vines were the pope's own vines. These were the holiest of holy wines.

Still a mile or so from the castle, Antoine pulled over into a dusty turnout on the edge of a vineyard and turned off the ignition. We squeezed out of the car so we could feel the crunch of this ground so hallowed by religious believers and the wine faithful. The late afternoon sun had chased off the rainclouds and was burning softly. The mistral must have stayed home that day.

The Mediterranean heat and the ferocious wind are two formative features of the area, but there is an even more famed terroir signature of Châteauneuf-du-Pape. The ground is covered with rocks. I don't mean gravel or pebbles. I mean big, round, flat, hamburger-bun-sized rocks, perfectly shaped for a giant to skip stones across the sea. They are called *galets*, which is the same word for the savory crepes served up in bistros across France.

Antoine explained to us how the galets came to be there. The Rhone region is a massive valley that collapsed between the Massif Central, the mountains to the west, and the Alps to the east. The ground under our feet was something like 250 million years old. Two million years ago glaciers covered much of this region, but as the earth warmed the glaciers retreated north. As they did, in their last act of defiance, they ripped huge chunks of quartzite off the Alps. Over the ages the rush of the Rhone River, which was once eighteen miles wide, broke the quartzite apart, smoothed the stones, and carried them down to the valley below. Now the *galets* play a supporting role in the vineyards, trapping moisture below them and reflecting heat to the vines, contributing to Châteauneuf's reputation for lavish, blockbuster wines.

From where I was looking, there was not one piece of dirt to be seen. I was immersed in a sea of crepes, surrounded by goblets of grenache, with the ruins of the pope's chateau looming in the background.

"It's incredible to me that vines can grow out of rocks," I marveled.

Antoine responded, "That's why the local expression here is that making wine is like squeezing blood from a stone."

"I know, I just—wait. What? Say that again."

"Making wine here is like squeezing blood from a stone," he repeated.

I wobbled on the smooth stones beneath my feet. These words struck me with a force I didn't understand. It was as though a thousand Champagne corks had popped inside my head at once. My brain whirled, until I felt a little dizzy.

*Blood from a stone.* This phrase came to me like the voice of someone from your past calling behind you, when your heart leaps out of your chest before you can even name the voice. It felt like some sort of conversion experience. This was my Damascus Road, my "take and read," my vision at Mecca, my "by this sign shall you conquer," my "holy shit!" moment. The jolt of that phrase was enough to wake the dead.

There was life in the stones. There was life in the stones! Somehow, these smooth, rounded, ancient corpses were giving blood, coursing under miniature trees of life. Had they been listening to the centuries of holy mass performed in this place? Here at the pope's altar, when the bread was transformed into body broken, the wine into blood spilled, had the stones also been changed? A deathbed of rocks was now beating and bleeding like hearts.

I wanted to stand there forever. The rocks were alive. I was alive. This valley of dry bones had a pulse.

I have seen more than my share of death. I am drawn to wine because of the life in it. The French have a saying: *La vie en la vigne.* There is life in the vine. Grapes should rot, juice should spoil. Yet life refuses to surrender, and wine is the resurrected heart of the grape. Some people use wine to deaden their senses. Wine was made to enliven the senses.

In every civilization blood is the sign of life. Lifeblood fills you and warms you, coursing through you even when you are still. When it dries up, life is extinguished. And wine has long been associated with the blood of gods. The stories of wine gods are often violent, with deities torn limb from limb like branches ripped from vines, since that is how you release their blood and receive their life. You have to squeeze the stones to get the blood out. For believers, we drink a wine that reveals blood shed for forgiveness, a cup of suffering emptied for love. As we partake of the blood of crushed grapes, we discover union with the life of Christ in the deepest places. We experience not only the God of wine, but the God in wine. More than the God *of* us, we meet the God *in* us. We share the same blood, and we are family. To drink wine is to participate in a divine life.

The stones shared their secrets with me. I never would have heard them if wine hadn't drawn me there. The more I discover about wine, the more I learn how much it involves hidden mystery. The story of wine is a chain reaction of transformation, carried out under a veil. Roots reach for water and nutrients in invisible places. Microscopic yeasts lurk in juice, prepared to carry out their work of secret change. Aromatic compounds are hidden in long equations, their wild fragrances masked until yeasts break them apart in fermentation, and then they rush for the air. In dark bottles wine changes and evolves, taking on new textures and flavors that taste like nothing you have ever had.

That's always been the nature of sacraments, hidden mysteries of grace and life squeezed out of ordinary objects. Baskets of bread and goblets of wine, vials of oil and pitchers of water, even rocks can play host to heaven's surprise visits.

So can place. I have been thinking about this particular place among the stones ever since. I think this was my first experience of what the ancient Celts would call a "thin place." They would say that there is more than meets the eye to a particular piece of dirt. A thin place is where the ground you are standing on is elevated into an altar, where dirt becomes revelation. The Celts believed there are places where the veil separating the spirit and the soil is particularly thin, where heaven looms close, eager to reveal itself and pierce the skin of the world. Heaven is always nearer than we think, but there are some places where it feels closer. I think a thin place is where we are simultaneously grounded and uplifted, where we experience heaven at its most heavenly, and earth at its earthiest. The modern take on terroir says that a place has a climate, slope, and soil. A thin place says that a place has a spirit.

Celtic Christians spoke of another type of thin place. You would be summoned to take a long pilgrimage away from the security of home, and you wouldn't return. It was a type of martyrdom, because where you landed would be the place you would die, and where your bones would await resurrection. This was the *place of resurrection*.

When you encounter a thin place, it is not usually a restful feeling. I felt like my soul had been pierced, and that this place had taken a magnet to my internal compass. But I felt alive, for the first time in a very long time. Naked but alive. I was done denying the things and desires that make me feel most alive. This is my place of resurrection.

*Vive la France!*

*Seven*

# THE DARK NIGHT
# OF THE SOUL

As all pilgrims returning home discover, my reentry into life after France was full of contradiction. I was inspired, even hopeful, and hungry to keep writing. Though I still had to finish my book about how I used to listen for a living, a whisper of an idea for a wine book had also begun to haunt me. France had given me a fresh thirst for every wine that crossed my palate and new curiosity for each particular somewhere that grew it. But though I had new eyes, I was still looking at an old life. There were no navigation stars pointing me somewhere new after ministry, and I was quickly burdened with the thoroughly uninspired realities of subsistence, like paying rent. Yes, I wanted to drink in absolutely everything I could about wine, but from time to time, I also wanted to eat food.

I was spending my afternoons writing at a caffeinated nook called the Coffee Klatch, which sits forty miles east of LA on Foot-hill Boulevard in Rancho Cucamonga, a funny name that has been teased by everyone from Jack Benny to Krusty the Clown. For years I had written sermons there, not to mention filled out documentation for hundreds of hospice patients at the end of my shifts. What I had somehow overlooked all this time was that the cross street for the Coffee Klatch is named Vineyard Avenue. I had only vaguely registered the large redwood cask at the entrance to the parking lot, the tree-trunk-sized vine curling up a post on the back porch, the lime-green grape leaves hanging down from the eaves. It had never occurred to me to ask why these vestiges of wine production lingered here. It required a special display of inattention.

Wine books rarely follow chapters on Champagne and Châteauneuf-du-Pape with a discussion about the wines of Rancho Cucamonga. But, now that I was looking for wine wherever I went, I was flummoxed to learn that Rancho was at one time the heart of the California wine industry, with more vineyard acreage than Napa and Sonoma combined. At its peak after World War II, Rancho Cucamonga had over fifty wineries and thirty-two thousand acres planted to vine.

It is astonishing because the Cucamonga Valley—the name means "sandy place" and is derived from the Kukamonga tribe who settled in this area—is scandalously, inappropriately hot. If you crack an egg on the sidewalk at high noon in August there, it turns into a chicken. If you manage to survive the summer, October rewards you with the Santa Ana winds, the sinister exhale of hell's breath that whips eighty-mile-per-hour desert air through the valley and rains fire on every hillside. This hardly seems a suitable climate for growing grapes, or children for that matter. There is a smattering of wineries that still make wine in the area, but the weather is so scalding and dry for half the year that the only wines they can make are dessert wines or zinfandel so jammy you would be better off schmearing it on toast. And something called Chocolate Port, when you are searching for that perfect wine to complement the Ding Dongs and Goldfish crackers course.

Somehow Rancho Cucamonga, now a suburban jungle of tract homes encircled by green belts, big box stores, and palm tree strip malls, was once described as a marshy oasis, with creeks tumbling down from the mountains, and a habitat for cottonwoods, sycamores, and willows. In 1839, a Mexican merchant/smuggler named Tiburcio Tapia successfully petitioned the governor of Alta California with a hand drawn map of a thirteen-thousand-acre land grant called Rancho Cucamonga. One of the first things Tapia did to celebrate was plant 565 vines on his new property. This was the opening gambit of what would become a prolific viticultural history over the next century. Seventy years later, an Italian named Secondo Guasti of the Italian Wine Company owned a five-thousand-acre vineyard in the Cucamonga Valley, which he boasted was the largest vineyard on the planet. It must be hard not to overcompensate when your parents name you "Second."

The Italian Wine Company survived Prohibition by selling grape bricks called Vine-Glo, which were carried by rail across the country to home winemakers capitalizing on a fuzzy exception in the Volstead Act. The Volstead Act was passed to enforce the Eighteenth Amendment, which declared the national prohibition on alcoholic beverages, but section twenty-nine allowed for each household to make two hundred gallons of "nonintoxicating cider and fruit juice" per year. Nonintoxicating, but not necessarily nonalcoholic, or at least that's how some crafty California wineries interpreted it.

Two hundred gallons is almost one thousand bottles of bathtub wine a year, and Americans were so thirsty for it that vineyard acreage in the United States doubled during Prohibition. California wineries like the Italian Wine Company packed dehydrated grapes into the shape of bricks and included a package of yeast and instructions such as this: "After dissolving the brick in a gallon of water, do not place the liquid in a jug away in the cupboard for twenty days, because then it would turn into wine." Another Cucamonga operation, The Virginia Dare Winery, made "wine tonic" during Prohibition, a

20-percent solution for your nerves that required a pharmacist's prescription. Our local wine community also did its part during the war. They offered pomace—the grape skins and seeds leftover from harvest—to the military, who used it as fuel to make bombs. I have tried a few Cucamonga wines, and that sounds about right to me.

Local amateur historians believe that the long rectangular building at the corner of Vineyard and Foothill, with its rusty tower that once housed a brass still for making brandy, was the original 1839 site of Tiburcio Tapia's winery. They also claim it as California's very first commercial winery. While that feels like civic pride more than historical fact, it does appear I had been drinking coffee for years in one of the original California wineries, and I had no idea. Wine had been there all along.

⬥

I felt like I had been reborn in the vineyards of France, called out to a destiny unknown. But the thing about resurrection is that it first requires a death. You can't have a new beginning without an ending.

My writing career wasn't going well, at least from a financial point of view. There were sidewalk lemonade stands that were more profitable. I had also been collecting unemployment checks since my layoff, but I discovered that the government cheese board isn't served with wine pairings. Just as I was getting close to desperation, with tensions again rising in our household, an old colleague called, late on a balmy December afternoon. It was Hospice. The midnight to eight shift was open again. Hospice asked if I would consider coming back.

I think the blood might have retreated right back into the stone. I believed I had left the ministry for good. It's possible ministry hadn't yet left me. I was sure my Reverend McHugh name tag had washed clean on the wet cobblestones between Vincent's easels, but apparently you could still make out the faded letters.

I was under enough pressure that I agreed to an interview, where I took a seat at the same conference table I had once skipped my beeper across as a glorious gesture of finality. The competition for the graveyard chaplain position was less than fierce. Just like that, Reverend McHugh was placed back on hospice.

⁂

The whiplash of returning to hospice was jarring, but it was nothing compared to the shock I suffered when I first entered hospice. I originally found myself a hospice chaplain after my marriage fell apart the first time. Before that, I was in what I considered at the time my dream job. I was a college pastor at my alma mater in Claremont, a tree-shaded, ivy-climbing intellectual oasis on the outskirts of the creeping urban sprawl of LA. I was living in the place where my happiest memories resided, each night offered free lectures by renowned scholars with cheese and bad wine and Rice Krispies treats, and I loved working with college students, with their soaring curiosities and grand passions. Some of my students called me "The Irreverend" because I used words like *kickass* in my sermons, but they are the only audience who has ever listened to most of what I said.

But when I moved out of the house for a few weeks in the summer, when long simmering conflicts bubbled over, my bosses said I couldn't go back to campus in the fall, even though my wife and I were working to reconcile. I was devastated. There are few places more terrifying for your marriage to fall apart than in an evangelical Christian community. I was defiant, determined to show they were wrong to disqualify me from ministry. A Presbyterian colleague suggested I apply for an open chaplain position with a local hospice. I was the most surprised person in the room when they offered me the job. They were even more desperate than I was.

Yet I found myself right at home, because chaplain work often seems to be a sanctuary for disenchanted church ministers. I will never forget the hospital chaplain who told me that his previous church job ended after his wife left him, when "some guys came to my house to defrock me," which is disturbing on so many levels. Our team of hospice chaplains was a scrappy bunch of church outcasts, burned-out PhD candidates, divorcees, and recovering alcoholics. Just who you want praying at your bedside. In fact, we just might be. We were people who knew pain. We were all intimately acquainted with things ending badly, and with the internal hurricanes that can tear up everything. I never planned to be there, but it was the right place for me at the time, as I grieved the loss of a job I loved and all the expectations I had for how my life and career would go. It cracked me open on the inside and created space for grief.

I don't know why human life seems to require suffering for growth to take place, or why things have to be taken away from us if we are to expand. The pattern branded on the human heart seems to be that only pain brings lasting change, that we must learn how to grieve if we want to truly celebrate, that we have to get lost in order to be found again. The lesson of the grape seems to apply here: in order to get the life out, something has to get crushed.

<hr />

I had resumed my role as the Grim Reaper's wingman. For the next two and a half years, my world revolved around grief, loss, and death in the middle of the night, much of which belonged to me. I was back, but I had a strong feeling that these were the dying breaths of my ministry.

I started reading a book called *Transitions* by William Bridges. Let's first all pause to appreciate that a guy whose last name is *Bridges* is a leading expert on *transitions*. Bridges says that when it comes to beginnings and endings, many of us mix up the order. We turn the page when the last chapter isn't finished. We leap to the next job, the next relationship, the next title, the next phase, whatever is next, without coming to terms with the end of what came before, and the end of who we were before the change. I had tried to fast forward out of ministry without genuine closure. But internally, says Bridges, you are not ready to step into a new beginning until you have acknowledged the end. You can only get from fall to spring through winter.

In the language of a hospice chaplain, you must grieve what you have lost, or what you are losing. Grief isn't reserved exclusively for widows and survivors. Grief accompanies the small deaths as well as the Big One. I was learning that even if the loss is one I choose, it doesn't mean I won't, and shouldn't, experience grief. I had poured so much of my life into becoming an ordained minister: years of education and internships, libraries of books read and prayers offered, hundreds of sermons preached and classes taught. I had attended so many meetings for interviews that I could have become Chief Justice of the Supreme Court. My last test was to stand before a legion of skeptical theologians and defend my written statement of faith, just like Martin Luther at the Diet of Worms, right before he was excommunicated and sentenced to, well, a diet of worms. They ordained me Reverend Adam McHugh, Minister of Word and Sacrament, and all fell before me and despaired. It was awesome. But now, I knew he was dying. I was letting go of more than a role. I was losing an identity. Sometimes I felt like I was losing myself.

It was also hard to let go because I was doing meaningful, strange, and important work, and I knew there weren't many other people to do it. I was listening again for a living, and I would sit for a while with people suffering the loneliest hours of their lives. That happened more when I was working the day shift in years past. There was Kathleen, dying from advanced-stage lung disease, who lived alone in a senior high-rise overlooking the horse track in Arcadia. We spent many hours talking about her experiences as a young girl living during the blitz on World-War-II England. Kathleen always served Earl Grey and shortbread cookies out of a silver tin. There was Olivia in an old, tree-shaded Craftsman in Pasadena, who was Italian and full of verve to the very end, even as her heart failed. She loved to cook but hated taking her medicine almost as much as she hated Mussolini. Dementia was sadly starting to overtake Olivia, but I learned to enjoy the same stories over and over again, and to go by whatever name she chose to call me that particular day.

Then there was ninety-nine-year-old Eulogia, a nurse who served her country in two wars, with a name I will never forget because it means "blessing" in the Greek I studied in seminary. She proudly lived alone in her house in Sierra Madre with a screened patio and mid-century armchairs. I would visit her on Wednesdays. Sometimes we would talk, and other times we would sit quietly. A few months after she was placed on hospice, her family moved her to a nursing home in San Gabriel a few miles away, out of fear for her safety. The anguish of leaving her home of seventy years almost killed her. When I arrived the following Wednesday at the nursing home to check in on her, Eulogia saw me and burst into tears, saying, "I didn't know if you would be able to find me!" Eulogia lived to see her hundredth birthday, and the nursing home threw her a party.

But hospice work wasn't all sitting on porch swings sipping tea with sweet old ladies. Often, when I set foot in a home or facility, I found myself in a tangle of grief, coping mechanisms, and entrenched family dynamics. Some people were exceedingly grateful and hospitable, but others saw me as an intruder and, even though I assured them I was there to listen and not to preach, they wanted no whisper of religion in their house. Sometimes I had to sneak in with a nurse in order to do my initial evaluation. Other times I didn't bother. It cut against my nature to force help on people who didn't want it, for the sake of completing a chart.

My first training day as a hospice chaplain perfectly captured the contradictions I would live in this work. That day, I shadowed a fellow chaplain on two home visits. In the first home, a man lay in a hospital bed in a beautiful, well-illuminated living room surrounded by loving family members, who were whispering parting words to him. A beatific smile on his face, he lay with his arms upstretched toward the ceiling, as though he was being welcomed into the heavens by ancestors who had gone before him. In the second home, we met a hostile, chain-smoking old woman who complained about her son the entire visit. She thought chaplain was a needless and intrusive job, and that government-supported health-care companies paying us was a violation of the Constitution. The next day, we found out she had tuberculosis. I drove twenty miles to a medical clinic three times that week to make sure I didn't have TB. Welcome to hospice, McHugh. Some people will call you an angel, other people will call you the angel of death. Some deathbeds will feel like thin places; others will feel like extremely thick places.

⬥

I inched along the 210 West in the mid-afternoon, creeping my way in traffic-without-end to the Death Office to sign the form for my written reprimand. It was a rare cameo for me in the daylight hours, and I squinted in the smoggy glare like a grizzly emerging from hibernation. The complaint had come in early that morning, from a death visit I never made the night before. I had managed to stir up a family's anger without ever actually meeting them.

This was a written warning because I had already received a verbal warning a few months prior. On that occasion, I had attended the death of a ninety-year-old woman in South Pasadena, who passed away after midnight with her two sons at her bedside. After a forty-five-minute drive, I arrived to keep vigil with them until the mortuary came to take her away. I disposed of the medication and listened to her sons recount the story of her last moments. Most people were eager to tell that story, often rehearsing it many times, as though they wanted to get the words just right and seal the memory in their hearts. As I prepared to leave, they asked me if I could remove the IV drip attached to their mom's stomach. *But I'm a chaplain,* I wanted to protest. *I have no training for that. I deal in matters of the spirit, not the body.* In truth, the idea of reaching under a deceased woman's robe to pull out a tube made me feel queasy. I declined as gently as I could and assured them the mortuary would handle that. The next week, after the family filed a complaint, I was awarded a verbal warning and an hour of training on tube removal. Though hospice is designed to make people as comfortable as possible in times of stress, this doesn't apply to squeamish hospice chaplains.

It was not uncommon for me to be on the receiving end of anger. Anger is part of grief, after all, and it feels powerful and protective. Sadness and worry make us feel small, but anger makes us big, and it keeps us safe until we can feel the more vulnerable feelings. I suspect there is a knee-jerk tendency in all of us to look for someone to blame when we lose something precious. In this job, I made a living of being the nearest person. People would get angry at me because I was there. Or sometimes they got mad at me because I wasn't there.

I closed the door behind me as I entered Pam's office. Pam was our bereavement coordinator, chaplain supervisor, and resident straight shooter. Years earlier, when we were both team chaplains, she announced in front of the office staff that I dressed unprofessionally.

Here's what went down the night before. Around three in the morning, my beeper shrieked me out of bed, stirring up that familiar cocktail of disorientation, irritability, and despair that I guzzled most nights. I resisted the ever-growing temptation to lob the beeper into the community pool off our back patio. Telecare informed me that a patient on our service had died. I threw on my unprofessional attire and called the family to offer my condolences and inform them I was on my way.

The woman I spoke with, whose father had passed, said they were waiting for more family members to arrive, and they didn't want to call the mortuary until everyone had a chance to say goodbye in person.

"Wonderful," I said. "Would you like me to come now, or to come later when you are ready to call the mortuary?"

"Why don't you check in with us in a couple of hours?" she said sweetly.

"I'll tell you what. Just call Telecare when you are ready, and I will get out there as quickly as I can."

She agreed, and I collapsed back into bed. Around 7:30 a.m., the call came. My nightly schedule was midnight to eight in the morning, and if I wasn't sealed back into my coffin by eight, I was a cranky vampire. I told her I would alert the day shift team, and one of them would start out at eight and likely get there before I could, since I lived an hour away. I went back to bed.

Later that morning, I learned, the family called and talked to Pam. They informed her that I didn't seem to have any interest in doing my job, and that "he either needs to do something else with his life or learn some goddamn respect!" I started to plead my case to Pam, but I knew it was futile. Sighing audibly, I signed the form. This was strike two. One more, and I would be making the long, sad walk back to the chaplain bench. That's when Pam said this: "Adam, have you ever considered another line of work? We all know you are not very good at this."

Pam's sledgehammer diplomacy had struck another blow. After my ears stopped ringing, my first thought was *I need to get to a pen and paper as quickly as possible because this is going in a book someday.* I have never been so offended by something I knew to be completely true.

There is no doubt the darkness was getting to me. My memories of those hospice nights are hazy, and during most of my midnight visits I was distracted by wild fantasies about being in bed asleep. I had coaxed myself into taking the nightwalker chaplain shift because

I thought I would be able to write during the day, but within a few weeks any predictable life rhythms had been unsympathetically interrupted. Until you have done it, you don't realize what a surreal thing it is, spending your waking hours while the world is asleep. There is something almost subhuman about living the nocturnal life. You start to understand why all the paranormal creatures and fairytale beasts occupy the night. The darkness is for ghosts haunting old barns, monsters lurking in closets, and overtired people making terrible decisions. That is the natural order of things, and woe unto you who disobeys the rule of the night.

I started to feel like I was living in an alternative universe, where everything had been inverted and the moon was now the brightest light in the sky. It's hard to tell time when the moon is your guide. I was in a foggy, in-between world. The majority of my job was not listening or praying but driving, and I spent my nights on LA freeways, en route from one place to the next. I would interact with a family just one time, and most of my visits lasted less than an hour. Many of the people I met were already absent. The rest were suspended between life and death, or else grief had brought their lives to a halt. I was far away, neither here nor there, increasingly detached from everything and everyone, including myself. It's hard to have a sense of place in the pitch black.

A weariness had crept into my soul that couldn't be explained only by sleep deprivation. The experts called it "compassion fatigue," but I felt even more weighed down by the feeling that I had become an imposter. Every time people made a hushed path when I walked into their home, I wanted to say, "There's been a mistake, I'm not supposed to be here. I am not who you think I am." I was running on empty because I was still acting out a version of myself that had departed. I was living on the fumes of memories of a past life.

For some lightness I started taking wine classes at UCLA, plowing through LA smog banks and braving the 405/10 Freeway interchange to get to campus on Wednesday nights, even though my hospice shift started at midnight. In class we learned the basics of winemaking and viticulture and tasted the classic wines of Europe and the New World. I bought a set of tasting glasses that I carried in a gray twill case, usually managing to avoid getting beat up by jocks on the walk to class. I don't think I have a naturally sensitive palate, but I was learning that I could train it, even grow it like a muscle, by storing up memories of unfamiliar aromas. The part of our brain that records smell also holds memories, and if you focus your attention on a particular aroma for a few minutes, it will help you recognize and name it in the future. One evening before class I was caught at the grocery store with my nose buried in a crate of black currants.

"Uh, can I help you with something?" asked the perplexed produce guy.

"No thanks," I said. "I'm just smelling."

I also rediscovered a portal into another world of wine, and I started taking that door as often as I could. A hundred and fifty miles north, just beyond Santa Barbara, there is a magic tunnel that appears where the 101 Freeway hooks sharply away from the Pacific Ocean and cuts through a jagged peak of sandstone. This dim tunnel is but a football field long, but when I reemerge into the light on the other side it is as though I am transported to a wholly different place. The climate changes dramatically; the chill, misty breezes of the coast are replaced by pointed sunlight in high-flying blue skies. I had come again to the Santa Ynez Valley, a wonderland of wine-soaked hills surrounding a fairytale, Pinocchio village with a year-round Christmas shop, populated by a wine-country folk seemingly unruffled by the urgencies and death visits of the world beyond their mountains. I had enjoyed visiting Santa Ynez for years, but it was beginning to take on new meaning for me. It was a lifeline of vine and sky. I never breathed more deeply than I did there. At least once a month, I would do the drive roundtrip in one day, leaving at eight in the morning and returning home right before my midnight shift began, just to smell the garden-fresh air and pinot noir.

Medieval pilgrims departed home in search of the relics and remains of saints in holy sites. I fled the dry bones of hospice for a land full of life. The Santa Ynez Valley was becoming my new sanctuary.

<hr />

I took my beeper with me to wine class each week, in case traffic was slow on the return commute and I wasn't home by midnight. One Wednesday night in February, the beeper screeched from the passenger seat at 11:40 p.m. A woman was dying in Altadena, and she had two old friends gathered at her bedside requesting a chaplain visit. I arrived, in a surprisingly energized mood, and we had a nice conversation. The patient had just been accepted into hospice that morning, and she had no family nearby, so her two dear friends had come to hold vigil with her. They had been neighbors for forty years and had all cried with each other when their husbands died. Widows to me are like war heroes, people who have seen their loved ones die in their arms, and yet picked up and kept marching up the hill. After we talked in quiet tones for a while, I passed on my condolences, and went to head home. One of the women ran down the driveway as I was pulling out and bid me to roll my window down.

"Adam, do you think it would be possible to get a priest to visit and pray for her?"

Even though I was an ordained minister, I knew from experience that when Catholics are dying they want a visit from a priest, not from a Protestant chaplain. I had left dozens of messages over the years with parish switchboard operators in the middle of the night, hoping that a local priest could be rousted out of bed to visit in a patient's last hours. I assured her I would do my best. I pulled over before I got to the freeway, and left two messages with nearby parishes, asking for a priest to come to offer the sacrament of the sick.

The next morning, Pam called. Pam never called to say hi or to congratulate me on a job well done. She requested that I come into the office that afternoon. With growing dread, I drove to the Death Office, where Pam asked me to close the door behind me as I entered her office.

"Adam, I will get right to it. The family you met last night called this morning to complain. They said they asked the chaplain to pray for the patient, but he refused and left, saying he would find someone else to do it. I'm sorry, but we have had this sort of conversation before. We are going to have to let you go."

I sat there in my chair, stunned, staring at Pam's desk. There were heart candies in a mug by her computer. It was Valentine's Day. This on-again, off-again relationship was over. In the end, I was fired from hospice for not acting enough like a minister.

⚜

Hospice had broken up with me on Valentine's Day, but in truth I was the one who got distant months earlier and then acted surprised when I was dumped. I knew the end was coming, but it still stung.

As I came out of shock over the next few days, I was slowly realizing I had been set free, and my redeemer was a prickly woman named Pam. The next week, I called our general manager to tell him thank you for my time there, and I meant it. When I sort through it all—the 2:00 a.m. phone conversations with suicidal people, the times when I held a patient's hand as she took her last breath, the honor of witnessing every night the outpourings of love and agony that may be the same thing—I do feel grateful. I am grateful I learned how to give room for grief, and how to listen without trying to control. I learned how to be still with people in pain. It may be the most human thing you can do. There is no less humanity in a person in a hospital gown, an IV dripping into their veins, than there is in an athlete in victory or a model on the runway. No, I am wrong. There is more humanity in the person in pain. We are all that person.

People love to ask me what wisdom I gained from my time in hospice, but I usually disappoint them when I don't deal out aphorisms. Personally, I have never found the idea that we should "live every day like it's your last" to be helpful advice. For every one person who spends their last day romping through wildflowers and bestowing tender messages on their beloveds, praying words of thanksgiving as the sun falls into the ocean, there are two people who on their last day will order everything on the drive-thru menu at Taco Bell and chase it with a bottle of Wild Turkey. Urgency never makes a good life, or a good death. No one flosses on their last day on Earth. But there is something to be said about realizing that stability is always a temporary situation, and that your dreams and plans will not pulsate within you forever. A life of denying them, for the sake of security and stability, won't get you where you think it will.

The good news about today is that for the vast majority of Earth's inhabitants, it is not your last. Today is the day for seeds to be planted, love to be pursued, changes to be made, wine to be poured, life to be squeezed out.

As I write my obituary for Reverend McHugh, I confess that my work as a minister and chaplain played neatly into my tendency toward detachment. The role kept me a safe distance from people, while giving the impression of closeness. As a minister, I could preside, instead of participating. I could be a counselor, without entering the fray of friendship. I got very good at sharing right up to the point of actual self-revelation, and I could offer compassion without approaching real intimacy and vulnerability.

I believe I had to leave the ministry in order to become myself. I never did laminate the ordination card in my wallet. But I am also convinced that Reverend McHugh wasn't a false identity; it was more that the name had served its purpose and was ready to give way to something new. It got me close enough to where I knew I wanted more. My temptation is to look back and reject or resent what came before, but that is like taking a cross-country trip and getting angry at Chicago for not being New York. It is a stop along the way, and you can't get to where you are heading without going through it.

That is the meaning of hospice, in fact. In the Middle Ages a hospice was a waystation for pilgrims on their way to the Promised Land. Pilgrimages back then were harrowing journeys, requiring great faith and courage. You didn't know when or even if you would return, and what dangers you would encounter along the way. Monasteries and religious orders built hospices for weary pilgrims, offering medicine to the sick, comfort to the dying, and wine to the thirsty. Hospice was a stop along my pilgrim trail, a retreat that provided healing and nourishment for the journey to follow.

This last shift in hospice was my opportunity to acknowledge and grieve the end. Grieving is so you can have tomorrow. Otherwise, you keep living yesterday, over and over again. You need to live yesterday for a while, to gather up all your memories of what was and who you were during that time. Grief is so agonizing not only because you have lost something, but you have lost someone, and that someone is the version of you that was alive before your loss. Your life has changed, and something fundamental about you has irreversibly changed. It will take a long time to let go of that person in order to meet the new person you are becoming. Grief is the treacherous but unavoidable path that takes you from the old to the new.

My old nametag had washed off. This leg of my pilgrimage was over. Next, I would learn that if ultimately you want to move forward, for a while you have to go sideways.

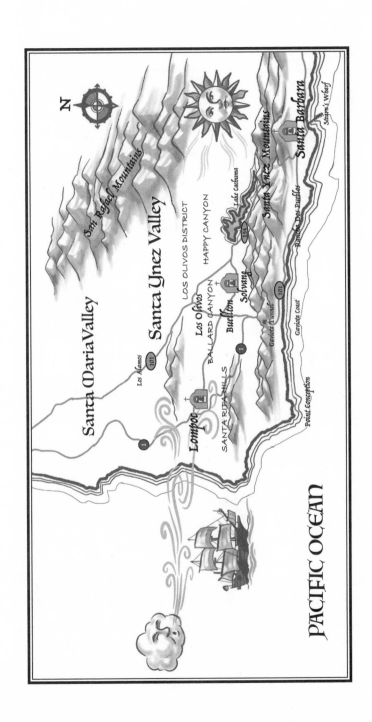

## Eight

# THE SIDEWAYS EFFECT

The first time I visited Santa Barbara, that Mediterranean seaside village that washed up on the shores of the Pacific, I set out to participate in the most sacred of western ritual: the grand, collective pause to bid the sun bon voyage on its nightly passage into the sea. On my way, I ambled along State Street, which pours down the center of town like a river on a direct course home to the ocean. State dips under the 101-Freeway overpass—where locals like to boast that the last remaining traffic signals on the route from Baja, Mexico, to San Francisco forced drivers to brake and admire Santa Barbara until the early '90s—and then meets Stearns Wharf at the beach, a former working wharf turned tourist pier that glides out a half mile into the water. The Pacific, frigid and tumultuous just sixty miles north, here in the Santa Barbara harbor is idyllic and unperturbed, with waves gentle enough to remind you of a baby splashing in a bathtub.

Stearns Wharf is a collection of trinket kiosks, ice cream shops, a tasting room known more for its views than its wines, and seafood shacks. I passed fathers and sons with fishing lines dangling off the wharf and interested seagulls plotting to snatch their catch or else deposit their displeasure on those refusing to share. I edged around the shack of lobsters and crabs at the Santa Barbara Shellfish Company, the saline aromas of steamed clams combining with the briny air, and claimed my viewing spot at the end of the pier. It was a sparklingly clear afternoon, and I could make out every ridge of Santa Cruz Island, the largest of the Santa Barbara Channel Islands that have been transformed into a pristine if unfrequented national park. What I didn't see was the sunset. To do that, I had to swivel my head to the right.

I double-checked my internal compass—and my sobriety level. This third-grade geography-bee champion felt reasonably certain that the Pacific Ocean is to the west of California and that the sun falls on the portside of the continent. It should be directly in front of the wharf's edge, I swear. What sort of wizardry is this? Is Santa Barbara so enchanted that a sorceress cast the sunset into the north?

The answer, I would learn, is this: the sun sets on the side here because Santa Barbara County is turned sideways.

<hr>

Allow me to get tectonic on you for a few moments. That's the only way we can get the sunset back where it belongs.

The massive plates sliding under the earth's top crust don't go long without having some sort of conflict with one another, and in the long history of California they have proven particularly hotheaded. Two hundred million years ago, the left edge of what we now call North America was the western border of Nevada. California did not yet exist, and no one had even conceived of spreading avocado on toast. A hundred and fifty million years ago, give or take fifty million years, the Farallon Plate, lumbering east under the floor of the Pacific Ocean, made contact with the North American Plate. What transpired is a process called *subduction*. Oceanic plates are thinner and denser than continental plates, and when they collide, the oceanic plate will usually slide under the thicker and more buoyant continental plate, melting into magma underneath. The downward force of the Farallon Plate was like a spatula under a hot pie crust, thrusting up the Sierra Nevada mountains on the eastern side of California and later the Coastal Range that runs parallel to the coastline along California's western edge. Ocean bottom was exalted to mountain peak. To this day, hikers find fossils of scallop shells in the Santa Barbara backcountry, miles from the ocean.

The North American Plate essentially ate the Farallon Plate, but it bit off more than it could chew. Some of the oceanic plate scraped off and crumpled into the continent instead of sliding under, extending the land westward and forming the basement of what one day would be called California. Further, all that hot magma produced by subduction would build steam and erupt through vents in the ocean floor, cooling and hardening, slowly raising the seabed to touch the sky. It was as though inch by inch the Great Tide went out, and more and more land was revealed.

Out in Happy Canyon, the eastern edge of the Santa Ynez Valley, scattered among the vines are green rocks called serpentinites, so named for their scaly, reptilian appearance. Serpentine rocks were formed where the ancient seabed melted under the continent and then were slowly uplifted with the mountains. To me they look like dragon eggs that have toppled down from nests in mountain heights, waiting for eons to hatch with a hiss on the valley floor. What sort of sea monsters were awakened in the deep when sea and land collided?

If you are struggling to follow this tectonic talk, know that I don't really understand what I am talking about either. My degrees in history and theology somehow didn't cover these topics I find myself flailing around in nowadays. You get into wine because you think it tastes good, and suddenly people are throwing terms like *convergent plate boundary* and *accreted terrane* at you, when you are still congratulating yourself for learning how to pronounce *viognier* (it's vee-own-yay). But what I want to show you is how two hundred million years of seismic drama in California formed the building blocks of a nursery for pinot noir, which would be grown and nurtured in an unlikely place. And how it brought me to live in an unexpected place, too.

Historians all agree that the next few million years were pretty boring, so we will fast forward. The Farallon Plate subducting under what is now Santa Barbara County has run out of material, having been thoroughly magmafied. But both to the north of Santa Barbara and to her south, Farallon still has more pie to serve, which results in the uplifting of the Coastal Range along most of the coastline. The Coastal Range has a long pause starting at the southern boundary of San Luis Obispo, just north of the Santa Barbara region, eventually resuming in the Peninsular Range south of Los Angeles, extending down to San Diego. What that means is that the Coastal Range will shield most of California from the coldest influences of the chilly Pacific, but not Santa Barbara.

Finally, when the Farallon Plate was completely exhausted under California, in its wake came the Pacific Plate, which collided with the North American Plate 135 million years ago and formed the dread San Andreas Fault. San Andreas runs the length of most of California and is the battle line where the two plates square off. This is the fault that gives California its shaky reputation in other parts of the country, and why my parents sent me to college with an emergency preparedness kit. San Andreas is called a *transform boundary*, or by a much cooler name, *strike-slip boundary*, meaning that instead of one plate subducting and one plate consuming, the two plates grind and bump and strike against each other, an aggressive dance that sends cracks and seizures in every direction. The Pacific Plate is traveling northwest, and the North American Plate is heading southwest, and they are both filled with road rage because they are literally going three inches a year. When ridges of the two unyielding plates catch on each other and their gears stall, an earthquake alleviates the pressure, and Californians check real estate listings in other states.

The San Andreas Fault is not a straight line. It runs in a roughly northwest direction through the middle of Southern California, but then above LA it swoops west for six miles before veering north again. Geologists call this the "Big Bend." Around twenty million years ago, basically yesterday in geological timelines, a portion of the Pacific Plate pushing north struck the Big Bend and the force was so great that a teardrop-shaped section of land broke off, except for its north-eastern point. The still-attached point acted as a hinge, and the rest of the broken piece would slowly rotate clockwise ninety degrees, from six o'clock to nine o'clock. It was like a gate swinging open to welcome into its paths the bracing, salty winds of the Pacific. Santa Barbara County turned sideways.

The location on the map we call Santa Barbara was once at about the same latitude as San Diego, which is now two hundred miles south. Geologists have discovered pinkish rocks called the Poway Formation in both San Diego and in the Santa Barbara Channel Islands, which were part of the ninety-degree swing. Santa Barbara and San Diego must have had a sort of falling out. My theory, slowly gaining support among geologists, is that because San Diego is the mecca of craft beer on the West Coast and Santa Barbara is home to three hundred wineries, those two just couldn't live together. Santa Barbara, classy lady that she is, had one too many over-hopped, palate-wrecking IPAs, and performed the slowest storm-off in history.

The massive pressure created by the land grinding northwards on its pivot caused the ground to fissure and fold. Mountains and foot-hills rumbled up and valleys collapsed down, like crests and troughs of ocean waves. Time and erosion shaped the brows, bumps, and wrinkles of Santa Barbara County's well-weathered face. Some steep and jagged, more rounded and polished, the one thing they all have in common is they are directed east to west. This is exquisitely rare. From the Arctic tip of Alaska all the way down to Cape Horn, you will find only one set of mountain ranges that rolls east to west where the land ends at the Pacific. They are called the Transverse Ranges, and at their heart are the Santa Ynez Mountains, which head due west until they fall into the ocean at Point Arguello near Lompoc. They run seventy miles sideways and sweep up the whole county on their way.

When I look at a map of California, I see what looks like an enormous dress sock, and Santa Barbara County is the heel of the sock. If you look above LA, you will see a piece of land that juts west, like a horizontal line. This is the coastline around the town of Santa Barbara. It is a perfect boundary between Southern California under the line and the Central Coast above. The sandstone rampart of the Santa Ynez Mountains stands above Santa Barbara, running beautifully parallel to her beaches, two dividing lines that say emphatically, "You are not in LA anymore, dude." This is the California Central Coast: home to frosty waters, university agriculture programs, the inquisitive brows of cypress and oaks so old they may have greeted the first Spaniards, and vines stitched on hillsides from Santa Barbara to Santa Cruz. We will have to pass over the mountains to see the rolling vinescapes of the Santa Ynez Valley. It is miraculous to me that a valley born of raging tectonic violence could be such an irenic place.

This is all to say that when you stand on Stearns Wharf in the afternoon looking directly over the Pacific Ocean, you are facing south. When you turn right, you are looking west. Santa Barbara is quite a magical place, but the sun does still set in the west.

I visited Santa Barbara for the first time after I watched a movie called *Sideways*. If you listen carefully, you may be able to hear the gathered voices of all the residents of the Santa Ynez Valley groaning in exasperation at the mention of this title. Though *Sideways* now feels like an old, obscure movie to the rest of the world, in Santa Ynez they continue to live it day after day after day. Its impact is called "The Sideways Effect." The film's influence on the once sleepy hollow of Santa Ynez was so momentous that now you cannot tell its story without *Sideways* as a character, and I cannot tell my own story without it either. The hills around Salzburg have *The Sound of Music*, the South has *Gone with the Wind*, and, for better or worse, the Santa Ynez Valley has *Sideways*.

*Sideways* is based on a book by the same name by Rex Pickett, which Alexander Payne restyled into a 2004 film that won an Oscar for Best Adapted Screenplay. It was a sixteen-million-dollar project that took in a hundred and ten million at the box office and snagged five Academy Award nominations, but sadly, not one for Paul Giamatti, who plays a divorced, fledgling writer—as though there is any other kind—carrying a residual itch for his ex-wife, a disheveled novel pending publisher approval, and a hangdog, bloodshot way in the world. To summarize, *Sideways* is a movie about a struggling and sardonic writer escaping to wine country from an unsatisfying life in Southern California. It's my life, except the movie has a lot of sex in it.

*Sideways* was set and filmed in the Santa Ynez Valley, a place that has about an acre of vines for each of its twenty thousand residents. Yet until I saw the movie, I had never heard of Santa Ynez, even though I lived three hours away. I used to drive right by on the way to Napa and Sonoma, another six hours north, when I could have been going west. The title of the film seems to rattle with several meanings, and I can't tell if Pickett or Payne intended a whisper of Santa Barbara County's epic westward slide in the name. In the book, the phrase "getting sideways" means getting drunk. I like to think that this wine-drenched valley got sideways a few million years ago and never got back up.

*Sideways* is a comedy when your life is going well. It is an Odd Couple story of two men in their fleshy, forty-something years, who lie a lot and drink almost as much. In the first scene bottles of aspirin and antacid are on parade when the leading character is jolted out of bed, at eleven in the morning, who then complains traffic made him late. Miles the oenophile and Jack the neophyte drive up to wine country for a weeklong bachelor send-off of wine tasting before Jack's wedding, as no two dudes have done—ever. When I first saw it in the theater, I was in my twenties, and my youthful dreams were still shiny and unwrinkled. I had never been fired; I had never been divorced; I had never had book proposals rejected; no publisher had ever called my prose "plodding and workmanlike but uncompelling"; and I was even sleeping through nights instead of spending them with dying patients. I thought *Sideways* was hysterical. I loved it so much, I went back the next week to see it again.

When I watch *Sideways* now, as life's wrinkles crease one at a time, I understand why some people have a visceral response to it. Yes, it is caustic and crassly voyeuristic at times, but what I can't miss anymore is how excruciatingly sad it is. I now see how much it is about grief and loss, and how the refusal to acknowledge endings can leave you in shadowy, hungover limbo. From the moment Miles declares, when comparing the merits of two wedding cakes, "I prefer the dark," the film is a downward spiral into a bottle of wine with all the sloshy emotions that accompany the next glass. *Sideways* is about drinking pinot in purgatory.

***

I didn't know any of that back then. I thought *Sideways* was a playful little wine romp with breathtaking scenery. I was transfixed by its portrayal of this wine country I knew nothing about, right down to the jazzy score that sounded like the soundtrack for a 1970s gumshoe. Two weeks after I first watched it, after a brief stopover in Santa Barbara for a slanted sunset, I crossed over the horizontal mountains and visited the Santa Ynez Valley for the first time. I wasn't the only one. It seemed like half of LA had shown up for what would be dubbed "The *Sideways* Tour," visiting every winery and restaurant cast in the movie.

The bell tower in the little wine village of Los Olivos struck drunk o'clock early on Saturday afternoon in those days. The bar at the Hitching Post, a local favorite steakhouse and winery that featured prominently in the movie, was three deep for three years, and their sales soared by 40 percent. Incensed locals had to start showing up at four in the afternoon to reclaim their bar stools. The Hitching Post is where Rex Pickett came up with the idea to write the book years earlier, and it seems that the character of Miles has some autobiographical echoes, just like the protagonist in Miles's novel mirrors his own life. No doubt the tales get taller every year, but the story goes that Pickett had been struggling with writer's block, but he found his muse in Hitching Post Pinot Noir and a corner barstool, and his book research was helped along by local winemakers drinking margaritas there after long days in their cellars.

Here are the statistics that truly capture The *Sideways* Effect, which reverberated far beyond this little valley. In the year after *Sideways*, a love letter to pinot noir, was released, nationwide pinot sales increased 16 percent. Merlot sales, on the other hand, went the other direction, because of one jolting line in the movie. On their second night in the valley, the engaged-to-another-woman Jack gives a very uncomfortable Miles a pep talk before they walk into the Los Olivos Café for dinner with Maya and Stephanie, two women they just met.

Jack: "If they want to drink merlot, we're drinking merlot."

Miles: "No. If anyone orders merlot, I'm leaving. I am not drinking any fucking merlot!"

Retail sales of merlot, historically one of the bestselling red wines in the United States, dropped 2 percent, and didn't recover its reputation for ten years. For merlot, it was the *Sideways* curse.

There is one more statistic I want you to know. One of the major tensions of the movie is whether Miles will get a book deal. Major publishers have already spurned his manuscript, and his agent has submitted it to a small, independent press as a Hail Mary. On their last afternoon before heading home, the boys are tasting wine at a commercial winery Jack dragged Miles to, fancifully called Frass Canyon. *Frass* means "insect excrement," and Miles says their pinot tastes like "the back of an LA school bus." That is where Miles gets the call. His agent informs him that the last interested publisher has passed on his book.

The slow simmer Miles has been burning the entire film boils over. He reaches over the bar to grab a bottle and empties it into his glass. The guy behind the bar snatches it away, so Miles takes the dump bucket, filled with the discarded and expectorated wine of the day's tastings, and dumps it over his head and down his shirt, downing all the bug spit that hits his mouth.

With all the well-crafted scenes in the film, why do I tell you about that one? Because in the year after the movie was released, the same thing happened three separate times at the Andrew Murray Winery alone. Maybe you can understand why some locals think *Sideways* desecrated the Santa Ynez Valley.

<hr />

As for me, I was bewitched. Like everyone hurtling out of LA smog, the first feature I noticed in Santa Ynez was the light. I am convinced this is a land graced with more photons than other places. Not only does the light sparkle in endless skies, but it seems to impart a little of itself in everything it touches. The hills glint in straw-gold fire, and the vines glow in greens so vivid they seem illuminated from within.

The air has a transparency and a purity here in this valley devoted to Saint Agnes, patron saint to virgins, that unveils the brightest days and darkest nights I have known since moving to California.

I felt I had hiked into the wine backcountry. I rumbled along gravel paths between vines and through dribbling creeks to drink chardonnay in tumbledown shacks. I tasted pinot in a corrugated blacksmith shop from the 1800s and syrah in a century-old gas station that had been relocated from Santa Barbara for ten dollars. I drank wine in A-frame barns and in weathered houses. I knocked on the unmarked door of a winery in a nondescript cement building adjacent to an auto repair shop, like I was slipping into a jazz-age speakeasy with a two-drink minimum and a complementary smog check.

Then, just beyond a tunnel of towering pines, there was the Hitching Post, perched on a bluff above an ostrich farm and the westward trickle of the Santa Ynez River, announced from the road by a high sign in school bus yellow. From the outside, the building looked to me like a mahogany red house popping up out of a wooden cigar box. Inside, on the wood-paneled walls were portraits of horses and flowery drapes that transport you to Sunday dinner at Nana's house, with the same beige tablecloths and low post-war ceilings built to withstand an air raid. The centerpiece of the dining room was the grill, on display behind glass, where generous cuts of steak, swordfish, garlic bread, and artichokes sizzled in butter over a fire of red oak harvested from the Central Coast.

They trotted out a multicourse menu of peculiar, nostalgic delights. Their best wines are named after fishing terms, like Highliner and Perfect Set, perhaps because after a day on the *Sideways* tour people were drunk like fish. The Hitching Post version of antipasto is a basket of crackers and a relish tray of carrots, celery, radishes, green onions, olives, and pickles. Then came the world's smallest shrimp cocktail and a salad assembled mostly as a leafy venue for their house-made blue cheese dressing. The basket of garlic bread was accompanied by a side of salsa, which violates all common culinary decency. Then, after you have tried it a few times, you will go to an Italian restaurant and say, "You forgot the salsa," when the server brings the garlic bread, and he will slap your face. Finally came a smoky, buttery filet with prolifically seasoned fries crisped in duck fat, served on old plates wreathed with burgundy floral patterns that I think match Nana's drapes. At the bar and around the crowded restaurant tables of people were sharing their wines with others at adjacent tables, the only place I have ever seen this happen. It felt like the entire valley was gathered in the dining room by the red oak fire for Sunday dinner. Everyone seemed familiar with each other or were just a charitable pour of wine away from knowing each other. Looking around, I thought to myself, *This valley is a strange and backward and beautiful place. I need to come back.*

The Santa Ynez Valley was once a stop on the stagecoach line between Los Angeles and San Francisco, but it seems that after those days were gone, Time's runaway stagecoach rushed right past on its way to meddle with other places. Standard Pacific chose to lay track in the early 1900s along the Pacific coast rather than cut inland, leaving Santa Ynez unspoiled by progress. There remains something wild and untouched about this valley of gnarled oaks twisting upon themselves and parched grass savannahs that are the Central Coast's answer to the Serengeti. Each time I visited I was intoxicated by the drinkable landscape, this countryside of grapes and horses, which rustled through the seasons at the pace of a lazy tumbleweed, and this community gathered at a long table with wine at the center.

Santa Ynez is the sort of place where you can get lost, which is exactly what I was looking to do in my last season of hospice, even if I wasn't conscious of it. In the valley I didn't have to play the role of

Reverend McHugh. I wasn't expected to carry the banner of faith or stand firm while others were falling apart. No one looked to me for answers they didn't have or prayers they couldn't express. I could be with my own questions there. I retreated to the valley again and again when hospice had drawn the life out of me, and when my nametag felt particularly heavy.

After I was dumped by hospice once and for all, I sought the therapy of Santa Ynez once more. I was able to go because a generous friend loaned me her house on a hill for a couple weeks. "The valley is a place to heal," insisted Kathy, when I protested her extravagant invitation.

Kathy was right. There is something deeply healing about this place where the skies have no ceiling but where nature's life cycle is close. The vines that run the lengths of hillsides like leafy pews are soothing to my eyes. They give an order to the chaos, a partnership between humans and Mother Nature creating beauty out of upheaval. They tame the hills but without taking away their wildness.

Everything in my world to the south seemed to be fading and dying, but the valley felt so astonishingly alive, a garden in continuous, irrepressible bloom, trees exploding in salvos of color, and vines dressed in fluorescence even on the baldest of hills. The springtime air was perfumed with peach and apricot blossoms, and the fresh grass rippled in the wind. Glossy new colts were getting their feet beneath them, stunted tails swishing feverishly, prancing and bucking and flopping on the ground next to their mamas. The cocktail of soil-replenishing seeds planted in the rows between the vines were flowering in lily-white and soft purple petals. Vineyards were coursing with fresh energy, sap dripping from the cuts of winter pruning, making pathways for tiny, wooly buds to appear.

The bucolic setting was a contrast to the world roiling within me, yet it seemed fitting to be there during budbreak, that fresh start in a vine's life that is also the season of the most vulnerable, unanswered questions. The survival questions that I find so distasteful and dry ate away at me: What am I supposed to do now? I have maybe two skills in this life and society isn't paying for them. I don't have the right degrees or training to be a teacher, or a web designer, or a forest ranger, plus I don't like being outside that long. Holding a Master of Divinity makes me sound godlike but thoroughly unequipped for a real job. Should I list that I can translate ancient Greek on my resume?

Those questions came with apprehension and a nervous thrill, but not surprise. What I didn't expect was the lack of relief I felt after leaving ministry, or after ministry left me. I felt untethered. I realized that one thing I could count on as a pastor was clarity. The role that I had so often found a hindrance to genuine intimacy had given me a way of acting around people. I knew the rules of behavior and what people expected of me, and there was comfort in that.

There was also a status and significance I had enjoyed in my role. When you are an ordained minister you wear religion on your sleeve, and any time you name your job, you are at risk of finding yourself in a confessional. Strangers will volunteer their regrets and their bad church experiences before they tell you their name. When a minister walks into a bar, all the jokes cease. As much as I detested that sometimes, I secretly relished the respect and prestige. I had experienced this treatment from the moment I considered ordination. When I played golf at the course next to the seminary I attended, my playing partners would apologize for dropping f-bombs after bad shots as soon as they learned where I was a student. Clearly, I am quite scandalized by cussing.

Suddenly the code of conduct had been suspended. And no one was falling silent when I walked into a room. I had surrendered the role and the robe, yet I felt adrift and unimportant. Can you relish the experience of blending in yet feel invisible at the same time?

I felt I had been cast out into the wilderness. The wilderness is where you find yourself when you are in transition. It's what William Bridges calls "the neutral zone." It's the place between here and there, the setting of historic wander and wait. It's also the perfect setting for a movie about going sideways in life.

In a rare scene of genuine vulnerability in the movie, Miles tells Maya the title of his novel: *The Day After Yesterday*. This is the line that interprets the entire film for me. Miles is suffering from grief's hangover. He is drifting in a haze cast by the past. He has defined himself by what he has lost, still bargaining that perhaps he can regain it. Bargaining is a recurring expression of grief.

Maya responds, "Oh, you mean *today*?" Today is the day that she is living, as the only character in the film who has acknowledged the end of a previous chapter of her life. But though his body may be living this day, the rest of Miles is still living yesterday. The "day after yesterday" is the day that grief lives over and over again.

Miles has a bottle of wine squirreled away at the bottom of his closet, a 1961 Château Cheval Blanc, arguably one of the best modern wines ever made. He had been saving it for his ten-year wedding anniversary, which never happened, so now it sits, fading slowly, reserved for no happy occasion. Cheval Blanc is from the right bank of Bordeaux in southwestern France, and it is a blend of 40 percent cabernet franc and 60 percent fucking merlot. The reason for Miles's aversion to merlot becomes more clear. Even cab franc, he confesses earlier in the film, is the varietal he "doesn't expect greatness from." It seems to me that this now middle-aged bottle of wine represents Miles, and the life he had planned for. The Cheval Blanc is a reminder of what he has lost. He can't bring himself to drink it because he still won't accept that his old life has died, the future he envisioned turned to vinegar.

I wasn't struggling to acknowledge an ending in the same way as Miles, as I knew my chaplain days were finished. But I was dealing with an aftermath that was messier and more painful than I expected. A huge part of my life had been subtracted, not to mention my livelihood, and a quiet grief lingered in me. Grief is always there to meet you in the in-between, in the transition between life's seasons.

I felt like I had lost my way. That's what grief can do to you. It casts you out into the middle, suspended between two places you can't reach, as though you teeter at the edge of a medieval stone bridge that stops halfway into the river. Impenetrable fog shrouds the way back, but there is no footpath ahead of you either, and you can't make out the riverbank on the other side.

Grief is raw and it is wild. The "stages of grief" that have become canon in our bereavement lexicon—denial, bargaining, anger, depression, acceptance—always sound so orderly to me. There is nothing orderly about grief. Grief is not progressing through emotional phases like hopping on lily pads over a pond. You don't feel a little bit better every day after your loss. That's not how Elisabeth Kübler-Ross and David Kessler envisioned it either when they conceived of the five stages, but popular culture has tucked them into a neat timeline of sadness.

To me, grief goes the way of a labyrinth. A labyrinth is a path or maze that slowly winds and turns its way to a center. History's most famous labyrinth belonged to King Minos of Crete, who ordered its construction to contain the Minotaur. The path to manhood and kingship wound Prince Theseus of Athens into the Minotaur's lair, where he slayed the horned man-beast and rescued the youth who had been offered as tribute. But in the Middle Ages, a labyrinth was a tool of pilgrimage for homebound pilgrims, a sort of spiritual enlightenment available in your backyard. The labyrinth path was the pilgrim trail in miniature, and the center was salvation, or the source of life, or God, or your truest self, or Home.

From a distance, a labyrinth looks like a series of concentric circles spiraling into the center like grooves on a record, a few gentle loops to the finish. It is anything but. The path turns and lurches and doubles back on itself, sometimes tilting you directly toward the center on the high road to glory but then exiling you out to the farthest edge. It thwarts and it wanders and it disorients. The labyrinth is a path of unraveling. Before you can reach the center, you must be undone.

Surely this is life's path, but is it not also the way of grieving? You have lost something, including yourself, and you are cast into the labyrinth of grief, saying farewell to the life you have known, unaware of what lies ahead, unsure if you will return or who you will be at the end. Maps aren't clearly marked. There are bandits along the way. You walk alone, wrested out of time and space, because time always stops when you are grieving, and there are deep chambers of grief you must face alone. You don't know whether you are journeying toward healing and acceptance or toward a Minotaur with you on the menu.

Most of the labyrinth path goes through wilderness. The wilderness is where your name tag is blank. Reverend McHugh was gone, but no new letters were appearing. Bridges was right: I was tempted to scribble on it the first thing I came up with. It is so much easier to leap to the next phase or career or relationship than it is to wait for your new name.

My wilderness wander would last much longer than I thought, persisting even well after I started working again, but I guess wilderness periods always do. If you knew the way out, you wouldn't be in the wilderness. Grief takes the long way.

The best path between two places might be a straight line, but we will never know because no human has ever taken one. Even this land under my feet on my Santa Ynez retreat seemed to be on its own labyrinth journey, ever since it flung itself athwart and reached west for the sea. It took twenty million years to get there.

On our crooked paths, there are moments we are offered glimpses of the center—like when I stood among the stones of Châteauneuf-du-Pape—only then to be jerked back out to the limits, farther away than ever. Or at least that's how it seems. The truth is, on the labyrinth path, even when you are veering sideways, you are still moving toward the center.

❦

Pinot noir gets called "the heartbreak grape," and it is fitting that our heartbroken friend Miles is smitten with it. He rhapsodizes about pinot even while bemoaning his own life. The attachment is so personal that when Miles describes pinot, he seems equally to be describing himself:

> Maya: Why are you so into pinot? I mean, it's like a thing with you.
>
> Miles: I don't know, I don't know. It's a hard grape to grow, as you know, right? It's thin-skinned, temperamental, ripens early. It's not a survivor like cabernet, which can just grow anywhere and thrive even when neglected. No, pinot needs constant care and attention. And in fact it can only grow in these really specific, little, tucked-away corners of the world. And, only the most patient and nurturing of growers can do it, really. Only somebody who really takes the time to understand pinot's potential can then coax it into its fullest expression. Then, I mean, oh its flavors, they're just the most haunting and brilliant and thrilling and subtle and ancient on the planet.

He's right. Pinot turns wine drinkers into poets. If you catch it at the right moment, pinot noir carries a perfume from on high. It has all the silk and expression of heaven's own vintage. But both in the vineyard and in the cellar, pinot is high maintenance. It's those thin, sensitive skins that offer it so little protection from this bad world. It seems to take every little bit of weather personally. Pinot likes sun, but not heat. It turns to raisins in a heatwave and shivers in the cold. It lets almost everything in too close: frost, mildew, bugs. If you are lucky enough to get a good crop pressed into barrel, you may still have to endure its theatrical mood swings. My winemaker friend Brandon calls its histrionics "the death and resurrection of pinot noir," when a barrel will go from bursting with aroma and complexity one week to tasting like nothing at all the next. You can only place it in deep hiding and wait for it to come back from the dead. André Tchelistcheff, the famed winemaking pioneer who made California's first great pinot, said "God made cabernet sauvignon, whereas the devil made pinot noir."

The Santa Ynez Valley has no business growing pinot noir. Santa Ynez is south of Spain, south of Greece, south of Sicily. It is the same latitude as Tunisia. It is the last great wine region of the Northern Hemisphere as you plummet toward the equator. The fact that the valley can grow wine grapes at all is remarkable, but that it is hospitable to pinot noir is miraculous. The motherland of Burgundy sits at about the same latitude as Seattle, a thousand miles north of Santa Ynez. But when the gate of Santa Barbara County swung open, it received the Pacific Ocean as its guest. The average water temperature throughout the year off the coast of Lompoc is fifty-eight degrees, and that makes all the difference.

On their first stop in the valley, Miles takes Jack into the Santa Rita Hills. This is the westernmost part of the Santa Ynez Valley and the most willing subject of the Pacific's cold reign. It is high-class real estate for pinot noir. A fog bank forms over Lompoc almost every night on the calendar, and then drifts inland along the transverse hallway toward Buellton, covering pinot and chardonnay vines with a thick marine layer in the mornings. The daytime air heats up slowly, like water out of the refrigerator. Then, when the sun has burned off the fog and the air reaches a simmer, the fan starts to blow. Right around lunchtime, the ocean winds blast off from Lompoc, fittingly called Rocket Town, and rush down the east-west throat of the valley, buffeting the Santa Rita Hills on early spring days with frigid, knock-you-down winds. But, if the pinot manages to flower properly in the wind, it is contented in the chilled sunlight, producing a unique style of lush and vibrant pinot noir.

As for Miles, if he has any chance of thriving in his own little tucked-away corner like his beloved pinot, something has to die. After Jack's wedding ceremony back in LA, he meets his ex-wife in the parking lot. Earlier that week he had been jolted to learn she had remarried, but now he discovers that she is also pregnant. As he turns left out of the parking lot when everyone else is turning right to the reception, I am left to wonder if he is going to end his life. Instead, he takes the life of his 1961 Cheval Blanc, drinking it unceremoniously at a diner out of a Styrofoam cup. His old life has passed.

Our last glimpse is of Miles, months later, driving back up to Santa Ynez to knock on Maya's door.

⁕

Several weeks after my Santa Ynez wilderness escape, I attended a conference in Napa about wine and spirituality, which I was thrilled to learn is a thing. I have always loved Napa, but it looked different to me this time. Driving Highway 29 through Napa Valley felt like driving Main Street at Disneyland, fitting because Napa receives more tourists than anywhere in California besides Disneyland. That week I navigated a hedge maze to get to the winery bar. I considered a museum of modern art while tasting a hundred-and-fifty-dollar cab at another winery. I ate at Michelin star restaurants. It all felt so impressive, so polished, so opulent.

I desperately missed the Santa Ynez Valley, which felt like Mayberry at happy hour compared to this. The valley I had visited so many times seemed like it was now visiting me. I didn't know how to identify my new self yet, but I was starting to identify with that place. I felt that I was coming to know it, and just maybe it was starting to recognize me, too. Could it be turning into my own little tucked-away corner of the world, my somewhere?

That week at the conference we talked about promised lands. Promised lands drip with wine and loom with giants. Usually the more inviting they look, the farther away they seem, and the more obstacles are in the way.

On the last morning of the conference, I received a call from the manager of a winery outside of Los Olivos, who knew I was looking for work. He offered me a job selling wine in their tasting room.

I was moving to the Santa Ynez Valley.

## _Nine_

# THE KING'S HIGHWAY

I awoke before daybreak on the morning I moved to the Santa Ynez Valley, and I could tell further sleep had already gone ahead without me. I double-checked my surroundings, one more time, to make sure I hadn't just dozed off during a hospice visit and dreamed this entire thing. The idea of working at a winery in Santa Ynez had just been a fantasy that sustained me through the darkest nights of hospice, or so I thought, right up there with bartending at a swim-up bar in the Bahamas or working as a roving hot dog vendor at Wrigley Field. But this was really happening.

I spent a few minutes listening to a dove cooing outside the window, while dreaming about what was for dinner. This is a recurring quirk of mine, that often among my day's first bleary thoughts is what I will be eating later that night. But I knew tonight would be special. In about fourteen hours I would be eating artichokes and ahi tuna seared over oak coals and drinking Cork Dancer Pinot at the Hitching Post, my first meal as a resident of Santa Ynez. What I didn't know was when I sat down to eat at the bar, Gray Hartley, the lanky, lovably oddball cellarmaster of

Hitching Post Wines, would assume the stool next to me, listen to my story, and say, "That's amazing, Adam. Welcome home."

There is no way Gray could have known how meaningful those words were to me. In the weeks leading up to my move, I had been thinking a lot about home. I was moving toward something new, but I was also leaving. It is unsettling when you leave home. It is far more unsettling when home leaves you. My experience ever since I returned from France was that I still lived on the same block, but home had fled the neighborhood. I was left feeling like a visitor where I once belonged, like I had worn out my welcome in the same place that once threw its arms open to me.

This idea of home is mercurial. Home seems to be a spirit that enlivens a particular place or community but is free to go whenever and wherever it wants. You think you have home under lock and key, and then it sneaks out the back door. When home departs, somehow *here* becomes *there* while you are still standing in the same spot. The place you knew, the people you knew in that place, and the person you were in that place to those people all become strangers to one another. I know no deeper loneliness than when a familiar place turns cold. Many of us have had the experience of returning as an adult to the house of our childhood and realizing it's not home anymore. The place has changed, and you have changed. There is a grief in learning you are homesick for a place that no longer exists.

Home and just about everything I had known for the last fifteen years uprooted themselves and moved away, leaving me drifting in the wilderness. After another several months of worsening tension, my marriage was hanging on by a lone tendril. Losing your job is a hard frost on an already tender shoot. We hadn't given up yet, but in retrospect, I think we were in anticipatory grief for the end. We were bargaining that we could live long distance, or that I could scout out a future life for us together in the country, far removed from her job. We were two people who thrived on distance, and in truth the decision for me to move and her to stay was far too easy for both of us to make. We were parting into separate lives, with some feelings of relief.

In the list of life's most stressful events, job loss, career change, marriage breakdown, and moving to a new home are always right at the top. Instead of tackling them one at a time, I thought I would knock them out all at once. The only one left was death.

⁂

I was on a pilgrimage to find a new home for my new self, or probably more accurately to find a new self in a new home. My winery job began in a few days, and Kathy had generously offered her vacation house to me again while I looked for a place to rent. My car had been packed for two days, with lamps and books and suitcases crammed into no particular order. A three-hour drive around LA and up the coast was ahead of me, so I headed to the Coffee Klatch one last time, taking in Tiburcio Tapia's old Cucamonga winery on Foothill Boulevard while I was there. Foothill Boulevard is the fabled Old Route 66, which Steinbeck referred to as the "Mother Road" in *The Grapes of Wrath*. Route 66 offered salvation to Dust Bowl refugees fleeing west and, decades later, became a symbol of mobility and adventure on the open road. Exodus and adventure. That all sounded good to me today.

Wine was at the beginning of my path that morning, and wine was waiting at the end. But if you live in greater Los Angeles, the in-between is where it feels you spend most of your time. The LA freeway system is an unforgiving, yellow-speckled monster flailing its wild tentacles of transportation all over the city. It is a purgatory of steel and asphalt. Or, when my metaphors are not fueled by road rage, it is a labyrinth: a world-between-worlds hemmed in by guardrails and sound barriers, where pilgrims weave through bends and straightaways and nonexistent shortcuts while threatening the whole time to give up and turn around. They sputter toward healing waters and sand or the promise of home, given occasional glimpses of future salvation but remaining yet so far away, despairing of ever arriving at all. Pilgrims of old faced churning seas and ominous skies, bandits and threats of violence, hunger and exposure. They never had to navigate the 101 and 405 interchange. That is the true test of faith.

A quirky part of the Angeleno dialect is to put a "the" in front of freeway numbers. It's not "I-5" or "5," it's "the 5." It's the secret code you must use to be initiated into these concrete rites of passage. So today my exodus out of LA would go the way of the 210 to the 134 to the 101. It was a drive I had done at least a hundred times, though the thrill and anticipation I felt for it never faded. The route would take me west past the Rose Bowl in Pasadena, cut through the glossy high-rises of Glendale where I might get a glimpse of distant downtown LA, and then hook north at the LA Zoo up the coast.

The 210 West follows the path of the San Gabriel Mountains, another one of those Transverse Ranges that rumble unexpectedly west. I keep thinking that our ancient Roman gardener friend Ampelos would have lost his mind if he saw all these south-facing slopes that westward slanting mountains create. He wouldn't have found the ideal climate until he discovered the Santa Ynez Mountains a hundred miles northwest, but he certainly would have planted on all these sunbathing hills.

That is exactly what happened in the first half of the nineteenth century. There was an era when Los Angeles was called the City of Vines and had no serious rival for wine in all of California. A French immigrant, the son of a Bordeaux barrel maker, is credited for the explosion of vines along the banks of the LA River in the 1800s. His name? Jean-Louis Vignes. That's right, his last name was "Vines." It seems terribly unfair that some people have their destinies embedded in their last names. This book would be a lot shorter if my last name were "Chapelbolt" or "Vindoosh."

Monsieur Vines planted a forty-acre vineyard around where Union Station now sits in downtown LA and built his winery in the shade of a massive sycamore tree, an *aliso* in Spanish, so he called his operation El Aliso. He renamed himself Don Luis del Aliso, in the style of the Mexican rancheros who had been granted much of Alta California in the 1820s and '30s after Mexico won independence from Spain. Don Luis poured his first vintage in 1837, and eventually he was making twelve thousand cases of wine and brandy annually and selling it up and down the coast—California's first wine and spirits distributor. He may have also been the first to experiment with French vines in California, though that is a historian's guess. We do know for sure that travelers and guests at El Aliso toasted the quality of Don Luis's wine, and new settlers in the pueblo of Los Angeles started planting grape trees everywhere they could.

We can trace the legacy of Los Angeles wine back even farther. There is a reason why a man named Vines thought to plant his vineyard there rather than Monterey or San Francisco. That reason is found a few miles northeast of his sycamore tree: a magnificent adobe-brick building covered in fired tile and crowned with bell towers and crosses, called Mission San Gabriel Arcángel. This is one of the oldest buildings in California, standing in its present location since 1775, and it was holy ground zero for what would become the pueblo of Los Angeles a few years later, founded by Spanish settlers ten miles to her west. The Mission and its surrounding rancho was called La Viña Madre—the Mother Vine, who gave birth to the commercial wine industry of Southern California in the 1830s. At her peak La Viña Madre stretched out 163,000 vines over 160 acres, and she produced ten thousand cases of wine a year. Settlers took cuttings from her bountiful vines and spread them throughout the LA Basin and the San Gabriel Valley. Our friend Tiburcio Tapia obtained his 565 vines for his Cucamonga rancho from La Viña Madre.

My personal encounters with Mission San Gabriel took place, perhaps not surprisingly at this point, almost exclusively in the middle of the night. Anybody can visit places in the daylight, but the ghosts of history are most felt in the moonlight, or so I told myself as I paced Mission Drive trying to stave off sleep. We had at least two Chinese patients that I can remember die at the Royal Vista Skilled Nursing Center a block away. Those were always memorable nights, as Buddhist chants on CD would fill the room of the deceased patient, and there would even be a webcam set up so that family in China could join the chorus, ushering the departing soul into the afterlife. It is a beautiful ritual that just took forever, and I would wander around the Mission neighborhood while waiting for the right time to call the funeral home.

A corner of the Mission garden next to the cemetery features a prehistoric-looking vine with a trunk the girth of an oak tree, which may be more than two hundred years old. The year 1774 was once scrawled on a fading wood sign at the base of the trunk. It would make for an incredible legacy and symbol of the Mother Vine, but in 1774 the Mission was three miles away from where it stands now, and it likely wasn't until 1778 that the first mission vines arrived in California. Some city records suggest it was planted in the 1820s, still quite impressive, especially because it still produces fruit! Thick branches creep hundreds of square feet along a tall red pergola, where translucent, marble-sized berries hang down to be collected each October by the LA Vintners Association and made into wine. That lovely old matriarch has seen some things. I was glad to know she was there when I made death visits nearby.

But today, I was wide-eyed on this beautifully smog-free April morning driving west toward the 101, passing just a little north of Mission San Gabriel. As I did, I found myself on a road that carries a much older name: El Camino Real. This is the Royal Road, or better, the King's Highway, that would take me all the way to Santa Ynez.

The King's Highway links La Viña Madre with twenty other historic, beautiful, troubled buildings up and down the state. I was a pilgrim on the original wine trail of California.

❦

In 1769, the same year Thomas Jefferson planted his first experimental grapevines at Monticello on the other side of the country, Father Junipero Serra set uncovered foot on the soil of Alta California as a member of the Portolá expedition, the first overland exploration of the northern half of Spanish California. The padre's foot was uncovered because, as a member of the Order of Discalced Carmelites, he either went barefoot or with feet exposed in open sandals, partly as a display of humility and solidarity with the poor and partly because the Carmelites thought sandals and socks looked ridiculous. It's possible he introduced the flip flop into California. A key leader on what was called "the Sacred Expedition," Father Serra carried a quiver of titles with him into San Diego: shoeless Carmelite, fashion trendsetter, Franciscan friar, first president of the Alta California Missions, and one that he would win later: founding father of California wine.

Before that time, what we now call California was considered part of New Spain but remained unexplored by land. Juan Rodríguez Cabrillo sailed its shores in 1542, in search of a water passage believed to cut through the continent and for Cibola, the fabled seven cities of gold, which wouldn't be discovered until centuries later by famed explorer Nicolas Cage. But in the 1740s, Russian fur trappers from Alaska made incursions into California waters, and the Spanish king, Carlos III, refused to let the Russians tamper with his election over New Spain. The king ordered a swift possession of Alta California.

His California conquistadors assumed three guises: soldiers, who built forts and armories called *presidios*; civilian settlers, who founded secular towns called *pueblos*; and Franciscan priests, who established *missions* for converting and educating native inhabitants. The

Missions aimed to be not only religious centers but self-sustaining economies, powered by the labor of the newly baptized members of the indigenous populations, who would learn agriculture, engineering, animal husbandry, and carpentry.

Fourth graders in the California public school system learn that over the next sixty-four years, Junipero Serra and his successors would establish twenty-one Missions, which were protected by garrisons at four presidios, including the presidio that became the foundation of downtown Santa Barbara in 1782. The first Mission was established in San Diego in 1769 and the last in the Sonoma Plaza forty miles north of San Francisco in 1823. There are three Missions in Santa Barbara County alone—Santa Barbara, called the "Queen of the Missions" with her classical Roman façade; the more modest Santa Inés, consecrated in 1804 at the eastern border of what is now Solvang, ushering in the modern history of my favorite valley; and La Purísima, pushed out toward the coast in Lompoc where pinot noir shivers in the fog, beautifully restored during the Depression as part of a New Deal project. These are postcards of a romanticized Spanish California, stunning buildings in Spanish colonial style where bells call out the hours of the day, fountains dribble, and rose gardens lead into holy chapels, all held together in cloisters of adobe, a sun-dried mudbrick that hardens to stone in arid climates but dissolves like sugar in wet winters and cracks at even the rumor of an earthquake.

The Spanish colonists introduced California as we now know it: multitudes of cities that grew up around the Missions and are all seemingly named after Catholic saints, groves of olives and orchards of oranges and walnuts and pears and olives and lemons and apricots, all brought across the border. They did not introduce the avocado, however, as the first avocado tree in the United States was planted by a Santa Barbara judge in 1871, founding a whole new California religion.

I wasn't en route to the Santa Ynez Valley on this morning for avocados or walnuts. Perhaps my move north was set in motion the day the Spanish introduced the wine-bearing vine into California. The pattern is familiar. Just as the Roman legions who pushed into Gaul brought grapevines with them as memories of the familiar, the Spanish couldn't conceive of making a life in the New World without wine. Wine has always been a sacrament of home. And it was the religious orders, once again, who were charged with tending the vines and making the wines, first for the purposes of the altar and then for trade. At Mission San José the annual treading of the grapes was accompanied by the singing of the choir.

❦

1769 is usually the date marked as the beginning of the California wine industry, and Missions mythology would have us believe that Junipero Serra himself toted vine cuttings from the Baja Peninsula and planted them in San Diego soil, as well as personally packing every adobe brick into its mold. But it was in 1778 that the Spanish ship *San Antonio* sailing from Mexico brought the first European grapevines into Alta California, which would be transported over land to Mission San Juan Capistrano, the birthplace of California wine. Capistrano's first vintage was 1782, perhaps the same year the first vine was stuck in the ground in Santa Barbara, and within a few years almost every Mission was growing grapes and making wine, except for those in fogbound locations, like San Francisco and Santa Cruz. San Juan Capistrano may have been first, but Mission San Gabriel would become Madre to the nascent California wine industry for the next fifty years.

California was actually awash in indigenous grapevines when the Spanish arrived, but they quickly discovered the native grapes made for terrible wine. This was a lesson North American colonies on both coasts would learn over and over again. Native American grapevines produced a beverage that resembled a musty, funky, flat strawberry soda. American colonists on the East Coast often referred to its scent as "foxy," which is less sexy than it sounds. They thought it smelled like a dead fox.

About the only thing the American vine has accomplished in the wine world was the proliferation of a yellow nightmare called phylloxera, a banana-peel-colored parasite indigenous to North America that feeds on grapevine roots and almost wiped out the French wine industry in the late 1800s. Botanists in England thought it would be a jolly good idea to collect and study grapevines from all over the world, but phylloxera stowed away on the sail across the pond as perhaps the first unwanted American vacationer. American vines had developed immunity to phylloxera over centuries of cohabitation, but the European vines had lived alone, and their first date was catastrophic. Six million acres of French vines were decimated, beginning with imported vines planted just north of Avignon in 1962. It looked like France was on its way to becoming a country of beer drinkers. But the solution was found: graft the European grapevine onto immune American rootstocks. So the American vine both created and solved the problem, establishing the definitive model for American foreign policy ever since.

California in the era of the Missions was isolated enough by mountains and deserts that phylloxera wasn't yet a problem for their imported vines. The European varietal the padres planted in California didn't inspire much song and poetry, but at least it didn't smell like roadkill. They selected a Spanish red grape called listán prieto, which in the eighteenth century flourished in the Canary Islands and Peru, two places the Franciscans would have passed through on the way to California. It became so synonymous with this undertaking it was renamed the mission grape. Mission was chosen more for its survival instincts than for its spiritual nature. It is hearty, prolific, and disease resistant. Mission cuttings endured international sea voyage and overland expedition, even burial during the snowy California winter of 1778, and yet still produced big clusters and massive yields of unremarkable but drinkable fruit. It thrived in the dry heat of Southern California in particular, helping Mission San Gabriel earn its status.

Mission grapes are actually better for eating than for drinking, as its berries are large and pulpy with high sugar content and low acid. Dry mission wines were syrupy and juicy, with the resemblance and concentration of cranberry juice, and only those with extraordinary faith could perceive this uninspired libation as a sacrament. People would take the cup at the altar and feel utterly abandoned by God. Fortunately, the padres quickly learned the trick every decent bartender knows: the best way to mask bad ingredients is to add alcohol. The most prized liquids of the California Missions were wines spiritualized by copper still into brandy, or a heavenly nectar known as Angelica, which involved adding brandy during fermentation to arrest the activity of the yeast. The result was a sensationally sweet and sultry dessert wine dripping with honeyed, caramelized orange rind and hazelnut flavors that could make angels sing and could age just about forever, even surviving hot and bumpy mule rides up the King's Highway. Angelica was the most pleasure a Franciscan priest was allowed.

<hr />

I was on my way out of LA, my home of over ten years. I was surprised to feel a pang of sadness. Places are storehouses of memories, and there were a few I wasn't eager to leave behind. Many of my best friends from college still live there, likely the only friendships I will keep my entire life. Since I am an only child, I have always considered them my brothers. I perused some of my favorite memories of them as I drove past Old Town Pasadena, where we met for burgers once a month or so after college to catch up. I thought about my southern friend Justin who would stay for a "second seating" on Sunday nights in our school's dining hall. He would eat and stay at the table for so long that the group he came with would finish and then a second group would join him. He was no doubt procrastinating from studying, but I think he was the first one who taught me about long meals and unrushed conversations around the table. One of the things I love about a good bottle of wine is its ability to make people linger at the table. No one hurries away when there is still wine left in the bottle.

Then there is my college roommate Sean, my best friend of twenty-five years. In our sophomore year, a few of us were walking back to campus with our glossy new local phonebooks, an exciting thing back before the invention of the Google machine. As some girls passed us, Sean held his phonebook up, saying, "Hey baby! I'll call you!" The rest of us just about fell over laughing. Fifteen years later, I officiated Sean's wedding. He didn't marry any of those girls on the quad. He never called.

The last LA landmark I took note of was Forest Lawn, the sprawling cemetery and park in the Hollywood Hills, which had become my personal symbol over the years that I was leaving hospice behind, on my way to hills that were still breathing. As I took the curve onto the 101, I was now on the main route of El Camino Real.

The King's Highway was originally a foot and mule path forged 650 miles up the coast to link the twenty-one Missions, which were spaced about a day's hard ride from each other. Legend says the padres planted mustard seeds along the way to mark the trail, and on this early spring day the roadsides north of LA exploded with yellow flower. From a distance it appeared to me like Mother Nature had highlighted her favorite sections of the hillsides.

Now the route of El Camino Real is marked by another sign: a Mission bell hanging on the curved handle of a walking stick, appearing every few miles. Every pilgrimage needs a symbol. Pilgrims on the Camino de Santiago in northern Spain carry a seashell as they trek toward the Atlantic Ocean. When they arrive in the Navarra region, seashells dangling off their backpacks, they can fill their water bottles with wine at Bodegas de Irache, a nineteenth-century winery that built a wine fountain for pilgrims on the Camino. The winery is a wing of the Monasterio de Irache, a thousand-year-old monastery established as a hospice on the Camino de Santiago, one of those way-stops to the sacred, offering rest and healing to pilgrims.

Wine is a pilgrim drink. Since the Middle Ages, when the routes to the Holy Land and Rome, Canterbury, and Santiago de Compostela filled with pilgrims who dared to leave home to go on holy search, wine has always been high on the sacred traveler's list of needs. Home may enfold you, but the way cracks you open, exposing you on arduous paths to the unfamiliar and the mysteries of God, and at the end of the day's journey you may well need a carafe of wine to sew yourself back together.

There are no wine fountains along the King's Highway, but the Missions played the role of the monasteries on the trail, establishing a California tradition of warm hospitality to travelers that would reach its zenith in the haciendas of the Ranchero era. The Missions were the first hostels of California, providing guest quarters and a generous public table of food and wine free of charge. If you brought news from the other Missions, or from Spain or Mexico, you might be rewarded with a pour of Angelica.

The symbol of the King's Highway is a bell and a walking stick, but it could just as easily be a grape cluster, since both the ancient and modern California wine trail follows the route of El Camino Real. I consider the modern wineries along this path to have assumed the mantle of hospitality established by the Missions. I may be the only person left who considers wineries to be outposts of heaven.

That is why I am deeply saddened that something as beautiful, convivial, and full of grace as wine was introduced into California by institutions haunted by profound tragedy and grief. Wine should give life and comfort and bring thirsty seekers together around the table. But the pilgrim path of El Camino Real is a trail of tears for the native peoples of California. There were three hundred thousand Native Americans when the Spanish arrived in 1769. Less than a hundred years later, there were fifty thousand. The Missions baptized eighty thousand neophytes; sixty thousand of them died from smallpox, syphilis, and other diseases, and a few lost their lives at the hands of the soldiers who were there to protect them. Four thousand of the local Chumash tribe died at Mission Santa Barbara alone. The most violent uprising in the history of the California Missions occurred at Mission Santa Inés.

Those beautiful buildings that offered such generous hospitality and founded treasured California traditions housed some ugly truths. Once baptized, a native convert was no longer able to leave of his own accord, and soldiers were sent to whip deserters back to the Missions. The padres called this "mortification of the flesh," but the rest of us just call it mortifying. I believe that Father Serra and his fellow padres genuinely thought they were doing good, and even that they bonded in love and faith with some under their charge. But you can't be a servant to all if you make a slave of another.

Laboring without wages, the native workers in the vineyards, called *viñaderos*, carried out California's first wine harvests. In the early years before brick vats and cellars had been constructed, *viñaderos* would stomp grapes on cowhides tied on a slope between four poles. Clay jars would catch the juice at the bottom, which they would transfer to another cowhide that was stitched closed for fermentation and a few months of aging. From what I can tell, the native peoples, like the Chumash tribe who populated the Santa Barbara coastal shelf, were California's first winemakers.

There is an epiphany waiting on the King's Highway for those souls brave enough to run the gauntlet of the Los Angeles freeway system. I was particularly desperate for it today. All through the LA labyrinth I felt like I was holding my breath while jostled through a narrow, crowded hallway. I kept a vigilant grip on the wheel while LA drivers wove their tapestry of chaos around me. Everything in me felt tight and squeezed, a little from the ordinary stress of the drive but mostly from the burden of starting over. My body knew I wasn't going on vacation this time. I felt like a spring coiled with nervous energy.

I was eager to join the Santa Ynez wine community, but I couldn't tell if the tension in my chest was from anticipation or terror. The last time I had a regular job was the summer after my freshman year in college, when I worked the salad bar at a Soup Plantation knockoff in our local mall. I spent three months refilling canisters of croutons and pepperoncini and wiping up ranch dressing that customers doused on salads like a cargo plane dropping water on a forest fire. I wasn't particularly good at that job, because I didn't particularly care. This time, I cared, which made it far more nerve-wracking. I couldn't blame poor performance on the fact that I was going back to school in the fall.

I passed the sign for Mission San Buenaventura, thirty-five miles south of Santa Barbara. Buenaventura was the ninth rung on the ladder of California Missions and the first of five established in Chumash territory. It was famous for its wooden bells, the only of their kind in the Mission system. They were later replaced with bells forged of the traditional cast iron—I imagine because with wooden bells telling the time, everyone was always late to everything.

Just past the Mission, as I came to Seaward Avenue in the city of Ventura, at the end of my narrow and congested hallway, the curtains parted and the world opened before me. There was the Pacific Ocean, secret until now, slate blue and roiling, vast and mysterious enough to absorb the troubles of the whole world. It was just a glimpse, and the waters soon hid themselves from the road once again, but it was a prophecy of future glory, a moment of consolation on this sometimes-disquieting pilgrim path. The salt air streamed into the vents. My soul took a deep breath.

The curtain dropped once more as the route returned inland, along steep rock walls scorched with the marks of recent fires, but the sandstone outcroppings of the Santa Ynez Mountains soon came into view. My anticipation was building as I arrived in the rustic beach town of Carpinteria, which means "Carpenter Shop," but always sounds to me like something that might require an antibiotic cream. Carpinteria was named by soldiers on the Portolá expedition that dropped off Father Serra in San Diego and kept trekking north toward Monterey. In Carp they saw Chumash master craftsmen building their famous ocean-going boats, called *tomols*, that took them all the way out to the Channel Islands and beyond. The builders would weave wooden planks together and seal the boats with the tar that naturally seeps up from fissures in the ocean floor. Those cracks are also why oil rigs menace a few miles offshore, now mostly dormant, but at twilight they look like the Spanish Armada has returned to reclaim her colony.

Carpinteria is the point where the King's Highway pivots sideways. Even though I was still on the 101 North, the compass pointed due west. It's easy to tell in the late afternoon, because it feels like if you keep going, you will drive straight into the sun. Santa Barbara was close.

On December 4, 1602, Spanish captain Sebastian Vizcaino, on maritime exploration of Alta California sixty years after Cabrillo, narrowly survived a violent storm in this channel. In thanksgiving he named the area in honor of Santa Barbara, who celebrates her feast day on December 4. World-weary travelers have been calling out to

Santa Barbara for rescue ever since. After the Mission era, once the golden spike had been driven into the transcontinental railroad, doctors in the east prescribed the sun and salty air of Santa Barbara to their convalescent patients. All year round, her south-facing beaches spend long and lazy hours watching the arc of the sun. It's the only place I have seen the sun both rise and set over the Pacific. The old pueblo became a health spa for the wealthy, a reputation it has maintained for 150 years. Even for the common people, the breezy Mediterranean climate and untroubled waters of the Santa Barbara Channel are enough to bring you back from the dead. In fact, the tiny hamlet of Summerland to its east was founded as a spiritualist colony, by people who believed they could communicate with the spirits of the dead. Santa Barbara beaches are still populated with mellow, health-conscious, sun-worshiping weirdos. They have grown on me.

All I saw of Santa Barbara that day were the palms and bougainvillea that soften the s-curves of the freeway through downtown. I had forty miles to go, and I felt like I could get out of my car and sprint the rest of the way. I passed the sign for Old Mission Santa Barbara, which sits in an amphitheater of hills overlooking the Santa Barbara Channel, and then the town of Goleta, where the old San José Winery building still gracefully crumbles. That is where the padres made wine for the Mission and her precocious pueblo in the young decades of the nineteenth century. UCSB flew by next, where students live in dorms with ocean views and must choose each morning between attending early class or surfing. Most flunk out.

The landscape started to change. Squat groves of orange trees spread out in neat rows to my left, and avocado trees climbed the foothills on the passenger side for miles. I was a little disappointed to see that the avocado trees were lush with foliage. In the winter, farmers prune them tight and lather their bark with white latex paint to protect them from sunburn, which, in my imagination, appear as thousands of massive skeletal fingers clawing their way out of the ground. It haunts me.

A few hundred yards beyond the orange groves hung a green wooden sign suspended on a tall, rusty metal gate, which read "Rancho Dos Pueblos." I will try to remain calm while I tell you that on October 16, 1542, the Spanish ships *San Salvador* and *La Victoria*, captained by Juan Rodríguez Cabrillo, the first European explorer to see California, anchored off the shore in this very spot, the shocking plot twist in the grand story of Santa Barbara. Dos Pueblos was home to two Chumash villages that faced each other on short bluffs across the mouth of the creek, and this incursion of tall ships and white men must have come upon them like an alien invasion. They handled it quite well, paddling out in their *tomols* with gifts for these overdressed newcomers, who themselves shared of their daily wine rations prescribed to prevent scurvy, the same friendly welcome the Portolá expedition would receive at Dos Pueblos 127 years later.

Finally, after a drumroll of local history and a few lanky puffs of eucalyptus, the skies cracked open and all the prophecies of the King's Highway were fulfilled. The Pacific Ocean reappeared, glinting in sapphire and emerald green all the way out to Santa Cruz and Santa Rosa Islands, which emerged like mountains in the sea on this perfectly transparent afternoon. Before me on the mainland, only a narrow grassy mantle hosting a few lucky cows and alpacas separated the ocean from the rocky face of the Santa Ynez Mountains, sparsely covered in chaparral and scrub oak on its south side. A blaze of mustard flower lit the way. This is the Gaviota coast, seventy-six miles of pristine virgin land, perhaps the last undeveloped section of California coastline that wouldn't fall into the sea if you tried to build on it. It is a pilgrimage site even for the butterflies, as one exit sign is marked Mariposa Reina—the Monarch butterfly, who flutters south for long winters in Goleta, massing together in eucalyptus trees along the bluffs in basketballs of orange wings and black bodies.

The silken surface of the water started to crease as I drove farther west. The navigators of old discovered the Pacific became much more threatening after their ships left the protection of the Channel Islands. The Gaviota coastline arcs in a way that reminds me of the curve between your thumb and forefinger, and the tip of this finger of land which extended ahead just out of my sight is called Point Conception. Point Conception is the corner where all the directions of the compass collide into each other. Here the western run of Santa Barbara is exhausted and the mountains collapse into the sea, and the coastline hooks north again. If there are four corners of the globe, then surely Point Conception must be one. It is the cape of California.

Geologists call Point Conception a headland or a promontory and navigators call it the graveyard of ships, which is why a lonely lighthouse shines out from her jagged cliffs, but the Chumash call it a gate. For them, it was the end of the world, and the beginning at the end. For thousands of years they have believed that the white-shale cliffs of Point Conception are the diving off point into the beyond, where the souls of the dead depart into the afterlife. It is the angle of ascent, a vertex swallowed up in vortex.

Thin places can be found anywhere, but there is something about the edges of the world, where the ancient elements of earth and water converge, that seem particularly exposed to mystery, especially in a place where the high places of the mountains meet the depths of the sea. Beginnings and endings blur in edge places. Ticking clocks and straight paths surrender to eternity. "This world" and "the next" seem dangerously close. Standing in an edge place can make you feel at once powerless and all-powerful, like you have appeared in the same moment that you have disappeared.

My pilgrimage was nearly complete.

The King's Highway takes a hard right turn at Gaviota State Beach, finally making its climb north over the Santa Ynez Mountains. Just past the dogleg I drove through the tunnel that is my own gateway into another world, and then climbed the Gaviota Pass, the only mountain pass in the Western Hemisphere that begins at sea level. It must have been placed there as a step out of the ocean for the wine god Bacchus, on his merry way to the Santa Ynez Valley.

At the top of the brief but steep climb, there is a short, flat stretch in the road that feels like a pause, as though it were designed for pilgrims to catch their breaths and behold the stunning view from above, before taking the plunge down into the valley. This vigilantly protected valley is cradled in the crook formed by two mountain ranges, which nudge each other a little east of here at a forty-five-degree angle. It is a fertile triangle. The Santa Ynez Mountains are the base, and the San Rafael range runs northwest toward the Santa Maria Valley. Both fall into the Pacific Ocean, the third side of the triangle, now back to the west after I rounded the bend.

Ahead on my path crossed hills on hills on hills, all rolling left to right like sentences on a page, a stanza of poetic slopes. The north side of the Santa Ynez Range is blanketed in the olive-green foliage of California oak, a striking contrast from the sparsity of the seaward side. To my left dense ocean clouds were drifting over Lompoc and the Santa Rita Hills, with spears of light shooting out from the setting sun behind them, but to my right opened a breathtaking corridor that ran the path of the Santa Ynez River all the way out to Happy Canyon and the San Rafaels. Hills of different sizes leaned in to feel the ocean breeze blowing through the riverbed on their faces. And down at the base of the mountains, just above a carpet of row crops, I could make out a small vineyard, the first grapevines of the Santa Ynez Valley.

After three hours and about 471 years of history, I made it home.

*Ten*

# THE FAIRYTALE

We are looking for someone to be an anchor behind the bar on the busiest days of the week," explained Chad, the tasting-room manager, when he offered me the job. "Someone who really knows their stuff, and who will be able to handle crowds and keep their cool."

*It's strange how I keep finding myself in such socially demanding jobs,* I mused to myself on the drive to my inaugural day of wine work. *The way I keep my cool is by* not *handling crowds. I wonder if I could get a job as lighthouse keeper at Point Conception?* First-day jitters were rustling me a little, but my new commute was helping. The Santa Ynez Valley truly puts the country in wine country. I found myself in a bucolic splendor that only extravagant wealth can afford in California. In these parts, quiet ain't cheap.

Rising above me in the San Rafael foothills was a triangular hill they call Grass Mountain, flaring up at this time of year in an inferno of orange poppies. *It kinda looks like giants had a picnic and wiped their Cheeto dust on the grass.* A few cows in varying shades of brown, my fellow commuters, ambled in my direction behind

a barbed-wire fence, and bales of hay scattered one by one in no com-
prehensible order looked like rectangles grazing in the meadows. *This
looks a little different from the 210 Freeway.* On the country roads of
Foxen Canyon, I would sometimes have to slow for ungainly packs
of wild turkeys or broods of pheasants scampering by, and in the
evenings I would pass grazing deer and waddling skunks, even a slow-
blinking owl on the road surveying prey. I had traded in a pastoral
calling for a pastoral setting.

***

Just a few cracks of the whip into the backcountry and I found myself
transported from the Mission era to the Old West. If El Camino Real
is the pilgrim path, then Foxen Canyon is the pioneer trail. Stage-
coaches trundled up Foxen Canyon Road beginning in the mid-
1800s en route to San Luis Obispo and slowly on to San Francisco.
We were only halfway into spring as I drove to my new job, but the
hills were already turning the color of brown sugar that looks just like
a spaghetti western backdrop. Most of the structures I could see were
A-framed barns pouring down from central silos, their doors crossed
with white boards in the shape of Xs. Even the wineries and tasting
rooms around here have a look that might be called "barn chic." On
my way, a few clicks down the road, I had passed through the town
of Santa Ynez, established 1882, where on creaky boards in western-
style storefronts and gabled houses they serve up not firewater and
cactus wine but grenache rosé and Bordeaux blends. Nowadays, no
one catches the consumption, but they do occasionally suffer
from overconsumption.

Up in Foxen Canyon, it wasn't hard for me to imagine wagon
trains of plucky pioneers on this trail shooting at shifty squirrels and
dying of dysentery. Folk around here still sometimes saddle up their
horses to head into town. Now, the herds of cattle that once ranged
these hills and prairies in the lucrative hide and tallow trade of the

Ranchero period have been whittled down to just a few amicable milk cows and an occasional kingly longhorn.

In 1833, the Mexican government passed a decree secularizing the Alta California Missions, meaning that the Missions were converted to local churches and its ranches, lands, and vineyards were granted to military officers and pueblo officials who had demonstrated loyalty to the crown and skill at raising cattle. California shifted from the Age of the Padres to the Days of the Dons, the honorific granted to these new landholders. This is known as the Ranchero era, the most romanticized period of California history, a time of haciendas, horsemanship, and hospitality, when Mexican cowboys called *vaqueros* sported broad-brimmed hats, silver-cuffed pantaloons, and gold-buttoned vests; all-night dances known as fandangos starred *señoritas* in dark braids, crepe dresses, and lace-edged petticoats; and seemingly every door, table, and brandy bottle was flung open to travelers making their way between ranchos.

If I were to keep driving for another twenty miles north on Foxen Canyon Road, I would come to one of these historic land grants, called Rancho Tepusquet. In 1837, Tomás Olivero, who had been superintendent of the three local Mission ranches, was awarded nine thousand acres on the banks of the Sisquoc River, borrowing the Chumash name Tepusquet, which means something like "where the trout bite." Rancho Tepusquet became the heart of the Santa Maria Valley, which is the northern perimeter of the county and the garden of Santa Barbara. On the Santa Maria lowlands, strawberries, broccoli, and cilantro stretch as far as your eye can see, nesting happily in the cool and fertile soils of the river overflow. Hanging on the incline of the San Rafael Mountains, which bow low here toward the ocean, are orchards of oranges and avocados. But on the mesa just north of the river, sitting atop the Santa Maria Bench, an undulating step rising out of the riverbed that was carved by once surging waters through a layer cake of sedimentary rock, are the first vines planted in Santa Barbara County after Prohibition. The Santa Maria Bench is where the Santa Barbara wine industry was reborn. Foxen Canyon Road is also the pioneer trail of wine.

Tragically, almost all the local vines were ripped up during Prohibition, and the memories of a prolific Santa Barbara wine industry in the previous century all but disappeared, even here at Rancho Tepusquet, where grapevines were first planted in the 1850s. The California wine business began to migrate north after gold was discovered at Sutter's Mill in 1848, and soon Northern California was swarming with Italian, German, and French argonauts, who, of course, thought it would be quite uncivilized not to bring some vines from home along with them. They didn't mine much gold, but they did eventually find riches in "purple gold," the grapes that would transform the hillsides of Napa and Sonoma, with the first cuttings coming from the mission vines off the Sonoma Plaza. George Yount carried his mission cuttings over the mountains on the east to Napa, and Count Agoston Haraszthy took his just a couple miles up the hill to his Buena Vista Winery. Yount and the Count prepared the ground of the modern California fine wine industry, which for decades was focused on Northern California. Later, the Count was eaten by an alligator in a stream in Nicaragua. Surely a cautionary tale for anyone who wants to start a winery in California.

But in 1964, two unlikely heroes named Uriel Nielson and Bill Demattei planted the Nielson Vineyard on the Tepusquet Mesa in Santa Maria. Over the next ten years a ragtag insurgency of dusty farmers, bohemian dreamers, and rogue scientists, convinced you didn't have to be in Napa to grow stellar grapes, could be seen in disturbingly short shorts, Burt Reynolds mustaches, and *Napoleon Dynamite* glasses, sticking sticks in the crunchy ground on both sides of the Sisquoc River.

Though at first the pioneers of this wine backwater planted the varietals in demand up north, like cabernet sauvignon, they soon discovered that the ocean wind whipping through the riverbed in this wide transverse corridor created an exceptionally cool climate. The cab grapes they planted here tasted like a green bell pepper. Trial and error led to the collective realization that this is pinot noir and chardonnay country, with a little late-ripening syrah for cold winter nights. Incredibly, UC Davis viticulture professors classified the Santa Maria Valley in the same climate category as the Champagne region, which is fifteen degrees higher in latitude. If it weren't for an extravagantly long growing season in this coastal desert, Santa Maria growers would have the same struggles getting sugar into their grapes. As it is, Santa Maria Pinot Noir smells to me like someone sprinkled white pepper on an April strawberry and dropped it in the dirt. I don't know about you, but I love a little dirt in my pinot.

Meanwhile, a few miles south back in the Santa Ynez Valley, the heat was radiating off the asphalt as I turned past the syrah vines into the winery's gravel drive. Microclimates change in the blink of an eye around here. My new job was at the Fess Parker Winery, which the world met as the setting for Frass Canyon in *Sideways*, where Miles drank the spit bucket. But Fess Parker wines were pleasant surprises to people like me who first visited after seeing the movie, expecting a perfume of diesel exhaust wafting out of the glass. I even joined their wine club on my first visit.

To get from the parking lot into the winery you walk through a sprawling lawn and photogenic grounds into a wine-party atmosphere, with weekend crowds lounging on the veranda that surrounds a western-style hunting lodge. Inside, flagstone floors lead to a huge cobblestone fireplace flanked by brown leather couches, where you can warm yourself after the hunt, although it is usually about eighty-five degrees outside.

If you were an American lad back in the 1950s, you likely recognize the name Fess Parker, and you may still have the coonskin cap in your attic to prove it. Before buying up some choice Santa Barbara real estate in the '70s and '80s, Fess Parker played Davy Crockett and Daniel Boone in movies and mesmerizingly new color TV. The winery even sells miniature coonskin caps you can slip over bottles of wine. My dad insisted I send him a couple immediately after I took the job.

Fess died a couple of years earlier, so I never got to meet him. Around the winery, he was described as a strapping and charismatic Texas gentleman, who displayed some parallels to the characters he played. It seems fitting that the man who played a hero at the Alamo bought property in the frontier of Foxen Canyon, where Mexican and Yankee cultures overlapped and sometimes clashed here in Santa Ynez. This canyon even has its own namesake frontiersman and bear-tussling hero, an English sea captain named Benjamin Foxen, who bought Rancho Tinaquaic up the road in the 1840s.

Benjamin Foxen almost seems like the sort of mythological figure that poets write into the origin stories of a civilization. He married a daughter of Tomás Olivera's who spoke no English, and he, no Spanish. He ate four meals a day of only meat, bread, eggs, and black coffee, reclined at his table with a shotgun on his lap in case bears attacked during supper, and once fought off eleven grizzlies while his wife reloaded his gun. He ran a stagecoach way station on his ranch, fending off banditos and highwaymen. And the most notorious local legend claims that Captain Foxen helped John C. Fremont and his California Battalion to claim Santa Barbara for the United States, which did not bode well for Foxen's relationship with his Mexican ranchero neighbors. The details are historically suspect, but the story goes that Foxen guided Fremont and his roughriders away from the bottleneck at Gaviota Pass, where Mexican and Native soldiers had supposedly set a trap, and down the cattle path of the San Marcos Pass in a deluge on Christmas Eve 1846. Fremont lost men and beasts to that slippery hill, but on December 28 he raised the stars and stripes over Santa Barbara while her citizens were at Mass.

Benjamin Foxen is buried at the lovely little historic San Ramon Chapel looking out on the Santa Maria Bench, along with members of the Ontiveros family, who bought Rancho Tepusquet from the Olivera family and planted its first grapes. Foxen's great-great grandson makes wine at the Foxen Winery on his old Rancho Tinaquaic, with a label featuring the image of an anchor that was Captain Foxen's cattle brand. James Ontiveros makes wine on a property adjacent to his own ancestral home, overlooking the adobe structure his family built on Rancho Tepusquet in 1857. Here are two more people who found their destinies in their last names. Meanwhile, when I sought the wisdom of my ancestors, I learned that McHugh means "son of Hugh." You're not helping, Hugh.

❦

My favorite Fess Parker quote is, "When you are in Los Olivos, you're gonna have to learn to saunter." I don't think that applies to people who work at his winery. There was no sauntering on my first day. The first thing they did was hand me a dolly and point me to a pallet of wine cases. That's fifty-six cases, for those of you counting along at home. It's possible I had help, but in my memory I carted all of them from the loading dock to the storage room entirely by myself.

This was the most physical work I had ever performed in a job, and by the end of my first weekend, every part of my body ached. I asked a twenty-three-year-old tasting-room colleague if he was sore after moving cases of wine and outdoor tables and umbrellas and standing on his feet for eight consecutive hours a day. He looked at me like I was old. Fortunately, I did remember the hospice training videos that urged us to lift with your legs if a patient falls down. When you work at a busy winery, this advice is more spot on than you might think. I have seen a few overzealous drinkers crumple to the ground over the years.

Then they hustled me into the Reserve Room where a group of wine importers from Denmark were tasting through the new releases. They didn't speak much English, which was fortunate, because as I poured their wines, I had no idea what to say. I tried to smile a lot and say the word *transverse* as many times as possible. Good advice for all conversations, really. I could tell my answers to their questions were not going well, because they would interrupt and say, "How long have you worked here?" I responded, "About three hours." No one laughed.

Finally, as a Greyhound bus of tourists pulled up, this Anchor was dropped behind the bar in the main tasting room where I would be spending most of my afternoons. It was so crowded and loud in the room that I had little opportunity to talk to guests, and I wasn't complaining about that. I seesawed up and down the bar, dripping sweat, opening bottles as fast as I could, cutting my fingers on the foil, blurting at each customer, "Which wine are you on?"

At the end of the day, Chad drove me in his truck up to the vines on the plateau above the winery. Rodney's Vineyard, as they call it, is invisible from the road, and where their best syrah is grown. It has the peppery and leathery goodness of the Northern Rhone, with all the decadent black fruit the California sun has to offer. I was exhausted to my core, even a little disoriented from the loud din of drinkers, but the vines running to the base of the mountains breathed stillness into me. Some of the young shoots were flopping into the rows, and tiny clusters of lime-green BBs were appearing at their base, near the arms of the trunk. I knew these were called *inflorescences*, and though they look like miniature green grapes, they are actually closed flower buds that soon would open and bloom. As I cradled one in my hand, it looked fragile, but flush with new life. I felt grateful.

It took me just a few days to feel comfortable on the other side of the wine bar. Once I actually started talking I likely spoke more words in my first week in wine than I did in a year of hospice. Life in the wine business is extremely conversational. I would spend six hours a day asking guests where they were from, giving restaurant recommendations, and remarking on the weather. The Angel of Death had become the Sultan of Small Talk. At least in an agricultural setting, weather talk is not mere idle chatter or suburbanite hobby. Weather is serious business around here. Livelihoods hang in the balance of heatwaves and spring frosts. Each vintage of wine is a year's worth of weather sealed away under cork. Or at least that is what I said to soothe myself after one too many conversations about the weather.

I discovered I was good at selling wine. Behind the bar, I felt like I was on stage performing for a crowd, but I used to preach before churches of extremely sober audiences, and in comparison, selling wine felt easy. The wine bar was my new pulpit. Except now I wasn't trying to persuade people to change their lives. In fact, their lives, at least for that afternoon, seemed to be going pretty well. It was weird to work in a setting where people were happy and laughing. There was so much less at stake in this world. I guess when you have labored daily in the industry of the Worst-Case Scenario, everything else feels breezy. But I still couldn't believe that, this whole time, people had been going to work in places where they weren't surrounded by unending grief and darkness. And they got *paid* for it. Now I would pour a little wine, drop a little knowledge, and sometimes a customer would slide me a twenty-dollar bill for my trouble. No one ever greased me as a hospice chaplain. A patient never offered me a handshake with a bill in it, hoping for a smooth six months or less.

When they learned I was new to the wine industry, guests would inevitably ask what I did for a living before this. I would once again stammer out, "Well . . . I worked as a grief counselor and uh, chaplain, in, mmm, hospice." "Wow! What a career change!" they would marvel, with that familiar blend of praise and bewilderment. After a few tries, I found the right response. "Not really," I said. "I used to listen to medicated people for a living, and I still listen to medicated people for a living. They are just much happier now."

⟨ ⟩

After a couple of weeks, I reluctantly moved out of Kathy's castle on the hill above Solvang and rented a room in a small house in Buellton. My move north happened so abruptly that I didn't have furniture or a life plan beyond working at a winery. I had stowed away on the first ship out of port. On my first night in Buellton, I drove through the Santa Rita Hills to the Lompoc Walmart and bought an air mattress, a set of scratchy sheets, and a gray camping chair.

The house belonged to a nurse named Andrea, who worked at a clinic in Santa Barbara, and she rented out two rooms to help pay the mortgage. In the room next to me was a hairy winemaker named Dan, a friendly enough guy whose hair would clog the shower drain in the bathroom that we shared. From my room on the side of the house, I could hear every word emanating from the kitchen in the house next door.

My new neighborhood was a festival of beige in the Buellton flats, tucked off the 101 Freeway and across the road from a huge RV park, near a collection of small eateries. Each of the valley towns seems to revolve around a particular theme, almost like lands in an amusement park, and in that case Buellton, and I say this affectionately, would be the food court. I was a block from Pea Soup Andersen's, a treasured relic of a rest stop that was the unofficial capital of "Servicetown, USA," as Buellton was once called, when it was the only pit stop between Santa Barbara and San Luis Obispo on the original Coast Highway. Andersen's was made famous by newspaper reporters in the '20s and '30s, who would pull over their Model As for lunch on their way up to Hearst Castle. It is still recognized by its billboards featuring cartoon chefs Pea-Wee and Hap-Pea splitting a pea with a huge mallet and log splitter, the creation of a Disney artist, that run for a hundred miles along the 101. Those were simpler times, when split pea soup was a French delicacy and a newfangled electric lamp in the window was enough to make you pull off the highway.

Outside of work, my daily routine was solitary, even for me. In the evening, I would pick up a sandwich and walk for miles around Solvang or Buellton, and then camp in my little room with my laptop and wine books, turning in early more out of boredom than drowsiness. I would wake up early in the mornings, my back aching from the night on my air mattress, and quickly duck out to avoid more small talk. I would try to pound out some words at the Bulldog Café or peruse the shelves next door at the Book Loft. On my days off, I took afternoon-long drives north, usually ending up in Cambria or San Luis Obispo, where I wandered aimlessly. My wife and I weren't speaking often, but I would linger on the phone with my parents in the evenings. With all the long walks and days spent on my feet, along with my shyness to cook in the house, I was losing weight rapidly. I was quickly discovering that it is one thing to vacation somewhere, but it is something else to live there.

It came as a relief to go to work and actually talk to people. I was enjoying parts of my job, but I was beginning to suspect my job wasn't enjoying me that much. There were some questions raised about my attitude, probably justifiably so. I was frustrated to learn that on busy Saturday afternoons, this little cocoon of a valley, so quiet and cozy during the week, is transmuted into a loud, drunk, annoying butterfly. It's when the bachelorettes spill out of stretch limos in sundresses and floppy hats, or when people chug the spit bucket. I was failing at hiding my irritation when they sloshed into the winery. It's hard to be the only sober person in a room. Even from underneath their big hats, they could see my eyes roll when they asked, "Do you have any sweet wines?"

At the same time, there were some whispers that maybe LA had rubbed off on me more than I thought. There was a cultural collision I did not expect. Through my seminars with sommeliers and hotel ballroom tastings I had learned wine in an urban scene that was showy and glamorized, but now I found myself working at a winery with a heartland sensibility, where you are expected to roll up your sleeves, respect the chain of command, and not draw attention to yourself. I was a little too vocal when I made a big sale. And when I resisted lifting heavy tables one afternoon because of my persistent back pain, it was taken as laziness. I had always done the heavy lifting with my brain, and all this physical exertion was new. I was working alongside sons of farmers and ranchers, who had grown up hoisting hay bales and pounding fence posts into the ground, who thought that back pain was just part of a hard day's work.

Another Saturday afternoon a month later, when the winery was hosting a syrah and food pairing seminar, I joined a group of several others to serve courses to guests. I thought there were too many of us in the kitchen, bumping into each other and standing around waiting, so I retreated back to the wine bar where I thought I could be more useful. When I came in the following Monday, I was told I would be in the kitchen washing glasses that afternoon. Shortly thereafter, they reduced my shifts from four to three days a week.

You may have guessed this already, but I don't have a sparkling history with authority figures. There is a mutinous streak in my family that I suspect comes from my grandmother. My dad's mom raised him on her own in the 1950s, working as a bailiff in the Seattle court system to pay the mortgage and send him to college, in an era when single mothers defied convention. Grandma loved ragtime piano, vodka martinis, baseball games that were one-to-nothing pitchers' duels, and not doing what others thought she should. Every time someone in my family retorts, "I'm not going to this stupid meeting!"

I imagine her cackling from behind the keys of a smoky piano lounge somewhere.

⌐⌐⌐⌐⌐

On my lunch breaks, I would walk through the vines, which I probably wasn't supposed to be doing either. The unruly shoots of a few weeks prior had been thinned and tucked into the trellis wires, and each row sculpted into a thin, long, manicured hedge. Many of the flower clusters had bloomed, waiting for a warm, matchmaking breeze to waft pollen from the male outer parts toward the womb in the center of the flower. Some had even begun to set fruit, their hard green berries starting to swell. Other flowers were still closed. When the flowers refuse to open, the vine masters call it "shatter," which is a highly dramatic name for flowers that don't pollinate and fruit that doesn't develop. The shattered clusters are dropped as spring turns to summer. As I crunched through the rows, it looked to me like there is a thin line between vines that bear fruit and those that shatter.

People are often incredulous when I tell them the vines of Fess Parker back up to a place called Neverland Ranch. But it's true: my first wine job took place at the corner of Davy Crockett and Peter Pan. I was working next door to Michael Jackson's fantasyland, decked out with a Disneyland-style train depot, carnival rides, circus animals, bronze troll statues, and a full-size steam engine puffing around an ivy-covered Tudor mansion straight off the pages of a fairytale. There were rumors of a ghost train around nearby Los Olivos for a spell, when at dusk the hills would resound with the blare of a train whistle, even though a train hadn't chugged through these parts since the Depression. Michael's infamous trial took place in Santa Maria just six months after the theatrical release of *Sideways*, and this valley that prefers life behind its mountain curtains was thrust into an uncomfortable spotlight. Michael was acquitted on all charges, but the questions and accusations continued to swirl. Neverland Ranch had become the Haunted Mansion.

My own wine fairytale was starting to taste like poison fruit. I knew something was wrong for sure when I got sick in June. In my life I don't remember having a cold that late in the year, and it was a doozy. I had a hacking cough that just wouldn't go away, and I couldn't sleep. I missed several days of work. It summoned memories of my first month in grad school, when I agonized through insomnia and a cough that persisted for weeks, or my first week of college, when I dealt with a severe cold and ear infection. I don't think William Bridges would be impressed with my ability to handle transition. I like to think of myself as steady and unflappable in challenging times, but the truth is, I was being flapped, hard.

Within another month, they reduced my days even further at the winery and sent me on weekdays out to the little wine and beer outpost inside the ritzy Fess Parker Inn in Los Olivos. This was a quirky place. Seemingly intended as a convenient bottle shop for hotel guests, the racks were stocked with mostly international wines and craft beer. It was tucked into a shadowed corner of the inn, virtually invisible from the road, and even many Los Olivos residents didn't know it was there. I would perch on a high chair behind the register for eight hours, reading wine articles on the internet, sometimes spending the entire day alone. No one comes to Los Olivos to drink Bordeaux. The shop did have a cult following of beerdos, so when the bells on the door would jingle and jolt me awake, customers would ask to sample sours and farmhouse ales that smelled like Brett the sweaty wild horse. I didn't move to wine country to pour beer.

On the days I worked alone, I would post an "At Lunch" sign in the window around two in the afternoon, lock up, and meander over to the Corner House Coffee Shop for a half hour. For years, their beautiful patio in the corner of town, shaded by a large pine, had been my first stop as I rolled into the valley from the south. Now I was taking a book and a number nineteen on focaccia from Panino to the coffee shop on my lunch breaks, reminding myself to take deep breaths.

One lunch break, as I sat by the trunk of the pine reading *Cannery Row* and having a pleasant little afternoon, I felt a cold liquid splash against the side of my head and pour down my shoulders and back. Startled, I snapped my head in the direction of the spray. On the railed wooden porch above me stood an older couple, looks of terror in their eyes, their hands covering wide-open mouths.

"Oh no, Gary, there is someone down there!"

"Oh my God, I am so sorry!"

Gary had not seen me behind the trunk, ten feet away, and he thought it would be a fun idea to dispense of the dregs of his cold Americano in the tree branches.

I shot up from my chair, my arms jerked out from my side and my palms flipped up in a classic WTF pose. All I could manage to blurt out was, "Are you kidding me?!" To this day I maintain this was an impressively restrained reaction. I looked down at my striped-white shirt, dripping with leftover coffee. "Really?!"

"I didn't see you there!"

"Seriously?!"

"Yes, I swear!"

Gary was convinced I was taking this moment to ask if he flung his wet coffee grounds at me on purpose.

I was torn between crying, laughing, and taking an axe to my favorite pine tree. I stormed off to my car back at the inn. I had to drive to Buellton, at least twenty minutes away, to change my shirt, jeans, and socks, and wash the stale coffee off the back of my head. I clocked in more than a few minutes late from lunch.

Two days later, Chad called me from the winery. "Adam, you know that we put new employees on ninety-day probation periods. We are getting close to the end of your probation. We have decided to go in another direction. We don't think this is a good fit."

I was cordial and thanked him for the opportunity. I said I was grateful for the incentive to finally move to the Santa Ynez Valley, and that is true. I knew he was right, but I didn't fully understand what went wrong. They asked me to be an anchor for the winery, and they can't say I didn't play my role. Together, after all, we went nowhere.

*Eleven*

# THE LAST STOP

I was deflated, but not defeated. Sure, I had been fired from my last two jobs; I was sleeping on an air mattress in a strange house; I was barely on speaking terms with my wife; and my first winery experience was a cold cup of coffee dumped over my wine-country fantasy. But I was staying positive, dammit. I still had a little up in my beat because I had already interviewed for another job. I had seen the writing on the wall, maybe even scrawled a few of the letters with my own hand, and started circulating my one-line wine resume around the valley a couple of weeks before they dropped anchor.

I had started out in one of the more prolific and buzzing wineries of Santa Ynez, and I thought I might be better suited to a quieter, boutique-ier place. When the Sandhi Winery offered me a tasting room position a few days after the coffee dried, I accepted on the spot. I would still be in Los Olivos, but I was relocating from the Davy Crockett All-American Winery to a tiny wine house with a name in Sanskrit, the project of a man from Calcutta.

Sandhi was a small upstart at the time, but the name behind it, Rajat Parr, is big. On the red carpet of celebrity sommeliers, Raj is an A-lister. He is a walking encyclopedia of vintages and domaines, and his blind tasting abilities are legend. This is the guy who casually tasted a wine out of a brown paper bag while working tableside one night and called the exact vintage, vineyard classification, producer, and tiny Burgundian village of a 1998 Domaine Michel Lafarge Volnay Premier Cru. Oh, and he had a head cold at the time. Though somms on his level will tell you that their blind tasting performances are built on thousands of hours of tasting and memorizing subtle differences in the world's wines, often at two in the morning after their restaurant shifts, it still seems preternatural to me, like they are less Olympic athletes and more superheroes.

I thought this new gig could be my first bite into the upper crust of wine elitism. I wasn't sure yet what my ambitions were in this world of wine, and whether I aspired to the sensory heights of the masters. I didn't know whether their superpower was something I coveted, like the ability to fly, or whether the great sommeliers were the Incredible Hulks of the olfactorily gifted. Yes, a guy that turns green when he gets mad, swells and rips out of his clothes, and then smashes a bunch of stuff is impressive, but it's not necessarily the lifestyle I'm looking for.

Sandhi is essentially Sanskrit for *terroir*, that interplay between earth, sky, vine, and human creativity that tells the story of a particular place. Terroir was a big topic in the California wine industry at the time, owing to a movement Raj pioneered, called "In Pursuit of Balance." It began as a friendly side-by-side tasting of different styles of California Pinot Noir, from decadent and inky to spritely and crunchy, and an open conversation about ripeness, alcohol levels, and the best time to harvest. But sometimes the more wine people drink the more they like to argue. The balance team argued that the overblown alcohol of many California Pinots obscures the nuances of terroir, and if all you get is a blast of overcooked fruit then all wines taste the same. The ripeness team countered that we live in sunny California, not misty Burgundy, and that rich, fruit-forward styles of pinot are an authentic expression of California terroir. It was another one of those maelstroms in a magnum, but it was the most controversy a hotel ballroom had seen since the first wedding where the young people danced the Charleston.

⚜

All that noise was far away from the charming wine hamlet of Los Olivos, population 831, which in recent years had transitioned from a display of art and antique saddles into an outdoor mall of artisan wines. Locals will tell you this is now a drinking town with a horse problem. About forty tasting rooms line the two main streets, Alamo Pintado Avenue and Grand Avenue, which greet one another at a circle with a flagpole in the center that was first plunged into a cement-filled coffee can in 1918. This village of western storefronts and turn-of-the-century homesteads seemed quite taken off guard by the influx of the wine industry. Parking spots are scarce, the cell towers broadcast in lowercase g, and there is precisely one public bathroom—at St. Mark's in the Valley Episcopal Church, which leaves out an offering basket for toilet paper and hand soap. A thousand wine drinkers on a Saturday and one bathroom—what could possibly go wrong?

Personally, I was sitting pretty in the tasting room nearest the bathroom, across a gravel drive from St. Mark's, polishing sixty-dollar wine glasses in a 130-year-old house on the back side of Mattei's Tavern. It was the only tasting room off the main drags of town, but I was even more excited about Sandhi's location than I was about Sandhi. The Sandhi name was fresh with hipster shine, but Mattei's Tavern is old, and you probably know by now that I prefer old stuff.

At the northwest corner of Los Olivos, Mattei's Tavern is a Steinbeck novel come alive. I had been reading through the Steinbeck library in all my lonely hours since moving to Santa Ynez. If I wanted to do any writing about my time here, I felt I needed the permission of the man who must now be the cringing muse of all inferior writers foolish enough to follow him in writing about the Central Coast. Steinbeck's Salinas Valley is 150 miles north on the King's Highway, and his images of iridescent ocean foam and wizened oaks reclining on the mountainsides could just as easily be set in the Santa Ynez Valley.

Exiting the front door of Mattei's Tavern, the words "Santa Barbara Stage Office" emblazoned in gold above, and stepping out from underneath the arbor adorned with wisteria and honeysuckle, late-nineteenth-century travelers found themselves at the crossroads of two eras of transportation nostalgia. There, a few paces from the white two-story inn, restaurant, and—rumor has it—brothel, the Concord mudwagon and the tally-ho ran smack into the broadside of the Iron Horse.

There was a brief but glorious era when every California explorer taking the coastal route between San Francisco and Los Angeles spent the night at Mattei's Tavern. It was part of a complicated travel itinerary. Standard Pacific linked the coast between the Bay Area and the Southland by rail in 1887, except for one fifty-mile gap in the tracks. Can you guess which mountain range was the biggest problem for the railroad engineers? It was the same set of mountains that would prove the last roadblock in completing the Coast Highway forty-five years later: that sideways wall we call the Santa Ynez Mountains. The gap in the railroad meant that passengers had to disembark the train at San Luis Obispo and board the Concord stagecoach, the Gold Rush-era vehicle that Mark Twain called "an imposing cradle on wheels," and try to stave off road-sickness as they were rocked to Santa Barbara, where they could board the train again.

But on November 16, 1887, the first pint-sized locomotive tooted into Los Olivos on the narrow gauge tributary line called the Pacific Coast Railroad, built to link San Luis Obispo to the Santa Ynez Valley. The track extension from Los Alamos, a one-horse and tumbleweed town fifteen miles up the line, which the conductors called "Lost Almost," had been completed just a few weeks earlier. The little engine unloaded its passengers in front of Felix Mattei's hotel, established the previous year in anticipation of this banner day. Los Olivos was the end of the line for the Pacific Coast Railroad, earning it the nickname "Lost Altogether," and the local kids would race to the turntable outside the railroad depot and grain warehouse to watch the train turn around. To this day it's the most exciting thing that has ever happened in Los Olivos.

Over the next fourteen years, travelers bunked in Mattei's upstairs rooms, caroused in the bar that was installed against the protest of Felix's wife, Lucy, who wore her white Women's Christian Temperance Union ribbon everywhere she went, and savored dove pies and corn fritters in the acclaimed restaurant just past the front door. Since Mattei's Tavern was the last stop of the Pacific Railroad, the next morning hungover adventurers would alight a Concord mudwagon led by a team of six, two more horses than the standard stagecoach because of the treachery of the path ahead. They would pitch their way through the valley, up San Marcos Pass, over the Santa Ynez Mountains, and admire breathtaking ocean views on their way down Slippery Rock to the Arlington Hotel in Santa Barbara. In total, it was an eight-hour trip with a pit stop at Cold Springs Tavern along the mountain pass for lunch and a change of teams.

In 1901, Standard Pacific finally plugged the gap in the tracks along the coast and built the Surf Station by the beach in Lompoc. Los Olivos had been bypassed, its boom town dreams dashed. The Overland Coast mail and express stage line was finished, and the passenger cars of the Pacific Coast Railroad were replaced by hopper cars and oil tankers, until its tracks were eventually removed, too. After the Overland stage closed, Felix Mattei purchased two stage-coaches for a biweekly mail and passenger run from Los Olivos to the steamer waiting at the Gaviota Pier, which carried on for thirteen more years. Then, as the historical plaque hung at the entrance to the tavern says, Mattei's stagecoaches were replaced by Henry Ford's horseless carriage.

It can be argued that the last drops of the Old West dried out by the massive fieldstone fireplace in Mattei's Tavern. There, in 1914, the driver of Mattei's Concord coach, or "the whip," as the drivers were called, warmed himself after his last mail run to Gaviota. Los Olivos stopped grooving to the percussion of hoof beats. Mattei's Tavern may well have been the last stop for the commercial stagecoach in America.

No longer a transportation hub, Los Olivos fell into a country slumber, but Mattei's kept hopping for one reason: people couldn't stop talking about the food. Felix originally named his spot "The New Central Hotel," but because of the fame of his restaurant and bar, everyone called it Mattei's Tavern. From the early days the quality of his wine cellar was renowned, and a bronze handle on the floor of the dining room led into a bootlegger's hatch during Prohibition. His star was a Chinese chef named Gin Lung Gin, who made a career change from laying railroad tracks for the Pacific line to running Mattei's kitchen. Surely when your name has two shots of "gin" in it, you are destined to work in a tavern, right? Gin was famous for his breads, flaky biscuits dripping with local honey, and his cookies, as light and thin as potato chips, dipped into his homemade ice cream. He dished up trout caught in Alamo Pintado Creek, which flowed right through the property. He served clams from nearby Pismo Beach, year-round Thanksgiving-style dinners, and his pièce de résistance, dove pie. Who, from time to time, doesn't relish a buttery, crumbly crust wrapped around meat from your nearby clocktower?

Gin Lung Gin's black and white visage had been emblazoned onto the tile of the new head chef's station a few weeks earlier, and that is how I found myself the captain of the back house wine bar. Mattei's Tavern, whose restaurant door had remained open for the better part of 125 years, was in the midst of revival. The new management was a team of first-round draft choices: the former owner of Screaming Eagle in Napa, who partnered with Raj to create Sandhi; a French Laundry trained chef; and an Alsatian-born sommelier who once served as the wine steward to the French minister of defense.

Los Angeles and San Francisco foodie magazines were atwitter, but the locals were suspicious. The tablecloths had been stripped away, the cozy chairs had been replaced with hard modern wood, and the old photographs of the Mattei family over the fireplace had been taken down. The wine list carried some local favorites, but there was a preponderance of premier cru Burgundies and a fourteen-hundred-dollar bottle of Bordeaux. As a wise man once said, no one comes to Los Olivos to drink Bordeaux.

But I thought the new menu was brilliant. Half of it offered comfort dishes from 1886, like wood-fired chicken and campfire trout, though no longer caught out of the stream on the property. Nowadays you would be lucky to hook an empty tuna can in that sandy creek bed. There was an avocado grilled over red oak, in that style of Central Coast barbeque that goes back to the Mexican Ranchero days, served with a citrus-infused soy sauce, a nod toward Gin Lung Gin's Chinese heritage. Then there were the dishes of historic whimsy. "Felix Mattei's Dirty Laundry" was charcuterie hung up on a miniature clothesline above grilled bread and tapenade, each piece of prosciutto and salami attached with a tiny clothespin. "Morro Bay's Greatest Hits" was local oysters on the half shell, shrimp, and yellowtail served on a vintage vinyl turntable. It took a special kind of history dork to see the wink in that serving platter to the Pacific Coast Railroad turntable, where the kids would watch the trains turn around.

<hr />

When I arrived for work each morning, this special history dork would take the long way around the tavern, past Gin Lung Gin's old bungalow, and under the water tower and palm trees to the house at the edge of the property, next to the cornfield the new chef had planted to make maize flour for his tempura. My winehouse had its own historical marker, as it was the first house ever built in Los Olivos, then relocated decades later to its current location. It had recently housed a museum, but now the kitchen featured a glass-top tasting bar, with windows that looked out on the memorial garden of St. Mark's and the walking labyrinth path inside its gates.

We called this old house the "Watering Hole." The living room and tiny dining room had been converted into a tasting lounge, decked out with wooden stools and high tables, leather couches, and brown and white cowhide rugs. Though I only poured Sandhi wines at the bar, there was a glass case in the living room that showcased all the wine labels owned by Terroir Capital, which ran a dozen or so wineries in California, New Zealand, and South Africa, and now a restaurant in Los Olivos. I preferred to say I worked for Sandhi rather than an international wine conglomerate, though there really was no danger of me being mistaken for The Man.

While Mattei's Tavern stands guard at the gateway to Ballard Canyon, my vote for the best syrah grown in California, I was exclusively pouring pinot and chardonnay from the Santa Rita Hills twenty-five miles southwest of Los Olivos. The Sandhi Pinots were admittedly a little sharp and green for my taste at the time, which must be why my invitation to "In Pursuit of Balance" was lost in the mail, but I thought the chardonnays were bottled lightning. The Bentrock Vineyard chardonnay, brandishing the highest price tag a white wine in this valley had ever seen, was easily the best chardonnay I had tasted outside of France. Too much California chardonnay is a gooey hug in a glass, thick with a sticky, buttery quality that always reminds me of movie popcorn. But this was electric and alive, with a current of acidity that crackled on my tongue. I could sell that, and the ninety-dollar sticker made it even more tempting forbidden fruit.

Raj Parr wasn't around the Watering Hole that summer, and he seemed more like a jet-setting myth to me, the celebrity somm touching down in a different country every week, who would send us tasting notes from a 747. So the entire Watering Hole team was myself and my manager, Caroline, a native of the valley from a well-bred local family. With a stack of bricks for a pizza oven and a white rock patio of picnic tables and yard games, Caroline was convinced the thirsty hordes were on their way to the Watering Hole. That is why I was hired.

The first three-day weekend I worked, we hosted fifteen guests. That would turn out to be a mad rush.

Over the course of the summer, high time for Los Olivos, I spent more than one weekend without seeing a single guest. Tasting rooms a block away were bursting at the seams, but at my bar, four people on a Saturday afternoon was a crowd. I don't think the clumsily scrawled chalkboard sign I posted at the end of the gravel driveway was helping. I know I asked for somewhere quieter to work, but this had crossed over into eerie. The outland location, the as yet undiscovered Sandhi name, and the local side-eye toward the hifalutin developments at their beloved Mattei's, all combined to make me the barkeep for the watering hole of a ghost town.

When fingerprints did appear on the glass bar, they usually belonged to somms from LA who knew the name Rajat Parr and were searching out new wines for their trendy lists. A few of them had an interesting habit of dropping their own names. Imagine starting a conversation like this:

"Good afternoon, my name is Preston Thomas. Here is my card. I am a certified sommelier and WSET Level 3, and I am the wine buyer for Mozza on Melrose. Before that I worked the floor at the St. Regis."

I would respond, "Okay."

I could tell by his miffed expression that my reaction was insufficiently impressed. What am I supposed to say to that? Should I answer with my own credentials? "Hi there! My name is Adam McHugh. I have two master's degrees, but now I pour wine for a living. I was third-chair alto sax in my high school jazz band, and one time when my family went out for Easter brunch, I went back to the omelet station five separate times."

Fortunately, those types were the exception. Most of the somms who visited weren't the popular kids in high school who didn't invite me to their parties, who after graduation traded out Natural Light for natural wine. Most of them were the kids who volunteered for chemistry extra-credit projects and who watched *The X-Files* on Friday nights in their parents' basements with the lights off. Now they spend their free time memorizing the grand-cru vineyards of Alsace and flipping through their hand-written note cards of twenty-five hundred indigenous grapes of Italy. They asked me questions about pinot clones and pH that I couldn't answer, and they said things like, "The mouthfeel has this really firm tension in it," without understanding why I was giggling. I thought I can hang with *these people.* They are not superheroes. They are *nerds.* In the words of another wine writer, they are *cork dorks.*

After discovering me alone at the bar sampling chardonnay one too many times, Caroline said, "You know, Adam, you can do other things here besides taste wine."

"Like what?" I asked innocently. I would come to regret this question.

The next morning a prolific checklist of daily cleaning tasks appeared on the bar. I think Caroline was feeling the heat from the kitchen next door, since without guests we were pouring oxidized pinot down the drain every weekend, and she needed to justify her hiring request. Plus, when the new owners of Mattei's looked up each night into the transparent skies over Los Olivos, they were seeing Michelin stars. They were insistent that no pebble from under the water tower should lodge in their treads, no scaly bathroom drain should sink their chances at culinary immortality. I was beginning to understand my role on this quest. I was the spare tire on the drive to a Michelin star.

For the rest of the summer, I spent my afternoons sweeping under the water tower, mopping bathrooms, wiping down tables and chairs, organizing supply closets, and chasing trash blown in throughout the day on the blistering winds of Los Olivos. I fought a losing battle with smudges on a glass bar. I waged an epic war with a platoon of massive country spiders and their webs. I feel like everyone is talking about how peaceful and quiet the country life is, but no one is talking about the bug situation. There are spiders here that make their penthouse-dwelling relatives in the cities look like fluffy house pets. Country spiders are color coded, and your ability to recognize the color scheme of an individual arachnid usually determines whether you live or die. You need to know whether to crumple him up in a paper towel, conflagrate him with a caramelizing torch, or pack only what you need and never return. And let's not overlook his farmhouse friends: weird flat bugs with butt pinchers that creep into anything you place on the floor, a prehistoric race of warlike fire ants that could easily take over the world if they were one centimeter longer, and some sort of evil that was making clicking noises in our broom closet. I was convinced the Predator was lurking in there with the mop and dustpans.

It's possible the heat of the Los Olivos summer was getting to me.

This tucked-away valley was starting to feel very isolated. My loneliness was reaching critical levels. Now I didn't even have guests to talk to during the day. I was spending all that I earned on burgers at Los Olivos Café or flatbreads at Industrial Eats, just to have something to do after work and maybe stumble into a conversation. "Nightlife" in the Santa Ynez Valley means "early dinner." The valley collectively shouts "Last call!" at about 8:15.

My feeble stabs at new friendships over the summer had all missed. I was hopeful when the new Mattei's chef brought with him an army of prep cooks and servers from the Tennessee kitchens he had most recently run, but they seemed to be counting the days until they could move back home. I wasn't so sure about the locals anymore. My relationships with them had changed, even with the people I knew before I moved. I wasn't a tourist buying their wine anymore, and they were treating me differently. My living situation seemed an apt metaphor. I felt like I had gone from warmly welcomed houseguest to that weird older guy who rents one of your spare bedrooms. You have your friends over and you throw dinner parties, and that guy is there, eating toast in the kitchen, but he is not invited. Everyone keeps it cordial and awkward. Occasionally you say hello when you run into him in the hallway outside the bathroom. The whole family is nice to him, but you are always a little relieved when he leaves for work in the morning and the house feels like yours again.

I fall in love with places much more easily than I do with people. But it turns out that somewheres always come with somebodies. I found I had almost no interest in the grindings of the local rumor mill, around which most talk in these little towns seemed to revolve at the time. This was before the glowing rectangles in front of our faces had begun to thoroughly pummel us with news of the outside world. Conversations here were starting to feel very small and commonplace. I just don't care what your neighbor Slim thinks about the height of your olive trees, nor what happens in dark cellars other than making wine.

Steinbeck would show all these local characters to be beautiful and quixotic representatives of the human race, but I don't have his gift. I had always appreciated that the people who live in this valley love to talk about where they live and that they intimately know the dirt under their feet. They had always seemed so deeply placed. Now I was beginning to wonder what the line is between being grounded and being stuck.

I didn't know it was possible to feel so disquieted in such a quiet place. Everything I once loved about the valley felt like it was turning against me. After work, I sat on the Watering Hole porch and seared an entry into my alcoholic's diary:

> What happens when a pilgrim decides to settle in the holy place? What happens when you don't just visit your temple and leave your offering at the altar, but you move in? You start to see the dirty baseboards and the spiderwebs in every corner. You start to notice that after their long journeys not everyone there smells so great. You realize that maybe you are in a holy place, but you are still the same dude with the same problems.
>
> I wanted a big life in a small town. I dreamed of moving to wine country, of diving into a community of passionate and adventurous friends where we all feasted on nectar and ambrosia like a pantheon of wine gods. Instead I wound up in a cave with six other dwarfs, and I just mined coal, day after day.

Was it ridiculous to think that I could advance in my retreat place? At what point does settling into your retreat become an all-out surrender?

I was artfully assembling a colorful variety of word-bouquets about how much my life sucked. Another harsh internal voice wondered if I was the problem. Was I continuing to stand at arm's length so I could say they pushed me away? Was the way I had chosen to live here—never eating at home or buying groceries, sleeping on an air mattress, living out of a suitcase, wandering the towns alone at night—a way of circling the runway without ever landing? I was living in the valley like I was still a tourist. I moved here because I wanted to come closer. My body had come closer, but my heart and mind had kept their distance. Big parts of me were still in the wilderness.

<hr/>

I knew I was in big trouble when I drove back to LA a week later for dinner. My college friends were reuniting to celebrate my old roommate Sean's birthday, with our buddies Mark and Charles flying down from San Francisco. It aimed to be the hottest social event I had attended in six months. I retraced the seaward paths of the King's Highway until my Honda was recaptured by the asphalt tentacles of the LA freeway monster. I leaned on my brakes as I approached the 405, and as I did I let out a deep exhale. This was nothing new, except my breath sounded less like a groan of exasperation and more like a sigh of relief. Had things turned so sour in my promised land that I was now nostalgic for my old, bitter captivity? I did miss the smells of carne asada and Korean barbeque—and the Korean taco truck.

I lingered with my friends until well after midnight, even though it meant scant hours of sleep before work the next morning. I didn't want to go back.

At dinner, Mark asked, "So McHugh, how is life in small-town America?"

"Small," I replied.

My dreams were crumbling like a dry cork.

<hr/>

The following Thursday, in addition to my daily list of chores, I was tasked with a new project. On the gravel patio by the picnic tables stood two "cabanas," as the Mattei's team called them. Everyone else called them storage sheds. Mattei's wanted to repurpose them as playhouses for the many children who frequent fine dining establishments. No kid in his right mind would go into those things. They looked like the sheds where we store children. But my day's assignment was to assemble mobiles of stars and planets and string them up in the cabanas with fishing line and hooks.

It was the hottest day of the summer, with the red on our outdoor thermometer pushing 105 degrees. For hours I fumbled around in the windowless cabanas, lightheaded and drenched in tropical sweat, trying to hang the universe on a fishhook. My big fingers fumbled through a dozen or more attempts at running the fishing line through the circles at the tops of the hooks. I attached the sun, which I was particularly resentful of that day, and a constellation of stars. The crescent moon was my last skylight left to lasso. After what must have been twenty minutes, I finally managed to string the line through the hook attached to the moon and, with salty sweat dripping into my eyes and mouth as I reached up, suspend the mobile from the ceiling. Just as I did, the entire galaxy came crashing down on my head.

I was tangled in fishing line and shooting stars. I think the moon turned to blood. I let loose a war cry and punched the wall of the shed with all the pent-up rage of the summer. And then with my fist on fire, my eyes burning with sweat, I came apart. All the protective layers of snark, grape tannins, and my grandmother's defiance collapsed, and my heart spilled out. I wailed like a baby until I couldn't breathe, and then I sobbed silently, sprawled out on the floor of the shed where we stored the children. At once I felt all the loneliness, the lost love, the crushed dreams, the broken promises of my promised land. I felt entirely forsaken. I was a failure.

⌐◦═◦─◦┐

After work I walked across the gravel driveway and under the pepper trees to St. Mark's. I had attended a few of their Sunday services since the beginning of the summer. It was the first time I took the sacrament with real wine and not grape juice. I enjoyed how the priest would turn to face the cross behind the altar and lift the consecrated wine and bread toward heaven, like we were raising a glass to the Provider of the feast, whose lifeblood now filled the cup.

I had long admired the beautifully timbered building wrapped around a cozy central courtyard that could be just as easily at home in the English countryside. But tonight I was headed through the iron gate behind the church that guards the gravestones of the memorial garden and the adjacent labyrinth path. I had read a good amount about labyrinths, but this would be my first time walking one. I didn't know what I was seeking or what compelled me that night to enter the labyrinth, but I didn't know what else to do. I had no words left to pray.

I walked as slowly as I could through the winding path that twists and turns, curves closer and doubles back, teases and casts out. I tried to release the feelings and sinister accusations of the day, imagining myself breathing out dark clouds of smoke with every exhale. As I moved closer to the center, I felt my pace quickening. I reached the clover-shaped opening, where fellow pilgrims had left a few smooth stones on the rose-colored dirt. I picked one up and turned toward the gravestones to face the sun setting beyond the mountains. I closed my eyes, and almost immediately a voice spoke within me.

"I love you."

More tears streamed down my face. There was a gentleness and a certainty in this voice that my inner world does not carry. It didn't offer answers. I was still in the midst of a spectacular failure that summer, an epic collapse. I was torn in pieces. And I was loved.

There was love and life among these stones, too. There are no dead ends in a labyrinth. You just keep walking the path.

✦

A few days later, after another sweltering afternoon of picking up trash blown in from town, I climbed the creaky steps to Caroline's office and gave my notice. She didn't seem surprised. In the end, my contribution to the storied history of Mattei's Tavern was a handful of cobweb-free windowsills and a few less fingerprints on a glass bar. And I never met Raj Parr.

No place has broken my heart like Los Olivos. I had a couple leads on new jobs in town, but I didn't know if I wanted any of them. I was lost altogether. The wine of the Santa Ynez Valley wasn't tasting very good to me anymore. I spent a few nights in my camping chair, drinking beer, feeling again tossed out into the wilderness.

Then, my wife called. With a quivering voice, she told me her father had died unexpectedly.

I decided to move back to LA. I went into exile from my promised land.

## Twelve

# THE BEAST OF BURDEN

I had returned to LA to attend a death. I think my life's labyrinth
path flipped a U-ey. It was as though an old script had been
found buried under a pile of wine receipts, and Chaplain McHugh
thought he was paged one more time. I am not sure that he was. I
think he may have made things worse.

My in-laws and I were not close. I had kept my characteristic
distance from my wife's family for all the time we were married. I
don't think the twenty-three-year-old version of me who said "I
do" fully understood that when you get married, you marry a family and not only an individual. From the beginning her family and
I were not a good fit. They weren't happy about us getting married,
and throughout the years we were often at odds and only stiltedly
cordial in the best of times.

Nevertheless, I tried to resurrect my old bedside manner for a
while. The memorial service had been postponed for six months.
I didn't know how long I would be staying, or how long I would
be wanted there. Part of me was relieved to feel needed somewhere, and part of me wondered if it was, in fact, possible to go

home again. It didn't take me long to realize that I was back, but I wasn't home. I wasn't sure where I was. I think my heart was somewhere in the dirt along the side of the King's Highway. I was now on a pilgrimage to Mount Indecision, via the Way of Oscillation.

I may have given up on the Santa Ynez Valley, but I had not given up on wine. I quickly found a position at a wine store in none other than the historic wine capital of Rancho Cucamonga. Gold prospectors taking the southern route into California once tromped through here on their way to the Sierra Nevada mines, filling their tin cups with Cucamonga red and dreaming of future riches. As for me, I was working part-time at a behemoth alcoholic warehouse called Total Wine & More. It would, quite unexpectedly, turn out to be one of the more enjoyable jobs I have worked in the wine industry.

There I was, in a tropical-themed parking lot across Route 66 from a large outdoor mall, selling every wine on the face of the earth next to El Pollo Loco. The façade of our building was in a southwestern adobe style, more Albuquerque than Santa Barbara, and even though it was autumn on the wall calendar in our fluorescently lit break room, outside it was torrid, dusty, and windy. Palm Springs was an hour east, and the 15 Freeway that zoomed past the iron bench where I ate my lunch would get you to Vegas in four hours. This was the wine desert.

It's probably obvious by now, but I should clarify that even though I told wine tasters in Los Olivos I had moved from "LA," no true resident of LA would call Claremont or Rancho Cucamonga "Los Angeles." I found it easier to say LA than try to explain where all these quirky places were to people who only asked to be polite. On every level, LA is to Rancho Cucamonga what New York City is to New Jersey. It's about fifty miles away, but it might as well be another planet. For the record, I went to grad school in New Jersey, and I enjoyed it. Once you get off the turnpike, it's a beautiful state. Yes, some residents of New Jersey are a little boorish and spend much of their time tailgating, shopping at malls, and playing Bon Jovi on a loop, but they pump your gas for you there.

Present-day Rancho Cucamonga is not known as a hotspot of wine sophistication. A disturbing number of wines I sold went to their deaths in water glasses bobbing with ice cubes. The most popular wine in our store was a fizzy fruit punch that some of us referred to as "She Who Must Not Be Named." People bought it by the pallet. Overall, the "& More" departments of Total Wine & More were more frequented in this particular location. There was the Beermuda Triangle, where once you were surrounded by beerdos pensively stroking their beards and inquiring about international bitterness units, there was no escape. And there were the hard-alcohol aisles, with enough liquor to stun a herd of wooly mammoths in its tracks.

The uniform was white shirt and tie, black slacks, and black dress shoes, and according to the style of many of my esteemed colleagues, a dazed, unshaven look. It was corporate from the collar down, retail from the neck up. Every morning I clocked in and donned an operator's headset, dropping the bulky battery pack into my front pocket. The headsets were essential because no one could ever find anything in the store. The inventory was massive and overwhelming, stacked three cases high, three rows deep on the top of each aisle, and back storage contained skyscrapers of wine and booze. We all spent eight to twelve hours a day looking for stuff, asking each other continuously through our headsets if anyone knew where stuff was. I would be in the Italian wines, talking to a customer about Brunello di Montalcino, while getting barraged through my headset by three coworkers asking if I knew where the Fireball was. I would politely excuse myself from the conversation, take a few steps away, and speak gently into my microphone, "Do I seem to you like someone who knows where the Fireball is?"

After months of working virtually alone, I enjoyed working on a team of wine bros. We had all given up a little, like high school seniors in April, and we bonded in a way that only underpaid retail workers under middle management can. There was Daniel, who had been laid off from his veterinary tech job a few weeks before, who thought this job was more fun than high school. There was Felipe, the oldest and grumpiest member of the team, who said he was "retired" but worked fifty hours a week and every weekend. There was Mark, who had worked there the longest, but whose tenure would abruptly end in January when he was caught drinking on the job. There was Brandon, a recent liberal arts graduate who lived with his mom. He drove a scooter to work and took daily naps in the back corner of the warehouse where the store cameras had a blind spot.

There was the barrel-chested shipping receiver Tommy, who got to wear a short-sleeved shirt but also had to wear spandex sleeves to cover up his ink. He advised me, "Dude. If you want to get ahead in this job, you need to be throwing cases all day long." "Throwing cases" meant stocking wine in and above the aisles, preferably in places none of us could find. And there was my favorite, Drew the assistant manager, who went home every night to his garage arcade of '80s vinyl and Ms. Pac Man. When he was in charge of the store soundtrack, we could count on Duran Duran and the Cars all night long. Before this job, he used to be locked into grocery stores overnight with a team of stock boys, who would hurl snowballs sculpted out of ice chips at each other through the aisles. Together, we were the most average any group of men can look wearing ties.

I had signed up to take the first-level sommelier exam through the Court of Master Sommeliers in the spring. When I wasn't throwing cases or singing "Hungry Like the Wolf" into my headset, I was walking the aisles of Bordeaux, Barolo, and Rioja, trying to memorize the classic wines and appellations and minutiae that might appear on the exam. I learned that the cocktail of sugar and wine added to

Champagne after the yeast has been removed and just before the bottle is corked and caged is called Liqueur d'Expedition—or, as I wrote on my flashcard, "one for the road." I studied the different types of sherry and how a yeasty film called *flor* forms on the top of the liquid and protects it from oxidation in partially filled barrels. I learned about the "noble rot" that attaches to berries in the humid southwestern corner of France, which leeches out water and deeply concentrates the sugars to make the most prized dessert wine in the world, perfected by Château d'Yquem in Sauternes. The German name for the high sugar levels in their own elegantly rotted grapes is *Trockenbeerenauslese*, which is fun to say but more fun to announce with Teutonic aggression into your work headset.

One story of the German discovery of this noble rot, called botrytis, is that medieval monks were not allowed to start harvest until the presiding bishop of the village permitted, but one fall the bishop was delayed while traveling. Harvest was postponed, and the grapes in the river valley started to brown and shrivel. When the bishop finally arrived and the feared spoiled fruit was harvested, the grapes were perfumed and heavenly sweet. The bishop's delay was seen as divine serendipity.

❦

Things at home were less sugary. One of the first things I noticed after moving back was that our old apartment smelled different. It didn't smell like home anymore. Because we store aromas as memories in our brains, a whiff of something familiar can summon vivid recollections of people we love or experiences we cherish. There is no smell more evocative than home. The smell of home should slow our breathing and our heart rate. It should make us feel safe and comforted and at ease. I have always believed that home is where we take the longest, deepest breaths.

My breaths in my off hours were shallow and uneasy, and I don't think I was alone in that. Once the initial shock of her father's death had worn off, both my wife and I seemed to be wondering what I was doing there. The memorial service was still three months away, and instead of serving as family chaplain, I had been assigned the task of choosing the wines for the reception. Reverend McHugh truly had been buried. No one was looking to me for spiritual guidance in a crisis anymore. No one here needed a hero.

My wife and I were making tepid attempts at reconciliation, but we were also fighting a lot, over everything and nothing. This was not new. It was an ominous sign early in our relationship that our favorite song was called "Something's Always Wrong." We were arguing bitterly in our honeymoon suite an hour after we paraded out of our wedding reception, while our best friends were still at the bar downstairs toasting us. It was a fight that would persist all the way through our honeymoon and our first summer of living together. The marriage books we read and the many counselors we saw individually and together over the years had a favorite quote: "Don't let the sun go down on your anger." We had long ago given up on that. Sometimes the sun set several times before we resumed speaking to one another.

Somehow the emotional intensity of arguing through the years kept some semblance of attachment and togetherness between us. The alternative was acknowledging our deep loneliness, and that was too terrifying to face.

We still loved each other, but it seemed that we were both very tired. Now that I had been back for a few months, I noticed that she was coming home later and later from work, and I was eating a lot of dinners alone. I asked for more evening shifts at work.

One quiet Thursday night in November, I was wandering down the whiskey aisle, and a customer stopped me to ask for help.

"Could you help me choose a good scotch for my husband?" she asked sweetly, her eyes roving the shelves.

"Sure. What does he—oh. Hi." I trailed off when I recognized her.

"Oh!" she recoiled. "Hello. Uhh, how are you?" She looked from my headset down to the company logo on my shirt, and back up to my eyes again, perplexed.

We are gonna need clean up in the brown liquor aisle. Someone just spilled a whole lotta awkward. I couldn't immediately recall her name, but I knew her as an elder at a nearby Presbyterian church where only a few years ago I had been part of the preaching team. We also served for two years together on an important church committee that prepared seminary students for ordination.

We sputtered through the exchange as briskly and uncomfortably as two exes bumping into each other at the grocery store—she looking a little embarrassed to be buying firewhiskey from a preacher, me looking a little embarrassed about existing on the planet Earth. As she walked away with her bottle of scotch, she turned back suddenly, and paused, before saying, "Good luck to you, Adam."

Once she was out of sight, I leaned against the shelf of Johnnie Walker, feeling every bruise from the hard fall my career and reputation had taken in the last nine months. I imagined her shaking her head at the next committee meeting while telling everyone where she had seen me working. "What happened to him?" they would all wonder.

I always secretly felt that there was something heroic about ministry. When the script you are reading has you saving souls, fighting evil and injustice, teaching the masses, rescuing the lost, and showing up in the very moments when others are fleeing, it's hard not to cast yourself as a hero in the story. When something went wrong, I was often the first call people made. I liked playing the hero. It made me feel important. It's not a job that a lot of people can do. It was also another way that I could keep my view from afar. The life of the hero is lonely. No superhero has a blissful and fulfilled home life.

The role of the hero is also exhausting, because it is built on an illusion. The world isn't broken down into heroes and those who need saving. We are all vulnerable, all flawed, all broken, all human. We are all lost, and we are all found. There is a strength we do not know and a weakness we cannot fathom in each one of us. I have seen bent and frail people in hospital beds fight for their lives with a power I never would have imagined they had. And I have seen them all eventually surrender.

This was the year I was relieved of the role of the hero. The fall hurt like hell.

I found myself once again, as the sun rose behind me, creeping along the 210 Freeway toward Pasadena, and the memories made me feel a little queasy. This time, however, I wasn't pointed toward death. Instead, I was headed for a luxury, two-story ecosystem of health and wellness, a spot that some people called "their happy place." Very few people said that about hospice. I now worked Wednesdays in the wine and specialty department of Whole Foods Pasadena.

The amount on my biweekly paychecks at Total Wine wasn't exactly stocking the wine cellar. Our particular branch rarely reached the sales goals that would win us cash bonuses. One month we narrowly topped a goal, and management threw us a pizza party. It was totally awesome, except we had to buy our own tokens for Space Invaders and Skee-Ball, and I had to go home early because my mom came to pick me up.

That's how I ended up working a day a week at Whole Foods. My new colleagues were a serious and zealous group, dedicated to the organic and sustainably sourced mission of the store and charging customers the price of the entire farm. They wore beanies and socially conscious t-shirts and were perpetually cold, perhaps from a lack of protein. They worked hard but always smelled good, because they knew where the free lotion samples were downstairs. The hand soap in the bathroom next to the lotions smelled like organic lavender and love for honeybees.

On my first training day, I sat in the back office and watched videos on recycling and the principles of organic farming, which I rather enjoyed. It felt like attending Green Church. Then they flung a name tag and apron over my head and hustled me up the escalator to my department on the second floor. One of the company values is "moving with a sense of urgency," which if you know me, you know I only do after a third cup of coffee.

A few Wednesdays into my tenure, my team leader, Ricky, sat me down for a chat.

"Adam, you are doing a good job here, overall, and you are helping the team out a lot on Wednesdays. But some of us are concerned that you're not moving enough with a sense of urgency."

"Yeah, Ricky, that's kind of my thing," I said. "I always thought it was one of my best qualities, to be honest."

I had been hired mostly to move with urgency in the spacious wine section, but the specialty department was vast, including a menagerie of cheeses and nitrate-free meats, vegan sausages for those who enjoy Cajun-spiced cardboard, olives bathing in oil and pickles in brine, a craft-beer aisle catering to the particularly well-oiled beard of the Pasadena beerdo, and a darkly lit wine bar that was being converted to a full-service restaurant.

Only a few of the hundreds of wines in the store were truly organic, meaning, for American wines, that no sulfites are added aside from the small amount produced naturally in fermentation. Some of them tasted very fresh and alive. Some of them, especially from the wineries that filtered out all naturally occurring sulfites, had a shelf life of about a month. I had more conversations about sulfites in one Wednesday afternoon of working at Whole Foods than I did in six months at Total Wine Rancho Cucamonga. Just so you know, there are a lot more sulfites in dried fruit and French fries than there are in wine, and unless you break out in a skin rash, you probably aren't allergic. The headaches you get are either from histamines, or from drinking a whole bottle of grocery-store wine last night.

⁕

On Wednesdays I stocked a little smoked turkey and vegan cheese, but my primary role was to move cases of wine for a few hours, and then move some more. This is something they don't tell you when you set out to become a sommelier. A sommelier's main task, whether you are grandmaster somm or the shiftiest of cellar rats, is to move stuff from one place to another. Manual labor is deviously embedded in the historical origins of the word. The word *sommelier*, disappointingly, is not actually French for "professional wine douche" but instead derives from the old French word for "herdsman." In the Middle Ages, the *somerier* was responsible for the *somier* or the *bêtes de somme*—the beasts of burden. He loaded the cargo and drove the pack animals on their heavy treks to French villages. He was the medieval mover.

Later, he was promoted from herdsman to butler for the royal palace and given an *l* in his title to distinguish him from a pack donkey. The sommelier toted the king's luggage on his journeys, and was in charge of provisions, including his wine. Eventually, they hung a silver saucer from his neck, called a *tastevin*, and dared him to taste the king's wine first to see if it was poisoned. Ancient Egypt had a similar job description for Pharaoh's cupbearer, whom we encounter in the first book of the Hebrew Bible, whose role was to organize and select the Pharaoh's wines, and always taste it first. The book of Genesis tells us that the cupbearer's job was to "place the cup in the king's hand,"

and he may well have been history's first recorded sommelier. The ancient Egyptian hieroglyph of the cupbearer was a dude carrying a large jar of wine on his head.

I tried to remind myself, as I herded wayward cases onto my wine cart again and again and again, that I was fulfilling the historic tradition of the noble sommelier, the cupbearer who placed his life on the line for king and country. Bearing the load on my aching back and knees, working up a lather like an ox while trying desperately not to drop any bottles, I was taking the poison so others could live to rule their kingdoms and drink wines untainted by excessive sulfites. The role of the hero dies hard.

I didn't have a silver saucer around my neck, or a gold-plated wine key in my pocket, but I did have a boxcutter. Whole Foods likes to showcase wines in displays of artistically carved case boxes. When you stack three cases high at the end of the aisle, you can't leave the wine to dwell in its dark boxes like troglodytes. You need to draw the bottles out to dazzle in the daylight.

I was no mere stock boy; I was a wine box architect. I carved off three-fourths of the top-floor box and pulled it up like a veil to reveal twelve acid blasts of New Zealand Sauvignon Blanc sitting on a little white shelf. Next, I carved display windows on both sides of the two boxes underneath, just to flourish my design aesthetic. Then I would reconstruct each three-story masterpiece, gently placing the penthouse shelf on its two-story foundation, and finally stand back and admire my craftsmanship.

Actually, they looked like crap. Children would take one look at my work and burst into tears. I couldn't cut the thick boxes straight, and my crooked windows would compromise the structural integrity of the boxes, so that more than one crumpled, toppling the bottles on display to the ground like statues of ousted dictators. Even worse, customers throughout my shift would come and desecrate my work by buying the wines still standing on the top shelf. Whole Foods does not tolerate half-empty displays, so I would have to continually disassemble the stacks I had built, bringing up wines from the bottom boxes while leaving the corner bottles as support beams so that the entire showcase wouldn't implode.

⚜

Armed with hundreds of hours of looking for stuff at Total Wine and a couple dozen Wednesdays moving stuff from one place to another at Whole Foods, along with my well-loved copy of *The Wine Bible*, I was nicely prepared for the introductory sommelier exam when spring arrived. The two-day event was hosted at the Sheraton in Pomona, the same place where my parents had taken me for dinner after my college graduation ceremony years ago. On the short drive to Pomona that Friday morning, I wistfully reflected on the high hopes that people once had for my career.

The stipulated dress code was "smart casual," but a few candidates showed up in three-piece suits with pocket squares. The most important dress requirement was that you don't wear cologne or perfume, so it wouldn't interfere with the nose of the wines we would be learning to evaluate. The first-level exam comes at the climax of a two-day crash course on every major wine region in the world and the basics of winemaking and grape growing, interspersed with a show-and-tell introduction to the deductive tasting method of the Court of Master Sommeliers.

The class was taught by four master sommeliers. There are several different certifications for wine geeks out there, but master somm is the most prized. There is another hard-to-achieve honorific called "Master of Wine," which makes you the equivalent of a tenured professor in wine, but the master sommelier pin tells people you are a wine wizard first class. You are blessed with a reaching, magical nose, the mastery and concentration of Dumbledore, and an air of superiority we will choose to call charming.

I think it's fair to say that master sommeliers are the best wine tasters in the world. They can see a Montrachet coming from a kilometer away, detect a corked wine from across a crowded restaurant, and airily differentiate between a chenin blanc from Savennières and a riesling from Rheingau over breakfast. They can open a bottle of Champagne without making a sound. They are the all-stars of the liquid world, so much so that one of the master somms teaching our introductory course—I swear on the giant fennel wand of Bacchus—was named Michael Jordan.

There are four levels of sommelier credentials. The difference between a master somm at the top and an introductory somm at the bottom is like Gandalf the white wizard versus a hobbit who just won his first drinking game at the Green Dragon. You don't even get to capitalize "sommelier" in your title until you pass the second level. The sort of basic question I could expect on my multiple-choice exam was, "What is the permitted grape varietal of Beaujolais?" (Answer: gamay. The Duke of Burgundy banished gamay from his pinot noir kingdom in the fourteenth century, calling it a "disloyal" grape, so it ended up a few miles south in Beaujolais.) The sort of exam question a master somm could expect would be, "What are the designated growing regions and all the indigenous varietals of Romania and Bulgaria?" (Answer: No clue. Where is Bulgaria?)

I was nervous as I stood up with my tasting group on Saturday morning to evaluate a wine we were blind tasting out of a paper bag. In these practice sessions, you taste the wine and then spit it rather unceremoniously into a cup, so the wine doesn't dull your senses. Blind tasting is an important discipline of the somm life, as it is intended to eliminate preconceptions and to heighten your ability to perceive and interpret a wine on its own merits. But I think it's more fun to think of blind tasting as searching for clues and slowly building a case to solve a great liquid mystery, in which the skilled detective reveals at the end the origins, age, and identity of the masked bottle.

Throughout the weekend, our instructors had been walking us through the steps of their deductive tasting grid, which involved dissecting a wine according to sight, smell, feel, and taste, and then drawing conclusions based on what we observed. They were eager for us to build up a storehouse of sense memories and a vocabulary of descriptors, for quick recall in the future and to share a common language with other professional drinkers. Apparently, in the trade, throwing back a wine and saying "Ahhhhh!" is an insufficient description.

Now it was our group's turn. My colleagues ahead of me noted the color, clarity, and brightness of the mystery wine in our glasses, and my role was to tell everyone in the class what I smelled coming out of the glass. I had been dreading this moment ever since I learned it was part of the introductory course. But here is a little trick if you are ever put on the spot to name what you smell in a wine: if you are drinking a white wine, say "citrus," and if you are drinking a red, say "cherry." You will never be wrong. Ours was red, and I was fairly certain it was a young Bordeaux, so I rattled off, "Black cherry, plum, licorice, pipe tobacco, vanilla," because I had read all those descriptors on Bordeaux wine tags at Total Wine & More. It was some fanciful BS, but the master somms nodded their approval. I fell into my chair, relieved. Now that the spotlight had moved on, it would be easier for me to focus on the lecture.

<hr />

Later that afternoon, Master Somm Peter Neptune—arguably the coolest name of all time—started talking about Cistercian monks in medieval Burgundy, and I was probably the only one in the class on the edge of my seat:

These guys in the brown hoods weren't spending all their time looking down at their iPhones. They had time to *notice*. They noticed the different soils, the unique growing patterns of each little patch of vines, right down to the tendencies of every single branch. They saw that some fruit ripened earlier, and some vines produced darker, sweeter fruit, but not a lot of it. They didn't always know why, but they observed and recorded all of it. They paid attention, and that's why we have this whole notion of terroir.

Did I just hear a master sommelier, in the middle of wine class, drop a contemplative spirituality on us? He might not put it in those terms, but I believe I did. As I thought more about the discovery of terroir and also the method of wine evaluation they were teaching us, I started to wonder if there just might be a spirituality of wine tasting. To love wine, or anything, is to pay attention to it. A casual glance is not enough. True love compels us to go deeper, to know everything we possibly can about the object of our affection. Sometimes I get restless breaking down a wine into its constituent parts, but I remind myself that to love wine is to bring all our senses to bear on the experience, for a little while to give ourselves wholly to it and to drink until we understand. We look, we smell, we taste, we feel, and we fall silent as the wine lingers on our palates. We listen to the story each wine is telling our senses.

I hope I never get over the miracle that fermented grape juice smells like everything but grapes. At first it seems odd that we swirl and smell a wine and promptly list all the *other* things it smells like: fruits and flowers, earth and spice. Wine's kaleidoscope of aromas is a fancy trick of organic chemistry; there are hundreds of aromatic compounds released from their molecular bondage during fermentation, and many are the same elements present in other fruits and vegetables. If you smell bell pepper in a cabernet franc from the Loire

Valley, for example, it's not because someone stewed a green pepper in a wine barrel. It's because the pyrazines in a pepper are also present in the organic makeup of the wine. The clinical breakdown of a wine can sound like a chart in a chemistry lab: terpenes, esters, aldehydes, rotundones, and don't forget the vanillin that comes from a toasted oak barrel.

But then there are the personal and subjective aspects to wine tasting, and these are what return my attention to wine again and again. I like to think of opening a bottle of wine as a revelation of secret mysteries, both hidden in the wine itself and in those enjoying it. Smelling great wine can be an evocative experience, summoning powerful memories of people, places, and experiences, stirring both intellect and imagination. Your memories are different from mine, and you never know where the aromas and sensations of a particular wine will take you. It can heighten our sense of delight, sometimes remind us of old griefs, and even deepen our spirituality, as we let its heady aromas lift our spirits.

I will always side with Robert Louis Stevenson, who called wine "bottled poetry," rather than with those who treat wine mostly as a specimen in a science lab. A lot of the experts these days are trying to demystify wine. Personally, I am leaning toward wanting to remystify it. Wine helps us, for the time we focus on it, to cast away distraction and to truly stop and smell. It is a tantalizing way to pay attention and to heighten our awareness of what we are experiencing in this present moment. It unites all our senses in the thrill of discovery. It helps us taste more deeply of life's gifts. Good wine is a reminder that life is full of abundance, not the imagined scarcity that we all try to survive on. And it is a way to use our earthiest, most tactile senses to connect with something otherworldly.

That is why I love wine. And why I spent two days sitting in a ball-room in the Sheraton at the Pomona Fairplex. I think the only question I missed on the exam on Saturday afternoon was about the river that flows through the Wachau region of Austria, which makes the best riesling and grüner veltliner in the country. It's the Danube River, for the record, and I won't ever forget it.

After a slightly uncomfortable wait, one of the master somms called my name and gave me my pin. Another handed me a glass of bubbles from Mendocino. I resisted the temptation to analyze it and just downed it victoriously. I was a lowercase sommelier.

# Thirteen

# VINEGAR

I want to tell you about my divorce about as much as I want to pound a magnum of white zin. Not only is divorce excruciating and embarrassing, but it is an impossibly complicated story to tell. The back and forth of our story convoluted things even further, but there is no such thing as a tidy divorce story. I found that some of our friends were looking for simple explanations so they would know who to blame. We were both to blame; we were neither to blame. We each sustained a lot of damage and inflicted a lot of damage.

I will leave most of the dirty laundry to air out on Felix Mattei's charcuterie board, but our story wasn't simply two people drifting apart over time. We tried so hard. The couch cushions of the therapists we saw privately and together over the years were well worn. Early in our marriage, when many young couples we knew were settling into a season of domestic bliss, we found ourselves thrown in over our heads, drowning in conflicts we were unprepared to handle. It may have been the wounds each of us carried that kept us together back then. Over the years, while we got better as individuals, as a couple we did not. Through all the therapy sessions we became so articulate about what we needed for a healthy and intimate relationship. We just couldn't have one.

A week after her father's memorial service that spring, we were embroiled in yet another argument. Since I moved back, I had been having a hard time feeling relaxed in our apartment. I was habitually biting the inside of my lower lip, sometimes until it bled. I was struggling again with insomnia, always a warning signal in my life that something is wrong, and if I did finally fall asleep, I was having a recurring dream of being trapped in a room with no doors, or in some situation with no way out.

I would stay out at night after work, not wanting to go home, taking dark walks through the Claremont Colleges, searching out my happy memories there. My wife was working until eight or nine at night and spending a lot of time with friends on weekends. One night, around ten o'clock, she stood in the kitchen with her hands on her hips and I sat on our olive-green couch with my arms crossed.

"I just can't believe how little time you want to actually spend with me," she scowled.

"What about you?" I scowled back. "You work all day and night, and I'm eating dinner alone every night like I'm single."

"Why don't you just wait until I get home?"

"Because I don't want to eat dinner at ten o'clock like your family does!" She let out a dagger of breath and glared at me.

"I am sorry," I conceded. "I don't want to eat dinner right before bed." I paused and took a deep breath. Then I said quietly, "At what point do we acknowledge that we just don't like being around each other anymore?"

She didn't protest. We both fell silent. I went to bed.

I have always believed that in a good marriage two people should be softened and deepened, their hard edges polished, their separate parts coming together like wine mellowing in a barrel, creating something richer and more beautiful. Unfortunately, not all wines age well. Some wines fall apart prematurely, their components break down, and they turn to vinegar. Once a wine goes to vinegar, it can't turn back. Love may never end, but some love stories turn sour.

Our friendship lasted for almost twenty years, beginning the first day of my sophomore year in college. We were always better friends than we were romantic partners, and I hung on to our friendship longer than I should have. I regretted moving back when I was, admittedly, running away from the Santa Ynez Valley more than I was running toward a new beginning for us. I convinced myself I was returning because I was needed. My wife was a strong and resilient woman, and she didn't need a hero. I made a hard situation worse. But it was agonizing for me to let go of our friendship, and the grief of losing it kept me awake many nights, both before I moved out, again, and after.

In good marriages, partners help bandage each other's wounds. More often we seemed to squeeze lemons over ours. We were battle-weary war survivors at this point, scarred and limping. I didn't want to live like that anymore. This was a war that likely should have ended years before, but we had a religious determination to stay together, and I felt frozen in the righteous spotlight of ministry. The shame heaped on a pastor getting divorced was too frightening for me to handle at the time. I knew there were some religious people whose only concern about the state of my marriage was that I was still married by the State. Now that I wasn't a pastor, divorce sounded less threatening, and a lot more liberating.

I think about all the counsel I received over the years, whether about marriage or ministry, to *stay*. Everyone seemingly had a plant analogy at the ready. Bloom where you are planted, water the grass under your feet, dig down not out. But I like to think about grapevines, and how they are vigorous enough to survive just about anywhere, but how some places, no matter how well you farm them, will produce thin, sour fruit that makes your mouth pucker. And then other places, maybe not even that far away, will offer up ripe, luxurious fruit that brings joy and abundance. I was still in the wrong place for a life of abundance. It was time to go.

⁕

My head was once again spinning with the recurring question that seemed to have no answer: Where is the right place to plant? I knew I didn't want to stay in LA. The end of my marriage had torn up the last roots of my life there.

I considered returning to my ancestral lands of West Seattle and taking a job on the ferry to Vashon Island, another life I had fantasized about in my darkest nights of hospice, when I just wanted to drive north and fade into myth. But so much of divorce involves going backward in life, as you slowly undo so many life decisions and joint accounts, and that move was a little *too* backward. I know my labyrinth trail had doubled back on itself a few times, but that felt like I would be exiting the way altogether.

I wanted to stay in wine. In my big adobe warehouse I was working at a wine pit stop, in a designer parking lot alongside a buzzing freeway. It all felt quite placeless. I had fallen in love with wine when it became more than a beverage to me; I came to see it as a symbol of a particular place, representing the shared life of the land, skies, waters, and humans that brought it into this world. I longed again to drink at the source with the creators who lived near, and not only with the consumers who drove away.

I drove up one weekend to Napa and interviewed at Duckhorn, but I don't think my references from Los Olivos were all that sparkly, and I could tell my heart wasn't there anyway. Napa still feels to me like the royal palace of California wine. It's a glamorous place to stop and admire, but I would rather live with the farmers outside the castle walls.

So my thoughts turned again to the secluded valley that people call "healing," something I was aching for. I didn't want to talk about it for the first few weeks after I moved back to LA, as the disappointment was too bitter on my tongue. But by the holidays, when customers would ask about wines from Santa Ynez, I felt my heart leap just a little. I started drinking those wines again, and I found they contained liquid memories of how that valley had once made me feel and the dreams it stirred. I even drove up for a weekend in February to study for my sommelier exam at Kathy's vacation house, and as I took in that panoramic view, I found myself forgiving the valley, even missing it. I wondered if I hadn't given it enough of a chance the first time around. It seemed like I had barely set one foot inside the valley the summer before, because I had been too divided inside to truly sink into home there. It's difficult to feel settled on a seesaw.

Now, I knew that Whole Foods would transfer me with a sense of urgency to the Santa Barbara store. On a whim, on my lunch break at Total Wine one afternoon, I responded to a job listing for a tasting-room position in Lompoc, near the Santa Rita Hills.

In all my years as a grief counselor I advised people who had just suffered great loss not to make any other big life changes, like moving or starting a new job, because piling more transition on top of loss can increase grief and burrow you deeper into depression. Screw that. Sometimes when God closes a door he opens a window, so you can sneak out of there when no one is looking. The grass isn't necessarily greener in Santa Ynez, as it's brown most of the year, but I still wanted to believe that the Santa Ynez Valley is a healing place, and I needed that more than ever.

With all I had lost in the last year, I sometimes felt like the grand marshal of the grief parade. Yet there was something truly exhilarating about choosing the possibility of happiness, even if I didn't know if I could achieve it. No trumpets sounded, no seas parted, no parade welcomed me home as I took the hook at the Gaviota Pass a few weeks later. But this time, I wasn't going back.

*Fourteen*

# THE HEALING PLACE

The air mattress was reinflated, leathery sheets reapplied, the
gray camping chair collapsed into the corner of the room,
record player and two small wooden speakers propped on a short,
wobbly nightstand. Everything seems low to the ground when you
are newly single. I think my coal-smeared friend Vincent would
have felt right at home in my ramshackle life. This time I was
camping out in the spare room of a weird dude named Herb, but
I did have my own bathroom. And I had a new muse, a lovelorn
nineteenth-century Danish storyteller named Hans, whose
statue pined in the town square next to the gazebo and the
Christmas tree.

You think you have a grip on the culture of the Santa Ynez Valley until you drive up a gentle slope to a town called Solvang.
Before that, as you head west from the stagecoach road, this valley
is a *paraíso* of rancheros and vaqueros and a left-behind pioneer
outpost, their cattle ranches now planted with grapevines, their
watering holes gentrified into wine bars and high-class honky-
tonks. Then, as you tootle along Mission Drive, admiring the

mountains in the near distance on the left, your gaze falls to the neighborhood at the bottom of the hill where, turning lazily in the reliable afternoon breeze, are the wooden blades of a Danish windmill. Rub your eyes and shake your head if you must, but when you look again you will still behold Solvang's oldest windmill, the nostalgic whimsy of a Dane named Ferd Sorensen, which will probably be the name of my next cat.

A little disoriented, you are relieved to see the belfry of Mission Santa Inés rising above the bluffs, which fall off into a pristine rural setting of olive groves, grapevines, and grassy fields easing down to the river. This Mission was the eighteenth rung in the ladder, almost a hundred years older than any other building in town, and the namesake of this beguiling and quirky valley, as well as the town of Santa Ynez, established four miles east in 1881. The nineteenth-century Yankee settlers did not know Spanish, so they went with the less common "Ynez" spelling, confusing people of all nationalities to this day.

You are ready to chalk up Ferd's windmill to architectural fancy, but then you see it. Past a long line of sycamores wrapped in white twinkle lights, a dreamscape of Danish gingerbread houses and windmills opens up before you, and on your right is a half-sized replica of the little mermaid of Copenhagen Harbor, basking in the sun on a gurgling fountain. Sixteenth-century-style half-timbered buildings with their eye-catching geometry of crisscrossed beams are crowned with storks' nests, spires, and green and white towers wearing what look like conical elf hats. The elves have their place too, in tiny little houses hanging off thatched eaves. Elven lore tells us that the *Julenisse* dwell there until Santa Lucia Day, when they gleefully emerge to give gifts or create mischief for those who don't offer them a bowl of porridge. Dormer windows framed by slatted shutters and flower boxes peek out of gabled roofs, and there is a Christmas shop open 364 days of the year. Indeed, if a December wind picked you up one afternoon and whirled you off to this little town, you might suspect you have been set down in a Bavarian Christmas Market, if not for the eighty-degree weather.

And there in Solvang Park in the town center is the bust of Danish fairytale master Hans Christian Andersen, as though this village was plucked right out of the dreams of his wintertime slumber. Welcome to Solvang, California, my friends, the Danish capital of America.

It's not hard to understand why Danish Lutherans living in the Midwest in the early 1900s would have been besotted with this valley when they first visited. They were drawn to it for the same reason the Spanish planted a Mission here in 1804: fertile farmland, plentiful water supply, and a warm and sunny climate. I would imagine that the Danes enduring winter after winter in Iowa and Michigan and Minnesota, not to mention the dark and frosty winters of the old country, had had just about enough of freezing their sweet *aebelskivers* off. Here the great steed pulls the sun across the sky in its chariot 340 days a year. The Danish-American colony completed the purchase of nine thousand acres of choice California real estate in 1911, for thirty-eight dollars an acre. They named it Solvang, which means "Sunny Field."

Their vision was to create a California Danish Valhalla centered around a high-minded folk school, which would teach children Danish language and culture and serve as a social and artistic center for the community. The Atterdag School was set on a hill north of town in 1915, and Solvang had achieved the heights of *hygge*, that delightful Danish term which wraps you and your loved ones in a cozy Scandinavian hug. Only one thing was missing. In their hustle to build on the sunny fields, the founders had settled for the wood frames and western storefronts of their neighbors in Los Olivos and Santa Ynez. But then, in 1947, *The Saturday Evening Post* ran a feature on Solvang, which they dubbed "Little Denmark, the spotless Danish village that blooms like a rose in California's charming Santa Ynez Valley."

That's when the Solvang Businessmen's Association resolved to honor the town's Danish heritage by creating the storybook Copenhagen look that now draws in two million visitors annually. The western false fronts were replaced by half-timber facades, Main Street became Copenhagen Drive, the annual Danish Days Festival was inaugurated and the presiding Danish Maid chosen, cafés started serving pickled herring and Danish meatballs on open faced rye with red cabbage, and three more traditional windmills were constructed to match Ferd's design.

A Danish windmill looks to me like an enormous, windowed saltshaker crowned in a winter cap, and its four decorative wooden blades are cut out in a pattern that resembles fingers of waffles. Or perhaps the mere thought of Solvang makes me hungry, because while there are four windmills in town, there are five authentic Danish bakeries. They keep on hand the flaky round pastries with fluffy fruit centers to appease tourists, but their shops are smorgasbords of strudels, eclairs, turnovers, and Danish waffles—long, sugar-coated pastry shells filled with buttercream and raspberry jam. Or, you can literally buy a bucket of Danish butter cookies. Then there is the magic window on Copenhagen Drive that serves up *aebelskivers*, which are tennis balls of fried pancake dough floating in a river of raspberry syrup, held down by an avalanche of powdered sugar.

There is no place like Solvang when it comes to eating your feelings. For the first time in over fifteen years, I was single, and I was ready to kringle.

<hr />

I was living in a one-story apartment complex coated with dirty white stucco, at the end of a cul-de-sac that must not have received the citywide memo on half-timbered design. Herb, a retired lawyer in his early sixties, told me he owned his condo, but I later found out he was renting it and charging me half the rent, even though he had the master bedroom and control of the space. He insisted I pay each month in cash, because "I have bank accounts on the East Coast that can't know I am getting income in California." There were some un-savory dealings going down in this corner of Solvang.

Each morning I got up early to make coffee, and he was already planted at the kitchen table with SportsCenter on TV and his laptop open to pictures of women on dating websites. "Check out this one, Adam!" was his regular morning greeting. "It's six in the morning, dude" was mine. Herb was a lonely guy. I think he rented out the spare room mostly for the company, and he wouldn't stop talking whenever I was in the same room with him. I stayed away from the apartment as much as I could. I think I was terrified that Herb was my future.

My daily rituals were holding my life together. Most nights I tromped through the well-lit streets of Solvang until nine or ten, sometimes stopping in for a drink by the fire at Root 246. By day, Solvang walks a tightrope between small-town charm and amusement-park kitsch. You wonder if some Vikings lost their bearings and oared their ship into the It's a Small World ride. But at night, after the tourist buses have departed, it becomes an enchanted European Christmas village, and I couldn't wait for my nightly walks, and not only because I was avoiding Herb. I would wander over to the Mission on the other side of town and sit on a bench under the pepper trees, or I would take a table in the park near the statue of my new friend Hans.

All I knew of Hans Christian Andersen before this was "The Ugly Duckling," apparently an autobiographical tale, and "The Little Mer-maid," which is quite different from Uncle Walt's cinematic version. In the book, the mermaid agrees to have her tongue cut off to gain human legs; each step she takes with her new legs feels like "walking on knives"; she sleeps on the floor outside the prince's door like a dog; and when he doesn't return her love, she contemplates murdering him. It's a heartwarming tale for children and feminists alike. I suspect that my friend Hans could have spent a little less time writing fairy tales and a little more time in therapy. But the more I read about him, the more I came to enjoy his social clumsiness and appreciate how nakedly and openheartedly he loved.

Hans idolized Charles Dickens, just like I did in high school, and after meeting Dickens on his first trip to London, took up a long correspondence with him. Years later, Charles invited Hans to stay with him and his family for two weeks. Hans stayed for five. On his first morning, he announced to the Dickens family that it is Danish custom for the host's son to shave their guest each morning. Dickens arranged a daily trip to the barber. Hans would venture out into London by day and get deep into the sherry, taking cabs around the city until he was lost. One afternoon during his visit, he read a bad review of one of his books, so he went outside and face-planted into the Dickens's lawn, weeping uncontrollably, while the family watched horrified at the window. Come on, Dickens, what writer hasn't done that, or at least entertained the idea? After Hans finally went home, Dickens left a note on the door of his room: "Hans Andersen slept in this room for five weeks—which seemed to the family AGES!"

All of that makes me like Hans and his puppy-dog ways even more. He once wrote, "My blood craves love, as does my heart," but he continually fell in love with unattainable women, and apparently a man or two as well. Here in Solvang Park, the long nose of Hans's statue does not point forward, but his head is turned, his gaze directed across Mission Drive to a second-story balcony bursting with flower baskets. I think he is waiting for a plump Danish maid to pop out the shuttered window and announce her undying love for him. Hans died wearing a pouch around his neck that contained a letter from his first love, penned decades before. He also may have died a virgin.

Hans's fairytales aren't typically the "happily ever after" sort. His stories brim with longing and unrequited love, often telling the tales of lonely and mournful creatures dwelling in beautiful, natural settings. I needed those kinds of stories as the silhouetted ridges of the mountains disappeared into the darkness of my Solvang nights. Time was passing slowly, as it does when you are grieving, since your loss still feels so near. Chosen grief is still an authentic grief. I wasn't in anguish, but my grief was quiet, and I kept most of it inside. There are some places of grief you have to go alone, and trying to describe it to people only cheapens it. At least I had Hans, and together we were lonely writers, sprawled face down in the Sunny Field.

<hr>

The next piece of my own advice I ignored was that when you are grappling with loss, you shouldn't over occupy your time with busyness to avoid your feelings. I was working six, often seven, days a week. Half the week I took the stagecoach route down San Marcos Pass, navigating serpentine twists through rocks rusted red from their time under the ocean, to the Santa Barbara Whole Foods. On my first day there, I found the small wine section and introduced myself to my new supervisor, Toby, who was stocking Malbec on the top shelf of the Argentina section.

"Toby—hi, I'm Adam, and I'm starting today. I just transferred up from the Pasadena store."

"Yeah, okay. Give me a minute here to finish," he said snappily.

"Take your time," I offered.

"Oh, I never take my time, and neither should you. There is far too much to do and not nearly enough time to do it."

*This will go well*, I thought to myself.

While Toby's impression of an overcaffeinated porcupine was spot on, he would soften over time, and overall, I fit in better at the Santa Barbara store than I did in Pasadena. I still got dinged for not wheeling my wine cart through the store fast enough, but Santa Barbara as a whole is not a place that moves with a sense of urgency very often. Rich people walk slowly, especially near the beach. I found Barbareños, as residents of Santa Barbara were known during the Ranchero days, to be overall more welcoming than my fellow wine-valley dwellers over the mountains. They didn't treat me like the weird guy renting their spare room. It was a relief to be on a large team with surfing cheesemongers and mellow beerdos, including one guy I swear was paid just to hug customers, when my life in Solvang could be so painfully solitary.

⁘

The other half of the week, I drove through the vines of the Santa Rita Hills to Lompoc on the western outskirts of the valley, the temperature dropping a degree per mile as the ocean drew closer. Babcock Winery on my route has a pinot named "Ocean's Ghost," in tribute to the specter of marine fog that clings to the late-morning chill even in midsummer.

There is no easy way to get to Lompoc. The big roads lost interest years ago, and no one just happens upon Lompoc. You have to really want it. It's way out on the salty and windswept edges of the western world, but there was something comforting about that. It felt safe and invisible, like I had fallen out of frame a little, and I could hide and heal out there in the fog.

Lompoc is home to a federal penitentiary, a space force base with the second longest runway in the United States, and world-class pinot noir. Delta rockets carrying spy satellites launch in a pillar of fire from Vandenberg Space Force Base, sometimes shattering the windows of nearby homes, and when an inmate at the Lompoc Pen is unaccounted for, flashing road signs advise you not to pick up hitchhikers. But as I approached town, passing a shaded walnut orchard and a rainbow of flower fields, I would see an arrow sign pointing me to the "Lompoc Wine Ghetto."

It's hard to believe that three generations ago in this part of town a group of axe-wielding mothers smashed every liquor bottle in a drugstore that was secretly selling it. Lompoc was a zealously guarded temperance colony, located halfway between the "wicked" cities of San Luis Obispo and Santa Barbara. These days, the eastern half of town is drunk with plucky little wineries.

The wine ghetto, a clever name as long as you are not a history major, is home to a crafty group of winemakers who found another way to pursue their wine dreams without building the luxury estate. Wedged between Home Depot and a power plant, it is home to two dozen family wineries that practice their heady science behind the roll-up doors of an industrial park. From the outside, it bears the insipid monochrome of a storage complex, but inside, warehouses have been transformed into cozy tasting rooms filled with the healing incense of wine wafting out of French oak barrels.

There are great stories tucked into these warehouses, and I have always been partial to the wine stories that don't start with an inherited pot of gold and a tax shelter. My new boss, Antonio Moretti, owned the Moretti Winery and a storefront called the Taste of Santa Rita Hills, which features wines from boutique producers in the area who don't have their own tasting rooms. Antonio is as Italian as his name sounds. His favorite joke was "How do you get an Italian to stop talking? Tie his hands behind his back." He had lived in California for about forty years, so I was convinced his persistent Italian accent was fake at this point, but customers, especially women of a certain age, swooned over every wine label he mispronounced. Antonio left the old country with his drumsticks to join the tail end of San Francisco's once-hopping jazz scene, but a motorcycle accident put an end to his jazz-drummer days, so he turned to every Italian's second true love: food and wine. He met his wife, Jeni, an importer of

Italian wines and yoga teacher, and together they moved south to Lompoc to open a winery.

I liked Antonio and Jeni. We shared a love of old-school jazz and pinot with just the right amount of funk in it. On my long weekends working for them, I poured some of the most coveted wines in the area, like Sea Smoke, which unleashed a style of pinot unknown on Burgundy lovers: a version so dark and inky it could stain your glass purple. It is a singular experience pouring 150-dollar wine while looking out on the lumberyard behind Home Depot and the ER parking lot for the Lompoc Valley Medical Center. Guests would ask me about the best food to pair with our ascendent pinots, and I would say, "Have you considered a hot dog from Home Depot?"

Since Antonio was insistent that "an Italian would never drink wine by itself," I was both lead wine salesman and proprietor of my own little Italian deli. Not only would I pour wine behind the bar, but I would dice up bread toasted on a panini press, thinly slice salami, carve Parmesan Reggiano into strips with a potato peeler, and—to go with the earthiest pinot we poured—cut a nibble of a cheese made with speckles of Italian black truffles. I think Antonio bought it out of the back of a windowless van in an alley somewhere. It was cheese crack.

People came for the wine, but stayed for the food, since we were the only tasting room in the wine ghetto that served any. They would camp out for hours on our patio, really just a white-picketed section of the parking lot, hoping I would pity them like the seagulls and toss them more bread and truffle cheese. As I came outside to pour their wine, I would try to direct their attention over the Fiddlehead Cellars warehouse to the east, where in the distance you could make out the tips of the White Cliffs of Lompoc.

"A winemaker gets excited when he sees this," said Ken Brown to me as we scaled the white coastal hills above Lompoc in early August. He handed me a rock that was unlike anything I had ever seen. It almost looked manmade, like a broken tile. It was flat and white and light as air, leaving a chalky residue on my hands after I handed it back to him. We were standing on a powdery dirt road probably seven hundred feet above Santa Rosa Road, looking down a treacherous slope at the young vines of the Radian Vineyard, in the extreme southwestern corner of the Santa Rita Hills.

We stocked some of Ken's wines at the Taste of Santa Rita Hills, and he was generous enough to take me along on his vineyard hike, to check on his fruit as harvest drew closer. Ken Brown is a legend in these parts, the first to plant syrah in Santa Barbara County and the founding winemaker of the Zaca Mesa Winery in 1977, where he also had an unofficial title: professor of Zaca Mesa University. In those pioneering days, most winemakers in this valley didn't have viticulture diplomas but instead learned through apprenticeship, and an impressive number of our historic wineries went on to be established by harvest interns and assistant winemakers who "studied" under Ken at Zaca Mesa U.

We were a couple weeks into *véraison*, a French term that means "ripening" or "coloring," the season in the vine cycle when the fruit swells from hard, green pearls to deep-purple or flecked-gold berries. The pinot clusters at Radian were so tiny that they practically disappeared when I closed my hand around one. "An ideal harvest for pinot," explained Ken, "is between two and three tons an acre. Here, there are years when we get less than a ton. The vines are stressed out all year long. Some of them don't make it." The vines looked stunted and a little scraggly. We were in the middle of a severe drought, a three-year stretch when Lompoc received no more than seven inches a year. That's a fifth of Burgundy's annual rainfall.

We braced ourselves both against the slope and against the merciless wind that batters these vines as soon as the morning fog burns off. I read once that this microclimate can be described as a "fog hurricane." The tiny berries here develop thick skins out of survival instincts, and the juice inside is incredibly concentrated, leading to some of the deepest and darkest pinots I have tasted. Next door was the Bentrock Vineyard, home to the lightning-in-a-bottle Sandhi Chardonnay that made me a convert the summer before, and I could feel the energy that those grapes seem to absorb from the air. I could smell the ocean in the wind, and I understood why people say chardonnay here smells like sea spray. But I didn't know until now that the wind stings like a jellyfish.

This savage corner of the Santa Rita Hills is called Rancho Salsipuedes. "Salsipuedes" is how an old Spanish mapmaker would mark a spot you did not want to be if it started raining. It was akin to drawing a skull and crossbones on the map. It means "get out if you can." The soil on these slopes turns to glass when it rains.

Why some guy thought, *This sure seems like a nice place to plant grapes, don't you think?* is beyond me. These hills are wild, cold, and barren. The masters of the vine call Radian a "marginal site," meaning that your two options here are revelation or ruin; there is no in-between. We were in the outer limits of grape possibilities, an edge place for pinot, where fruit only comes through the agony of the struggle. Another winemaker who works with Radian says, "I can see the vines cry sometimes."

As far as we know, this is the only place on the planet where vines are planted in the white talcum that coated my shoes. The rock that Ken held is called a diatomite, broken off the scaly cliffs above us, which would be eventually ground down to a snowy powder called diatomaceous earth. The gleaming faces of these hills are California's answer to the White Cliffs of Dover and the Paris Basin that lies under Champagne and Chablis, except diatomite is not limestone.

It's silica, the same element that makes up glass, and each grain of diatomaceous earth is like a tiny shard of glass. It all originates in microscopic sea creatures called diatoms, which are "algae that live in a house of glass." Diatoms are hard-shelled plankton, their cell walls made of transparent silica.

Ten million years ago, diatoms flourished in the waters of the Central Coast, teeming in the warm waters around volcanic vents like a Vegas hot tub. Even though the tectonic rollercoaster had surfaced the mainland long before that, beach-bum California decided to ride the waves one last time and dropped back into the ocean. That's when trillions of diatoms swam in shallow waters, photosynthesizing the sunlight that penetrated the surface, then dying and becoming a thick layer of fossilized sludge on the ocean floor. As California again crested the Pacific, diatoms became the building blocks of some pretty cool rocks: Monterey shale, which supports the white cliffs of Point Conception; chert, a hard and angular rock the Chumash used to make tools and spear points; and diatomaceous earth, which filters pools, kills ants, and makes vines cry.

We were so high up on this white hill that we had reached "the moon blocks" of Radian. From our extraterrestrial viewpoint, we could see everything. Ken gestured to the next set of hills to the north, where Rita's Crown, the highest elevation vineyard of the Santa Rita Hills, peaked above the fog line. Diatoms sparkled in her crown.

We couldn't make out the structure just below her peak that Ken had pointed out on our drive to Radian, and I wasn't sure I believed the story yet. There is an abandoned, half-completed monastery that sits on a gentle outlook under Rita's Crown, a wondrous and disastrous undertaking in the early '90s of an order of Carmelite nuns, a division of the same monastic order as Father Junipero Serra. The sisters named their home Mt. Carmel, but their visions were much grander than their resources, and it was never finished. It is a heartbreaking story. But their legacy has been preserved in wine bottles because they leased out a parcel of their diatom-rich land to be planted with cuttings from the Sanford & Benedict Vineyard visible from their holy overlook. It became the Mt. Carmel Vineyard, and it sits in the shadow of two white crosses perched atop the unfinished monastery.

Radian, Rita's Crown, and Mt. Carmel, these are the high places of the Santa Rita Hills, altars of glass that make for dramatic theaters of confrontation between rushing wind and cold sunlight. A few prophets are brave enough to call down fire from these hills and try to bottle it.

❦

To me, the Santa Rita Hills are the spiritual heart of the Santa Ynez Valley. The first to plant grapevines along the path of the Santa Ynez River were the padres of Mission La Purísima Concepción, founded in 1787 as the eleventh Mission in the chain. The original adobe was set in a foggy canyon along Santa Rosa Creek, where their mission grapes shriveled in the cold. After the violent earthquake of 1812, La Purísima was relocated two miles north to its present location, in the sunnier Canyon of the Watercress. It is my favorite of all the California Missions, a breeze-rustled, bird-chirping haven beautifully restored into a living history museum as a New Deal building project in the '30s. I loved to walk through its gardens in the evenings after work, talking to the pigs and goats in its stables.

At the Taste of Santa Rita Hills, we sold a pricey dessert wine that looked like it had been pirated from the stores of a Spanish galleon. It came in a hand-blown bottle stamped with a beeswax seal, and the label looked hand-made, with rough, browning edges. The story behind it gives me goosebumps. Twenty-five years ago, Deborah Hall bought an old lima-bean farm in Gypsy Canyon, four miles from the Mission. As she was clear cutting thick sagebrush on her property, she discovered fifteen hundred gnarly old vines hidden underneath them. A DNA test revealed that they were 115-year-old mission grape vines, dormant for a century, that likely began as cuttings taken from La Purísima, that were then hidden under sage and blackberries during Prohibition!

Miraculously, Deborah was able to awaken her vines, and they started producing a quarter ton of mission grapes a year. She went digging into the Santa Barbara Mission archives, where she found Mission San Gabriel's recipe for Angelica, the treasured, fortified dessert wine that was California's original wine, carried in mule carts from Mission to Mission along the King's Highway. She made twenty-five cases of Angelica a year, about half a barrel, from the ancient vines she coaxed back to life, the oldest vineyard in the county by ninety years. It is unlike anything I have ever tasted, a nectar oozing with caramel color and almost ethereal candied apricot and crème brûlée flavors.

There is healing and new life hidden out here on the margins. The modern story of the Santa Rita Hills began with one man's search for the therapy of place. In the early 1970s, Richard Sanford read viticulture books by candlelight in the old barn he was repurposing into a winery. After serving as a navigator on a navy destroyer in Vietnam, he felt rejected by the same society that sent him to war, so he sought healing in nature, in communion with the ground. He and his sailing buddy Michael Benedict planted the Sanford & Benedict Vineyard in 1971 on Santa Rosa Road, in spite of their neighbors who told them they were throwing their money away. Up until then, the western Santa Ynez Valley was reserved for beans, walnuts, and secret stashes of the devil's lettuce. It was far too cold and foggy to grow grapes, they said.

Richard Sanford had studied the climate of Burgundy, and he drove up and down these country roads with a thermometer taped to the windshield of his 1950 Mercedes. He discovered that the climate here was strikingly similar to maritime France, and the crunchy soils scattered with fragments of chert and shale drained well. So he and Benedict bought an abandoned bean farm with an old barn on the back of the property, and planted cabernet and riesling, the fashionable varieties at the time, but they also planted pinot noir. Sanford and Benedict were the first vintners to plant pinot in a region that would come to be known as one of the best places on the planet for pinot noir.

The first commercial release of Sanford & Benedict Pinot Noir came in 1976, the same year as the famous "Judgement of Paris" event when French wine judges declared Napa Valley wine entries superior to elite French wines in a blind tasting. It was depicted decades later in the movie *Bottle Shock*, which is no *Sideways*, but it did cast Hans Gruber from *Die Hard* as an effete wine snob, so it had that going for it. But it wasn't only Napa that had suddenly appeared on the wine map, because shortly after the release of the inaugural Sanford & Benedict Pinot, the LA Times ran a story headlined "American Grand Cru in a Lompoc Barn." The old barn and vineyard, which still has fifty-three acres of its original vines, has become a New World pilgrimage site for Burgundy lovers.

<hr>

Our mystic march completed, Ken eased his truck down the hazardous dirt path back to Santa Rosa Road, while we talked about the personality of the wines that come from this high corner of the Santa Rita Hills.

"I like how people say chardonnay from Bentrock smells like ocean air," I said. "The Radian Pinots I have tried all seem to have that 'wet stone' aroma. I love it because it reminds me of my childhood in Seattle. It smells the way our driveway would smell after a quick summer rain. The sun would still be out, but there would be one little raincloud that dripped on our house for a few minutes. Radian Pinot smells to me like summer rain."

"There is a name for that aroma," said Ken casually. "It's called *petrichor*."

"Petrichor," I repeated slowly. "Huh. I wonder where that comes from?"

As soon as we got back into cell range, about a half hour later, I looked it up. Apparently during prolonged dry spells, some plants secrete oils that inhibit new growth around them, out of self-protection. When it finally rains again, those oils are released into the air, and the scent is called petrichor. It means the essence or perfume of rock. But I suspected there was more.

I was right. *Ichor* is an ancient Greek word for "blood," sometimes referring to the blood of the gods, and *petra* means "stone." *Petrichor* literally means blood from a stone.

I couldn't believe it. Here was another miracle of stone and vine, and this time it was happening right where I lived. Out of the white ashes of that vast diatom graveyard spring the aromas of new life.

The stones are alive.

I am alive.

*Fifteen*

# THE PARADE

The founders of Solvang built their community around a folk school they named Atterdag, which means "return of the day," or "after darkness there shall be day again." My grief wasn't fully exhausted, but I was sleeping better, no longer rehearsing the past by rote night after night. My loneliness was beginning to subside, and the pit in my stomach was starting to fill in. I thought I might be ready to spend more time with people who weren't characters in books or statues in parks, or goats in a Mission.

One thing I was right about is that after significant wanderings of grief you do not reenter the world through the same door you departed it, nor do you reemerge as the same person you once were. It requires some time to adjust to the new version of yourself. I have always felt that labeling yourself "divorced" haunts you unnecessarily with past shadows, like I once was a whole person but now I am severed, so please speak in hushed tones around me. Whatever governing body first proposed "divorced" as a legal status should be the official sponsor of Miles's book *The Day After Yesterday.*

I was here to live a new day. I wasn't the same man I once was, but that wasn't a bad thing. I had reawakened as a happier and lighter person. I was taking deeper breaths. It was time to get up off the air mattress.

<hr/>

You can only go so far in the world of wine when you are pairing pinot noir with Home Depot hot dogs. I was grateful for my time working for Antonio and Jeni, but I knew that situation had an expiration. The fogged-in corners of the world may be good places to duck and cover in a crisis, but you don't necessarily want to be there long after the sirens have ceased. Teachers in Lompoc schools refer to "wind days," when the gusts off the ocean are so intense that the kids on the playground are stirred up to the point of being untamable. I was starting to go a little crazy out there.

Hence, I found myself a few weeks later sitting at a long wooden wine bar in the Presidio neighborhood of Santa Barbara.

"How much access would I have to the winemaker?" I asked, innocuously, as we neared the end of the job interview.

Jim Adelman laughed out loud. "Well, you might see him once a year."

That winemaker was another Jim—Jim Clendenen—and his winery is named Au Bon Climat, ABC for short. In a contemporary history of Santa Barbara County wine, Jim Clendenen would be on page one for his groundbreaking wines but also for his appellation-sized personality. Clendenen was in the first wave of wine trailblazers in the late '70s, along with Richard Sanford and Ken Brown and a few others, but as one wine codger put it, "Most of those guys were shrinking violets in a crowd, but Clendenen was a roaring lion." His lionized reputation was enhanced by his long, curly mane of dirty-blond hair that verged on a mullet in his youth and softened to silver waves in his later years. Yet for his thunderous voice, he made beautifully quiet and understated wines, a bombastic personality that boldly refused to make the fruit bombs the critics rewarded with big numbers.

Clendenen was elusive to the tasting room because he was either hosting long lunches at his airplane-hangar-sized winery on the fabled Bien Nacido Vineyard, sixty miles north of the Santa Barbara tasting room, or out trotting the globe, rousing wine rabbles on different continents. He was a celebrity in London, where Jancis Robinson nicknamed him "Wild Boy," and he was big in Japan, where he cut a prodigious figure and his lively, old-school pinots and chards played with every dish. He dressed like a rock star, in faded jeans and psychedelic t-shirts. He had the flamboyant, iconoclastic personality of a rock star. And for a half-century after he fell in love with wine while driving his VW bus through France, he partied like a rock star. He was an epicurean hero to many, a bon vivant, and the life of every party.

The assistant tasting-room manager position at ABC seemed out of my reach, especially with my professional history of killing the buzz of the party, so I was abnormally relaxed during the interview, my snark on a full display, which is usually best saved for six months into a job, or never. I rolled in ten minutes late because I had a hard time navigating the names of the southbound freeway exits, which read, in order, Carrillo, Castillo, and Cabrillo, surely the scheme of some nefarious city planner who hates tourists. Yet it may be that the best way to land a job is to think you can't. The next morning, if you squinted while peering out into the turquoise-streaked waters of the Santa Barbara Channel, you might have made out the silhouette of a vessel on the horizon, the letters on its approaching bow spelling *Adam McHugh*, lowercase *sommelier*. For his ship had come in.

My first long weekend with Au Bon Climat felt like some sort of wine fantasy. After my first day, I was invited to a barbeque on a boat. As the sun set to the side of our slip in the Marina, we ate tri-tip and drank syrah while watching sea lions wriggle nearby, as you do on a Thursday night. The next morning I parked my car a few blocks away and was walking to the tasting room, to discover that I was on a parade route. This would not be the last time this happened. State Street in Santa Barbara hosts more annual parades than any other street I know. There is a parade for old cars, for tanks and veterans, for the Fourth of July. There is the Christmas Parade of Lights, the Summer Solstice Parade of scantily clad middle-aged dancers, the "we haven't had a parade in a while" parade. I think after Santa Barbara gained its reputation in the 1800s as "the sanitorium of the Pacific," for the healing salt waters gently massaging its south-lounging beaches, the town lazed into a life of leisure and parade. Nineteenth-century deckhand and travel writer Richard Henry Dana, visiting from Boston, diagnosed our condition as "California fever" and said, "The people really hardly seem to earn their sun-light." Make sure to take your Protestant work ethic with you when you board the ship back to New England, amigo. We got naps to take.

The parade I stumbled on was the most anticipated of the Santa Barbara parade calendar and a tradition going back a hundred years. It was Fiesta Friday, the pinnacle of a weeklong August party called Old Spanish Days, which celebrates the Spanish heritage of this old but still shiny pueblo. I watched a kaleidoscope of flouncy dresses swirling past the crowds, *señoritas* in polka dots adorned with flowers and combs in their hair, and vaqueros in their sequined suits of light dancing their horses up State Street. De la Guerra Plaza had been transformed into a mercado of tamales, churros, souvenirs, and margaritas, and gleeful celebrants were breaking confetti-filled eggs over each other's heads for good luck. Just another Friday in Santa Barbara.

This was a tradition that Richard Henry Dana helped reignite through his travelogue *Two Years Before the Mast*, published in 1840. He took two years off from Harvard to join the cowhide-collecting voyage of the ship *Pilgrim* around the horn to Alta California, then the possession of Mexico, in what may have been the first ever Semester at Sea. This was in the heyday of the hide and tallow trade, California's first export, when rancheros raised so many cattle that the *Pilgrim*'s sailors ate fresh beef every day because it was cheaper than the salt to preserve it. Dana's first glimpse of California was the white-shale corner of Point Conception.

On one of his shore visits to Santa Barbara, Dana was invited to the home of the man they called El Capitan, the fifth Comandante of the Santa Barbara Presidio, the conductor of the Spanish-named train *Don José Antonio de la Guerra y Noriega*. Don José was basically the godfather of Santa Barbara—all business in the pueblo went through him—and his casa and plaza became the town marketplace and social center, with a generous bodega filled with wine El Capitan made himself. Dana attended the wedding of Don José's daughter, a three-day fandango of music, dancing, and shimmering pageantry, and noted that, being close to Easter, attendees were breaking perfume-filled eggs called *cascarones* over each other's heads, as a sort of fragrant anointing. Eighty years later, the founders of Old Spanish Days thought confetti was a better idea than perfume, which may not be the sentiment of the people who spend the next week sweeping it up on the streets of Santa Barbara. I hope it's biodegradable.

Au Bon Climat's tasting room sits on the border of the miniature Spanish village that now surrounds Casa de la Guerra, a maze of narrow passageways, bougainvillea-lined courtyards, and wine bodegas called El Paseo. In Spain, the *paseo* is the leisurely evening stroll you take through the town plaza for socializing and digesting. Finally, here is a wine building that gets me. No sense of urgency in here. In this building, in this part of town, I found myself unexpectedly at ground zero of Santa Barbara culture, both old and new. The clay and stucco of this neighborhood is etched with 250 years of beginnings.

A half-block away, the bells of the restored Presidio chapel rang clearly over red-tiled roofs. Junipero Serra was there to consecrate the Presidio on April 21, 1782, as the Spanish first broke Santa Barbara ground, and he may have planted the area's first grapevines nearby. The Presidio was the fourth and last fortress built by the Spanish as they colonized Alta California, since Santa Barbara was seen as a critical trading port between San Diego and Monterey. The Presidio was the seat of government and military might, once framed by walls nine feet high and four feet thick, and the center of worship until the Mission was completed up the hill in 1804. The adobes of the new pueblo grew slowly around it, mostly dwellings of soldiers and their families, the most important of which was Casa de la Guerra. A small soldier's quarters, called El Cuartel, still stands on the Presidio grounds in its untouched adobe form, now the second-oldest surviving building in California. Next door is the Pickle Room, the best dive bar in Santa Barbara, a tribute to the Chinatown restaurant that thrived there after World War II. It's now owned by the adjacent, pickle-themed deli, so patrons eat Reuben egg rolls and fried pickles while drinking pickletinis and viewing historical reenactments across the street at the Presidio. You didn't see that coming, did you?

In the early twentieth century, city planners were concerned that State Street looked too much like Main Street, USA, and that Santa Barbara had lost the Hispanic heritage that distinguished it from other small towns. So they proposed a Spanish revival, and their first project was El Paseo. There the grids and symmetry of Yankee design were restored to the covered arcades and blooming inner courtyards of the Spanish countryside, and it became the blueprint for the renaissance of the Spanish style. In 1925, a devastating earthquake decimated Santa Barbara, and the city was put back together not with the eclectic pre-earthquake architecture, but in the Spanish colonial revival style of low buildings of white stucco walls and red tile that are now the mark of El Pueblo Viejo, old town Santa Barbara. Over the next few years, I would come to love this Spanish garden-city ever in bloom, the fragrances of sage, aloe, and star jasmine wafting through the jacaranda, orange, and olive trees dotting the heart of downtown.

El Paseo was the birthplace of Santa Barbara County's first commercial winery since before Prohibition, when Pierre Lafond opened the Santa Barbara Winery there, in 1962. Lafond's wine and cheese shop drew a quirky group of bohemians from potholed Mountain Drive in the foothills above Santa Barbara. The Mountain Drive community "celebrated the spirit of Bacchus" and toasted his gifts while bubbling in the hot tub they claim to have invented. They made some wine themselves, in an annual harvest festival highlighted by a fully nude group grape stomp. I don't care how antibacterial the acid and alcohol of fermentation is, I'm not drinking wine that had naked hippies in it.

In the 1980s, the winemakers and enthusiasts who gathered again in El Paseo were still a scruffy bunch, but at least they were wearing clothes. One of the secret courtyards belongs to the Wine Cask Restaurant, which became the epicenter of Santa Barbara wine culture in the early '80s. At the time Santa Barbara County wine was still a fledgling experiment, and the valleys over the mountains sparsely populated and unknown. Much of America had just learned about the Santa Ynez Valley for the first time because of a mountaintop adobe called Rancho El Cielo, the Ranch in the Heavens, which was also known by another nickname: the Western White House. President Ronald Reagan spent fifty days a year running the country on his own peak of the Santa Ynez Mountains above Solvang, chopping wood and taxes. On one side of the ranch he could see boats cruising the Santa Barbara Channel, and on the other side a forest of oak leading down to the Santa Ynez Valley, which grew wines he served at state dinners in the other White House. The Firestone Winery near Los Olivos said their sales increased ten times when the First Wine Drinker started pouring them in his first term.

The Wine Cask Futures events of the '80s became a showcase for our pioneering winemakers and their young wines, as well as a springboard for a sophisticated local wine and food culture growing up with them. That brings me to a Friday night, thirty years later, still my second day of working for Au Bon Climat. All the Wine Cask legends were gathered again, this time at Jim Clendenen's ranch in Los Alamos for the tenth anniversary celebration of the release of *Sideways*.

Paul Giamatti was there, as was *Sideways* director Alexander Payne, surrounded by a who's who of Santa Barbara wine heroes, and somehow, me. The public charity event was the next evening, but tonight was the private party. There was a whole hog on the Santa Maria grill and a band playing classic rock in the corner. The local icons had broken into their personal stashes for large-format library vintages at least as old as the movie. Some of the bottles were so big it took two or three people to pour. Laughter filled the cool night air, which required heat lamps even in the middle of summer. All the vine whisperers were already talking about the upcoming harvest, or they were debating why Miles hated merlot so much. Some said California Merlot was an inferior product, others said it was because Miles and his ex-wife had enjoyed it together, and he directed his grief at merlot after the divorce. I noticed no one brought any merlot to the party.

Taking this all in, I felt like I had won the wine lottery. It was only six months ago that I had been selling fizzy wine in a desert warehouse next to the Crazy Chicken. After a couple hours, I steeled myself with some Bien Nacido and waded through a sea of adoring older women surrounding Paul Giamatti. I hovered near him for a few minutes, rehearsing my speech in my head, until I saw my opening.

"Mr. Giamatti, my name is Adam!" I blurted out as I jumped toward him and shook his hand. He looked about as uncomfortable as I felt, but I continued without taking a breath: "I won't take up much of your time. I just want to thank you for the movie. I used to live down in the Pasadena area, and I had never even heard of the Santa Ynez Valley until I saw *Sideways*. Now I live here and work in the wine industry."

"You moved here because of the movie?" he asked, incredulously.

"In a way, yes. It really did change my life."

He seemed genuinely moved by what I said. Granted, I think he had enjoyed a healthy amount of pinot himself that night, in true Miles fashion, but I swear I even saw a glisten in his eyes as he thanked me for telling him my story.

I knew then that everything was going to be okay.

⟡

I took the scenic route to ABC for the next three months, since I thought I could never afford rent in Santa Barbara. Dog houses appraise for eighty thousand dollars down there, and that's for a studio. But then a curly-haired angel named Ali appeared one afternoon to taste chardonnay and revealed that she was vacating her cheap downtown apartment in two weeks. The paint was chipping off the two-story Victorian down the western slope from the Mission, and the view from the kitchen sink looked straight into the shower of the house next door, through their bathroom window propped by an old shampoo bottle. But there was a lemon tree in the backyard that was pregnant all year round, and the kitchen smelled of cupcakes, because Ali was a cupcake champion and author of a book called *Sweet, Savory, Sometimes Boozy Cupcakes*. Unfortunately, she was also engaged.

In the late afternoon three weeks later, I took the exit for Mission Drive and tucked into my new narrow driveway with my fourteen-year-old calico Scout, who had been purring her contentment about retiring in Santa Barbara since I retrieved her from down south that morning. I had found my Domaine de la Solitude. I even bought a real bed.

❦

I had become a Barbareño. Santa Barbara has a reputation as a glossy-postcard resort town, but there are many different versions of Santa Barbara, depending on who you ask. There are the five-star resorts, the oceanfront mansions, celebrities escaping LA paparazzi, and royals in exile behind artistically sculpted hedgerows, but there is also a sizable homeless population. There is a large service industry of assistant managers and an immigrant population that makes the lifestyles of the rich possible, and a sandy residue of beach-bum colonies bedecked with wet suits hanging in old campers. There are huts for astrologers, palm readers, and tarot cards, and a psychic detective agency down by the beach.

I saw it all as I started walking to work, a life dream fulfilled, though I quickly learned to leave early. I never knew when a parade might break out and slow my progress. Of course my feet were involuntarily drawn to De la Vina Street, so named for the vineyard planted there in the 1800s after the Mission ranchos were dissolved and wine became a commercial enterprise in Santa Barbara. Mildew and disease hampered those vines, and I understood why when June gloom covered the old pueblo like a soft blanket for several weeks, depriving sun-starved tourists trying to avoid the midsummer crowds. Personally, I always thought Santa Barbara was at her most enchanting in the gray.

I would then cut across town to see the courthouse, the castle with the clocktower, surely the Platonic ideal of Spanish colonial revival

with its archway framing a view of the Santa Ynez Mountains towering above sunken gardens. On the way, I would greet the statue of the
Lone Woman of San Nicolas Island, called "Karana" in Scott O'Dell's
book *The Island of the Blue Dolphins*. I never said I wouldn't have *any*
statue friends, especially one who lived utterly alone on a remote
island for eighteen years. She was the last of her tribe, living in a hut
of whalebones and brush, subsisting on sea creatures and roasted
roots. In 1853, a passing ship discovered her, wearing a dress sewn of
cormorant feathers, and brought her to Mission Santa Barbara, where
tragically she died only seven weeks later from her radical change in
diet. She is buried at the Mission cemetery, and she is statuesque on
State Street.

Meanwhile, I was determined not to be the Lone Man of the Presidio, continuing my quest of befriending living people. I was relieved
to find that downtown Santa Barbara is an easy place to belong. I was
surrounded by a community of transplants who, like me, had moved
here to work in the hospitality and service sectors that make the tides
of this seaside village ebb and flow. They were an open-armed and
convivial bunch, and more sea salt of the earth than I expected for a
town of such luxury. It was like they came to Santa Barbara for a
parade and never left. Since the downtown parade route where many
of us lived and walked was so small, I saw them everywhere.

Inside Au Bon Climat, my new boss, Claire, was a novel human
experience for me. We were hired on the same day, and while I was
trying to learn every vineyard and vintage by heart, she burned sage
leaves, convinced the tasting room was haunted by the ghost of a
lonely conquistador. Claire was from Austin, with a Texas-sized personality. She had the booming, smoky voice of a speakeasy jazz singer,
and when she laughed, they could hear it in the tasting room next
door. She wore her long hair in an enormous bun that was really
more of a round of sourdough, and she taught me phrases like "The
bigger the hair, the closer to God," and "Honey, I'm gonna bake you

a pie!" She peppered her conversation with pop-culture references and kept insisting that my business card should read "Assistant *to the* Tasting-Room Manager." She would try to get us motivated before we did inventory, a monthly nightmare because we had dozens of different labels, by playing a country song called "Truck Yeah."

Claire believed that every wine-club party should feature a big hunk of meat "because these Santa Barbara folk need something besides quinoa and brussels sprouts." She would be up all night before the event cooking brisket or basting pork butt in Dr. Pepper. Once she figured out I wasn't angling for her job, we became unlikely friends. She would call me after *Game of Thrones* episodes, yelling and crying, and when I said I had to go she would say, "I am your boss, Adam! I will tell you when you can go!"

Most of my job was sales, or "slinging wine" as people in the business like to call it, which involves talking and standing for seven hours, a role I shared with a few younger tasting-room associates. One of them was Billie, named after Billie Holiday, an elementary-school teacher during the week who somehow still had energy to sling wine on the weekends. She would invite me to go out with her friends after work, but being fifteen years younger, she teased me for being so tired and usually opting to reunite with my couch and my cat. But the joke is on her because when I was twenty-five that's all I wanted to do after work, too. Still, she took me out to a quiet French bistro for my birthday, where I could be even older while eating escargot.

As predicted, I rarely saw Clendenen in Santa Barbara, but Jim Adelman invited me up to the winery in Santa Maria, affectionately called "The Shed," for a harvest lunch with the winery staff. We ate butternut squash ravioli along with pulled pork sizzling in Clendenen's homemade hot sauces, and sampled a dozen older vintages of ABC Chardonnay, Lindquist Syrah, and Hitching Post Pinot. How anyone does any work after lunch up there is beyond me, but they do.

They even let me do a punch down of Bien Nacido Pinot, which was brewing in one of a dozen open-top cauldrons. This is where you take a tool that looks like a giant potato masher, and push the grape skins, which the carbon dioxide produced by fermentation has lifted to the top of the tank, back down into the juice, to extract deeper color and flavor, like steeping a tea bag. Adelman then drove me up the hill to the vineyard, stopping every few hundred yards to unlock a deer-gate, and we tasted nearly ready nebbiolo grapes off the vines, spitting the seeds on the ground. Wine grapes don't pop in your mouth like table grapes, which are mostly water, and their skins are rubbery and thick and the juice much sweeter, almost candied at harvest time, which is why they can ferment to 14 percent alcohol.

Au Bon Climat means something like "a well-favored vineyard," or as I always put it in the tasting room, "a good place." I will never forget the first afternoon I spent there. I felt like I was coming closer.

<hr />

A wineslinger never knows what sort of characters will swagger through his doors. One young man walked in on a Monday morning carrying a bag of avocados. He said he needed wine because his girlfriend had broken up with him that morning and thrown all his stuff off the wharf into the ocean. He offered me an avocado. I didn't know whether to take it, since it seemed to be his only remaining possession.

Some of my favorite days were when cruise ships docked in the harbor, because I could count on a stampede of zany tourists in New Balance shoes. One Midwesterner with a tight perm strutted in from the ship one afternoon, in gleaming white tennis shoes; baggy, acid-washed jeans; and a blue Big Bird sweatshirt. She slammed her forearms down on the bar and exclaimed, "Mama needs her waaahnn!!" Which might be the funniest thing I have ever seen in my life.

Sometimes interactions didn't go as well. One spring weekend we added a third tasting list to our offerings, a lineup of crisp white wines for longer days and warmer weather. A young black couple walked in, and I cheerily explained our tasting options to them: "This list is our standard tasting, a blend of reds and whites, whereas this one here is our reserve tasting, all pretty special pinot noirs. Then we have a third tasting this weekend, which is *for whites only.*" I froze in place, eyes popping out, mouth agape. They laughed, but I lost a year of my life.

And then there is the visit that lives in Santa Barbara infamy. A somm walked in, flashed his card and dropped his own name, and started telling me about the restaurants he had worked for in LA and San Francisco, and I must have been wearing my suitably unimpressed face again. I poured him a taste of our rosé, which was made from an obscure French varietal called mondeuse.

"You probably know this," I said, "but it originates in the Savoy region in eastern France near the Alps."

"It's also grown in southwestern France as well," he comes back.

"Is that right? I didn't know that." I started looking it up on my laptop.

"Do you not believe me?"

"What? Oh, no, I am just curious," I explain.

I then poured him the next wine, a blend of pinot gris and pinot blanc, which I always said paired well with buttery clams tossed in linguine, or sunset.

"Do you know anything about winemaking?" he asked. "Tell me, step by step, how this wine is made, I dare you."

"Excuse me?" I scowled.

"You know what?" he said. "Forget it. I don't want any more wine. You clearly don't know anything about it anyway."

He then stormed out of the room while I watched, incredulously. At the door, he turned, and said, "This used to be a good place. But people like you are ruining Santa Barbara!"

In retrospect, I regret telling this story to my colleagues. Anytime something went wrong from then on, they would say, "This only happened because Adam ruined Santa Barbara."

The best task I have ever been given in a wine job was writing the tasting notes for the wines we poured at ABC. My first note was for our rosé: "If you know anything about wine, you will of course know that mondeuse is *not* made in southwestern France," but Claire nixed that one. Still, I was determined to write something that people would actually read. I didn't want to sound like I was trying to impress people with how many fruits I know. "This wine is bursting with aromas of dragonfruit, lychee, persimmon, red banana and a bunch of other fruit you have never heard of." Sometimes I am convinced tasting notes describe more fruit than there actually are. I don't think you can add another color to a fruit and create a new one. "Blue raspberry" is a snow-cone flavor.

One writer says that the wine descriptions that list all the fruit at your farmer's market are like standing in front of a great painting and describing it by rattling off all the colors you see. It doesn't show the experience in its fullness nor truly capture the art in the wine. Another article said those kinds of descriptions actually discourage sales, because the average taster feels their palate is inadequate to pick out such nuances. A better tact is to discuss wine and food pairings or to tell a story through the wine.

Clendenen was a colorful raconteur, who never told a story the same way twice, so many of the ABC bottle labels already told their own stories. My favorite was Hildegard, a white blend named in honor of the wife of Charlemagne, the first Holy Roman Emperor and catalyst for a great viticultural expansion at the end of the Dark Ages. The legend goes that the queen did not like how red wine stained the snowy white beard of the king, so she ordered that one side of the hill of Corton in Burgundy be replanted only with white varieties. That vineyard is now Corton-Charlemagne, a grand cru devoted exclusively to chardonnay.

We poured wines with classy sounding French names that shrouded slightly less classy translations. "La Bauge Au-dessus," one of our most elegant pinots, means the "wild, sloppy party upstairs," with "bauge" being a pigsty. "Nuits Blanches au Bouge," a chardonnay that could compete with premier crus, means "all-nighter at the dive bar."

Those stories told themselves. I came up with a few of my own. Probably my best ones were these:

> Our syrah grows next to eucalyptus trees in Los Alamos, and people swear they can smell the minty tree oils that stick to the grape skins. This wine pairs well with absolutely everything wrapped in bacon: filet mignon, dates, jalapeño poppers, shoelaces.

> This Pinot is our tasting-room manager Claire's favorite wine. She thinks the dusty, aged-leather aromas smell like Indiana Jones.

I liked to walk up the hill to the Mission on Sunday evenings. They call Old Mission Santa Barbara the "Queen of the Missions." She is adorned in a majestic Greco-Roman façade of column and stone, with two crowned bell towers serving as the arms of her throne. She once was the beacon that sailors used to guide their ships into port, and her altar candles have never gone out. The queen was baptized on December 4, 1786, on the feast day of Santa Barbara, located far enough above the Presidio so she wouldn't be tainted by the questionable morals of the soldiers, set in the amphitheater of hills that guard her cozy village below. On Sundays I would sit on the top step outside the sanctuary and look beyond the wooden cross on the lawn to the rose garden below, letting my gaze be swept out to the glistening waters of the Santa Barbara Channel and Santa Cruz Island floating on top.

The most successful Santa Barbara County winery and vineyard of the early 1900s was on that island, the Santa Cruz Island Wine Company owned by a Frenchman named Justinian Caire. A few descendants of his ancient vines still survive on Catalina Island, where the Rusack Winery of Ballard Canyon relocated cuttings of the Santa Cruz Zinfandel and Mission vines and still make wine out of their fruit. The history of our world here continues to dazzle me. The past is not dead as long as there are old vines and dusty bottles.

I lived in Santa Barbara for almost five years. She is an enchantress. My times with her were some of the happiest, most carefree days of my adult life. It wasn't all a parade. There was the torrid December when flames licked the foothills and the night skies blazed in orange apocalypse. The blood moon rising, I threw Scout and a suitcase into my car and we fled like a cat out of hell, driving through the Siskiyou Mountains out of California in the middle of the night. Fortunately, after a long Christmas in Seattle, we returned to an avalanche of ash but no damage. But two weeks later scorched-bare hills nearby collapsed under a dramatic rainstorm, and we were cut off from the rest of the world for several weeks while crews dug out the 101 Freeway. My affection for Santa Barbara only grew.

On those Sunday evenings at the Mission, as the red tiles of the old pueblo glowed softly in the twilight, I would think that Santa Barbara is the most beautiful place I have ever seen. Her only flaw is that she isn't the Santa Ynez Valley.

*Sixteen*

# THE STORY OF SOIL

I was a pilgrim on the King's Highway once more, but this time I was accompanied by a small band of thirsty travelers. I had traded in my wine retail outpost in Santa Barbara for a corner office in a Suburban, with a window view on mountains, seas, and vines. Leading wine tours from Santa Barbara to Santa Ynez had started as a Saturday hobby but soon became a driving passion, and when the opportunity to lead more tours arose, I took it. This wasn't your typical wine tour experience, where you're handed a sandwich in a brown paper bag as you board the Drunk Bus. In the morning before our tours, I and my fellow wine sherpas would assemble picnic baskets of aged gouda and triple-cream brie, apples and figs right off the tree, parmesan and cashew crusted chicken, and pasta salad tossed in garlicky pesto. My friends Matt and Ben, the owners of Coastal Concierge Wine Tours, had both served time in the restaurant business, and the picnic lunch we presented on Provençal tablecloths had become the centerpiece of our reputation.

Sometimes I took out larger groups in our Sprinter van, which looked like a giant toaster, and I would spend the day herding toasty turtles through the vinescapes of Santa Ynez. But usually I would pick up a couple weekending or celebrating an anniversary in Montecito, one town over from Santa Barbara, where Spanish mansions on grand-cru-priced hillsides tuck behind dense, two-story high hedges. If this wine business doesn't work out for me, I hope to land a gig as a hedge trimmer in Montecito. As I led my guests out from the hotel lobby, I would invite one of them, as I had been trained, to sit behind the driver's seat "so that way I can open your door all day," something I had a hard time saying louder than a mumble. Leading a private wine tour is a lot like going on a six-hour blind date, or like asking a couple you just met if they want to go on a road trip. Usually I could tell within a few minutes if there was any chemistry between us, or whether it was going to be an extremely long day.

For the first forty-five minutes on the drive along the sea and over the mountains to Santa Ynez, I would answer all the questions about wine, local history, transverse mountain ranges, and south-facing hills that my guests didn't ask, with gems of insight like "We are driving right now on the 101 North, but we are actually heading due west," which would blow their freaking minds. In truth, I felt deeply satisfied to be introducing people to the place that had captivated me so thoroughly that I moved there, twice. I had neglected the motherland of Santa Ynez while I was tasting-room manager in Santa Barbara, and I missed it. The more I talked about the valley, and the more times my guests said, "This is one of the most beautiful places I have ever seen," the more I remembered how much I love it. As much as I savored my time at ABC, it was still too far away. The thought kept nagging at me that I didn't move to this part of California to work in a downtown wine bar. My hands were too clean in Santa Barbara.

In the valley, it's the garages, with their dusty work boots and wine-stained jeans, that tell many of the best wine stories. My first tour stop was often Dragonette Cellars, essentially a large garage in a gritty industrial park that makes the Lompoc wine ghetto look like Montecito. As they liked to say at Dragonette, this is not the story of the tycoon who planted the vineyard and built the chateau. There was no sign anywhere on the building, and if it weren't for the wine barrels drying in the sun outside the roll-up door, you would have no idea you were at a winery. "I will get you to the wineries soon," I would tell my bemused guests as I pulled in, "but first I need to make a quick drug deal." More than one double-checked that I had locked the car door. Inside, the thick cement walls were decorated with a map of Santa Barbara County and a spreadsheet of weekly cleaning activities, and in the winter, the icy cold would creep through the cement floor into your feet and legs. One of the winemakers was usually climbing a stack of barrels, testing acid and sugar levels or sanitizing the barrel plugs with cheap vodka. From what I can tell, winemaking is about 95 percent janitorial work.

The French word for this type of winery is *garagiste*, an elegant term for people who make wine between their truck and their washing machine. Many of them seem to be disillusioned lawyers, like John Dragonette. Dragonette Cellars made their first barrel of wine in John's garage in Hermosa Beach, near LA. They stuffed clusters of syrah from a Los Olivos backyard into garbage bags, loaded them into Steve Dragonette's pickup, who had been recruited to help his brother and their friend Brandon because he was the only one who owned a truck, and drove it two hours through LA traffic to the garage. They spent the first night plucking each berry off the grape stems. According to John, that first barrel was "pretty terrible, and we absolutely sulfured the crap out of it." But they were all intrigued enough to uproot their families, move to the Santa Ynez Valley, and apprentice at local wineries. They stayed true to their roots by continuing to make wine in a garage, but this one holds two hundred barrels and once belonged to Richard Sanford. And now their wine is exceptional, with low amounts of sulfur.

My tour guests would go from vague apprehension to exuberance in just under an hour. They would have a great story to tell when they got home, how they ate dinner at Lucky's and got massages at the Four Seasons, but the highlight of their trip was the time they spent in a cold Buellton garage. These garages have a secret to tell: the ingredients are more important than the packaging. There are a lot of possible answers to the question "What makes the wines of one winery better than another?" I am convinced that one factor is how much sweat, blood, and tears goes into each barrel.

<hr />

For the rest of the day I would get my tour guests out into the patchwork of vines and beautiful buildings they had signed up for, often starting in the Santa Rita Hills, lunching in Ballard Canyon, and ending in Happy Canyon, trying to convince them it's unique to taste pinot in a heavy jacket and then cab in short sleeves two hours later. Usually their interest in wine talk would wane as the day lengthened, and after their grand picnic lunch the conversation in the car would change. The more wine they drank the more personal the questions would get. The morning questions were "Adam, what type of soil is this?" The afternoon questions were "Adam, what is your type?" Usually by the time we passed over Cold Spring Bridge on the way back to Santa Barbara, I was reluctantly immersed in a conversation about my dating life.

This had only recently become a topic worthy of conversation. For three years after my divorce, I was prepared to live out the remainder of my days in Domaine de la Solitude with Scout and a little porcelain owl named McHoo. Then some friends suggested I dip my toes into online dating, but unfortunately, they are no longer my friends. Whoever coined the phrase "Everything happens for a reason" never had to swipe left or right on pictures of strangers in a dating app. And downtown Santa Barbara is intimate enough that you may see those strangers on State Street the next day, or worse, they may see you. I did go out on a few dates but each night ended with a one-armed hug, the preemptive strike of post-date gestures. I learned that, for some women, telling them you used to be an ordained minister is like saying you just got out of prison. I also learned that the human body just isn't built for dating in your forties. It wants to be home falling asleep in your chair after dinner and tuning out your kids. The era of your life when you have to start getting up to pee in the middle of the night is not a sexy time.

Steadily losing interest in this conversation, my wine tour guests would reassume a glazed look or lapse into the occasional snore, until I told them about a message that appeared in my inbox one evening from a college professor. She taught writing classes, and a couple years back she had stumbled across my book about listening, which she assigned to her writing students to help them practice attentiveness. In her message, Kate thanked me for the book and told me that her students often considered reading it together the highlight of the semester. Gratified, I took one look at her profile picture and resolved immediately to stay in touch with her. You know, for the sake of continuing to refine my listening skills.

As we traded emails and talked on the phone through the summer, Kate seemed to think I was pursuing some sort of professional networking relationship. What man talks on the phone for two hours at a time with any other interest besides romance? I considered inventing a ruse for why I would be in her neighborhood, because of course she lived in the San Gabriel Valley, my old smoggy stomping grounds that refused to let me go. I could tell her I love LA and I get down there all the time for coffee, I thought. But an odd and wily plan presented itself. Months earlier, I had reluctantly agreed to speak on the subject of listening at a nonprofit leadership retreat taking place in Malibu in October. It had been years since I had spoken on any subject besides wine, and I don't know what compelled me to say yes when they invited me. Maybe this was the reason. I invited Kate to come.

The stakes were high the day I met her, since I was supposed to be a world-class listener, but also because I was giving three talks to an earnest group of nonprofit leaders that had no idea they were also paying me to impress a woman. My morning talk went better than I expected, given that my emotions were scattered all over Malibu, and I did my best not to look in Kate's direction too often. During the short break afterward, an older man approached me at the stage, and I readied myself for praise.

"I just want you to know," he said slowly, "that your fly is down." No wonder the group seemed so attentive during my talk. I think I was just really excited to meet Kate.

After that, things with us moved pretty quickly, though not *that* quickly. We took a long walk later that afternoon in Malibu Creek State Park, which, luck would have it, had recently reopened after a rash of grisly murders. By dinner that night, Kate seemed to have realized that I wasn't interested in networking.

On our second date, I introduced her to the Santa Ynez Valley for the first time. We walked through the vines below the old Mission and in the pumpkin patch and corn maze on Alamo Pintado. I even showed her the labyrinth in Los Olivos where, years before, a voice had spoken love into a storm. Kate thought the valley looked just like the Shire. That wasn't a surprise, since she loves and lives British literature, and has been known to star in a Victorian-type melodrama when she is tired. She is a poet and an amateur naturalist, part mystic, part squirrel. Verse spills out of her mid-conversation, when she may, in her soft voice, notice the red-winged blackbirds trilling as they dip in and out of the wild mustard, or the cold ocean air riding through the passes, ruffling a horse's mane in the valley below. When Kate was a little girl, she wore prairie dresses and sunbonnets, her hair in braids, imagining her grandparents' farm to be a pioneer settlement. She collects pinecones and sows wildflowers in burn zones. She used to store rocks from her favorite places in the cupholders of her car until I insisted she take them out. She replaced them with acorns. Kate felt at home in the Santa Ynez Valley.

<hr />

My wine tours often brought me back to the heartbreak town of Los Olivos. In the years since my wine fires had been snuffed out there by cold coffee, Los Olivos had become a farmer's market of artisanal wines. There are more tasting rooms than ever, and still no bathrooms, but it is now a goldmine for treasure hunters, those who love the pursuit of rare and unique bottles. Pinot noir may have put this valley on the map, but now it seems like the entire world of wine has come to play, with seventy-five different varietals planted on these slopes and a wine for every palate. Dragonette has a tasting room in Los Olivos now, and even Antonio and Jeni have relocated the Taste of Santa Rita Hills there. And in a little converted garage at the village edge, I met Jessica and Brady, a couple who own a microscopic winery called Story of Soil.

In her first year, Jess made three barrels of wine, about seventy-five cases. She had worked her way up to forty barrels by the time I met her, mostly pinot noir, sauvignon blanc, grenache, and syrah, but with dalliances into gamay, that "disloyal" grape exiled by the Duke of Burgundy, and a white Austrian variety called grüner veltliner, which I thought was tingly liquid gold. After her first vintage, one morning at the infamous Los Olivos coffee shop she met Brady, a screenwriter transplanted from rural Indiana to Hollywood, who escaped up to the Santa Ynez Valley as often as he could, the life trajectory of all great writers. Jess always cuts to the chase, whereas Brady takes the long way round a conversation, and they collided in the middle. They moved to an upstairs condo on a hidden vineyard of Los Olivos and became co-owners of a tiny winery, with grand dreams and diminutive cash flow.

Now that they had barely enough wine to sell to the public, Jess and Brady were opening their first tasting room, and they asked me to come work for them. I could lead wine tours on the weekends and sell their wines during the week. Do I dare give the town that broke my heart one more chance? The title on my Story of Soil business card would be "Wine Educator and Writer-in-Residence." Granted, they let me choose my own job title, but how could I say no to that?

⸎

We were a trio of wine artists and writers, probably not the dream team of small business, and I would say we were flying by the seat of our pants, but that would mean we could afford pants. We didn't have a dishwasher, so we handwashed all our glasses at night after work. We also labeled our bottles by hand, and sometimes we would get behind, so I would pour wine out of unlabeled shiner bottles. More than once, I had to ask buyers if they could come back in a few minutes so I could find time to slap labels on their wines while still talking to the other guests in the tasting room. Worse, sometimes our labels were backordered. When that happened, one of us would scrawl the variety and vintage on a shiner with a gold sharpie.

Instead of capping our wines with foil, we sealed the corks with wax, a classy signature move that's just a turd of a process. It involves warming the wax and then dipping and spinning the tip of the bottle into it, finally twirling it out and up at the right speed and angle so the wax doesn't drip down the neck, which it does anyway. And then you do it 11,999 more times. We would have three slow cookers of different wax colors simmering on the back deck, so when there was a lull in customers I would wax bottles out back, abandoning the project halfway if more guests arrived. Eventually, we gave up and left our bottlenecks naked. It was a natural, streamlined look, we justified, perfect for a winery making wines that Mother Nature served up.

It was the beauty of the wines that kept us in business those first years, though sometimes people would wander in thinking we were a garden center. The name comes from Jess's conviction that wine starts not in the winery but in the soil, and that the place, not the winemaker, tells the story of the wine. The unique temperament of a wine comes from being grown in a particular time on a particular patch of earth. She didn't filter her wines, and she used only native yeasts—the indigenous yeasts already present on the grapes at harvest—rather than the designer, lab-curated yeasts that are available now, along with a myriad of other additives for color, flavor, texture, and chemical stability. She didn't want to add or take anything away from a wine that would mask its sense of place. It's the ancient terroir story, born of love for the land and the purity of its fruit, that is also catnip for wine hipsters right now.

Speaking of hipsters, wines like Story of Soil or Dragonette bottles are, to me, the vinyl records of the wine industry. Holding it in your hands, you have something rare and special, a limited edition. Pulling the cork is like dropping the needle and hearing its gentle scratch as it searches for the groove. The wines taste slightly different on different days, because they are alive and changing, unlike mass-produced wines manufactured to taste exactly the same every year. There is an honesty and transparency to the small wines. They may have slight imperfections from vintage variations, but like the hiss and crackle of a well-loved record, they create a richer, deeper, more human experience. They may be more expensive, but you know that care and time have been poured into them, and that one bottle means so much more to the people who made it than it would to the company that made a million of them. And when I drink those wines, I feel a personal connection with the people who made it and a tangible connection to the places the grapes were grown. It's good marketing, yes, but it's also almost sacramental.

⟡

One Monday afternoon, a pretty, petite blonde woman with sparkling green eyes flitted through the door in leopard-skin heels carrying a carton of eggs wrapped in a fluffy bow and introduced herself as Sunshine. I looked down at the glass of our new grenache I was tasting, wondering what Jess had put in there. But this was really happening, and the story gets even more fantastical. I learned that Sunshine is a movie and television actress who moved from LA to Los Olivos with her dry-witted pilot husband, Nate, code name Tater, with winemaking aspirations of her own. Sunshine and Tater live walking distance from town, where they started a B&B and microfarm complete with a garden and orchard, goats and chickens. Those must have been particularly fresh eggs she left as a gift for Jess and Brady, because within a few weeks we had a fourth member of team Story of Soil.

No human has ever been more aptly named: Sunshine has enough energy to light up her own galaxy and a radiance that can warm the coldest heart caught in her beams. I knew I could never compete with her sparkle, so on the days we worked together, I took to calling myself Raincloud. I would stand behind the bar and introduce a wine with a straight, somewhat bored face: "This is our gamay, which comes from the Martian Vineyard in Alisos Canyon." Then Sunshine would pop in and say, "It's gamayzing!!!" This bit also played well for our syrahs, because, as I would learn, they were "syrahsome."

⟡

The wine conversations I have in Los Olivos are different from the conversations I had in downtown Santa Barbara. Down there I was a classy bartender and a concierge. I spent much of my time giving restaurant recommendations and suggestions for activities I have never done myself, like paddleboarding, or going out after nine at night. In Los Olivos, everyone wants to talk about farming, especially when your winery is called Story of Soil. We'll add farming to the growing list of topics my theological education did not cover.

As I tried to catch up, I found I was drawn to the small farmers who talked about their plants like they were raising children. They talk about nurturing life in the soil, about loving their land and ensuring its legacy, and about creating an environment where plants can grow and thrive. This is compared to some larger commercial farms that seem to view farming more like waging a war, their targets set on eliminating any enemies that threaten their commodities.

I was invited one early spring morning to accompany the Dragonette team on a tour of the Duvarita Vineyard, adjacent to Mission La Purísima in Lompoc. On the drive, we noted that a nearby dormant vineyard looked barren and monochrome, brown dirt under brown vines. This was in stark contrast to Duvarita, where in between sleeping vines was a jungle of green that reached past my knees. This is cover crop, a cocktail of seeds carefully mixed for the healing of the soil.

Clover, peas, barley, oats, and rye capture nitrogen out of the air and impart it back into the ground, not to mention hold moisture and break up the dirt for oxygen penetration. They create a haven for the ladybugs and lacewings I kept waving off my neck as we hiked through the vineyard. But these are beneficial insects, who will prey on aphids that would otherwise feast on new spring growth like Easter brunch. It all felt so sharply alive, the oxygen so fresh in this garden-vineyard, and this was before the sheep had been brought in to do their special weeding and offer their own gifts to the life of the soil.

Brook Williams, the owner, lives in a house among his vines and can talk about the unique growth pattern of each individual vine. I don't know many vineyard owners who do most of the farming themselves. He trains his vines low to the ground, to keep them out of the notorious Lompoc winds and to absorb some of the heat reflected off the sandy beach soils. "I am still getting to know my land," he told us, as though he was talking about a person who had come into his life. He is one of those peculiar people who seems to love nothing more than plunging his hands into a compost pile and pulling out a handful of dung and wriggly earthworms, smelling it all like a foraged truffle.

The compost pile is vital to his style of farming, which is called biodynamic. This was my first personal encounter with biodynamic agriculture, which is a fascinating blend of attentive organic farming and an ancient spirituality that invokes a little of the Force. It says that the vines on your property are one part of an ecosystem that emphasizes the interconnectedness of all things in, under, around, and above your farm. The life of the ground, the plants, the air, the animals and birds, even the bodies of the nighttime sky all interlap. There is some of the old magic in biodynamic farming, which, following ancient practices and even the *Farmers' Almanac*, is carried out in relationship to the lunar calendar as much as possible. The thought goes that if the moon can influence large bodies of water, like the tides, then it can also influence small bodies of water, like that in the soil and plants, so labor in the vineyard should vary according to the phases of the moon.

The "bio" part of biodynamics is the most uncontroversial. It is a proactive form of organic agriculture that finds farmers out in their vineyards on a daily basis. It builds healthy soils and supports wildlife. It creates vast microbe populations in the soil and helps vine roots dig deeper and absorb more nutrients. And, in theory if not always in practice, it has the smallest carbon footprint, since the compost recipe can be mixed from ingredients you grow or raise on the farm, and the goal is that animals do more work than tractors.

Many biodynamic farms have also adopted a no-till style of agriculture that sequesters carbon and retains water in the soil.

It's the "dynamic" (energy or force) part that introduces the weirdness. Even biodynamic devotees will admit there are things they don't understand about it. As we entered the vineyard we passed what looked to me like a three-story waterfall of bidets. It's a stirring machine called a "dynamizer," which stirs the water in one direction for a while, and then quickly shifts to stir the water in the opposite direction. It may make the microbes in the water more available to the dirt and plants when sprayed. But it is also a ritual that is supposed to create chaos, which energizes the mixture and makes it more sensitive to cosmic rhythms after it is applied. I told you it was weird. But it's not the first time I have seen images of chaos and grapevines together. In the ancient Mesopotamian creation myths I read in seminary, murky waters often represented primordial forces of chaos. In the biblical Noah story, the "rest" restored to the world came as the chaos of the great floodwaters subsided, putting heaven and earth at peace again, inviting the first grapevines to be planted in the dry ground.

The dynamizer stirs up the "preparations" that are central to biodynamic farming, which are homeopathic treatments for the soil, the plants, and the compost pile. The most famous is Preparation 500. Around the autumnal equinox, you bury cow horns filled with manure in a corner of your vineyard, let it ferment for six months underground, and then dig it up around the vernal equinox. Later, you dilute it heavily in water and then apply it to your soil. You do something similar with ground silica, which is for plant development. The compost pile mixes cow and sheep dung with ground-up vines, leaves, and grape skins, activated by a witches' brew of yarrow, chamomile, oak bark, and dandelion that have all been buried in sheaths of animal organs and then dug up. It's some weird shit.

Brook is no airy spiritualist, nor are most biodynamic farmers, who are deeply grounded people even when they are watching the skies. Many are reluctant to discuss their methods because of the skepticism they meet, and they will admit they don't know how it all works either. But they love the lifestyle—and the results. The results are why some of the most famous wineries in the world have converted their vineyards to biodynamic practices, including Domaine de la Romanée-Conti in Burgundy, arguably the most iconic winery in the world. When DRC goes biodynamic, other wineries are bound to throw their magic spirit fingers up in the air, too.

As for Brook at Duvarita, he considers this a smart economic investment. He believes his vines, farmed biodynamically, can live fifty years, thirty years longer than average, because of the healthy microbe population and the vineyard's strengthened ability to defend itself from pests. Personally, my favorite of his practices is that he stores some of his biodynamic preparations on a hill above Duvarita, in an old prayer chapel that once belonged to Mission La Purísima next door.

In retrospect, they probably should have taught farming in my theology degree program. I don't know what I think about the more metaphysical parts of biodynamics, but I do appreciate how it says that farming, and wine, cannot be boiled down exclusively to scientific formula. There is always mystery and wisdom beyond our understanding, and forces outside of our control and desire to dominate. But what I like even more about biodynamic farming is how close it gets you to your land. There are no absentee landlords in this system, only the footprints of caretakers who are deeply and personally connected to their farms. They are attached.

❦

The alarm screeched me awake at three thirty on a Monday morning in mid-September. I sighed heavily but dutifully got up and got dressed, almost falling over as I tried to work a leg into my pants. My eyelids were heavy, my eyes and skin dry and burning. I got in my Honda CRV and drove forty-five minutes in the deep black to my destination, listening to bad pop music to keep my eyes open.

By five o'clock, I was bracing myself on the back of a tractor high in the John Sebastiano Vineyard, squinting in the spotlights that illuminated the fog-shrouded vines. This was not another dark night of the soul. It was a harvest morning. I was there to help Jess and Brady harvest pinot noir. The crew was decked out in hoodies and headlamps, feverishly cutting clusters off the vines to the beat of the mariachi music playing from the tractor. They would dump their orange Home Depot buckets filled with fruit into the hard plastic bins being pulled behind the tractor, and then I would get to work. I was there for quality control, sorting out bad clusters and leaves as fast as I could to keep up with the pace of the harvesters. Jess had told me to look out for punctured, wasp-damaged berries and clusters covered by mealybugs and their powdery bright webs, as well as brown and dried-out berries ravaged by mildew. I tossed those bad clusters on the ground between the rows as the tractor moved down the steep slope, as well as clusters tainted with "hen and chicken syndrome"— a mixture of large berries with small and stunted berries, and what Jess called "water berries"—underdeveloped, shriveled grapes. I sorted out dozens of centipedes, spiders, silverfish, and at least one lizard. The early morning air was chill off the ocean, and the grapes felt like ice cubes in my ungloved hands. By the time we were done, two hours later, my trembling hands were red with cold and caked in mud.

Finally, my hands were dirty.

⟡

Maybe my name bears my destiny more than I ever knew. The first human being was formed out of the dust of the ground, as the ancient scrolls tell us. The ground was called *adamah*, and the first man was named Adam. Adam is the man of the dirt, the human born of humus. What if the new name I have been waiting for, after my old nametag washed off, was there all along, and it is as old as dirt? Soil is both cradle and grave, nurturer of life and receiver and transformer of death. Reverend McHugh has returned to dust, but Adam is born again, out of the dirt. The story of soil is my story, too.

*Epilogue*

# HOME

I t has become a ritual for me to sit under the pepper trees at Mission Santa Inés at sunset on New Year's Eve. The bluffs by the Mission create a natural amphitheater for taking in the year's last play of light. Behind me, Solvang is still lit up like Santa Lucia for the holiday season, enfolding horse-led carriages of tourists in a cozy Juletide hug. But before me is a view that has scarcely changed in two hundred years. A small gathering of olive and eucalyptus trees shelter a rocky creek bed and an old adobe grist mill built in 1820. A sprawling meadow stretches down to the plane trees gleaming in California gold by the river, where the oak forest that climbs up the north face of the mountains begins.

The arms of our two mountain ranges appear to converge in the distance in Happy Canyon, pulling this valley into their protective embrace. To my right, thick fog foams over the Santa Ynez Mountains like whitecaps, sparkling in amber rays as the sun falls into the sea somewhere near Point Conception. To my left, clouds over the San Rafael range glow with a pink hue that calls to mind that carafe of rosé in Avignon, the foothills in emerald shadow beneath.

There is a beauty here that makes my heart ache. I love the visual poetry of twilight on New Year's Eve, as the curtains close on the year but a sliver of light yet peaks out from underneath. It's a quiet moment between ending and beginning, in which a little wistful reflection takes me back, and a little hope pulls me forward.

❦

Three years after they first opened, Brady and Jess moved Story of Soil to the other side of Los Olivos, a distant block and a half away. Sunshine and Tater started their own iridescent wine label called Future Perfect, which features wines Sunny makes from a vineyard named the Joy Fantastic. Their new tasting room is across the street from Story of Soil and next door to our friends at Dragonette. All these wine boutiques work their magic in the shadow of that old pine tree that once concealed me from a man who tossed cold coffee on me during the worst summer of my life. This is now my favorite corner of the Santa Ynez Valley.

Kate and I were married at Kathy's house high on the hill above Solvang two years after our first date, surrounded by a couple dozen friends and family members. It was 96 degrees in late October, so it seemed like the perfect day to wear a suit. Sean and Brady stood by my side, and my friend Joe flew down from Seattle to officiate. Sunshine was our wedding planner, and our friends Chris and Gretchen, whom I met in the Whole Foods cheese department, created wood-fired pizzas and a massive, two-story cheeseboard. I was put in charge of wine. During the ceremony we celebrated the sacrament with a Ballard Canyon Syrah, and at one point, Kate mistook Joe's gesture of blessing for an opportunity to high-five him. Then we toasted with sparkling wine from the Santa Rita Hills, drinking Story of Soil the rest of the evening as we huddled around heat lamps, giving me a golden opportunity to explain the dramatic diurnal shifts of this valley, enthralling all. Kate is normally content with a half glass of rosé on a Saturday evening, but that night she was snatching flutes of bubbles out of people's hands, proclaiming, "This is mine, I'm the bride!"

We found a little rose-bordered cottage on a farm for horses who have been put out to pasture, right on the old stagecoach road near the tiny hamlet of Ballard, the first town founded in the Santa Ynez Valley. We call our farm the McShire. It's like being at home and on holiday at the same time, as Samwise Gamgee put it. Past the front gate is a long, white-gravel driveway that wanders to a Provençal-style circle courtyard with a central fountain emerging from lavender bushes and sunflowers. In the early evenings the farm smells of freshly cut hay and sounds with a croaking symphony of frogs. Many mornings I am awakened by horses snickering off our back patio. The cheerful lady who tends the horses speaks to them in a singsong Swiss accent, and sometimes it feels like we are living in the pages of *Heidi*. I can see vines from our bedroom window, and wisteria and apricot trees from our kitchen table. A horde of chickens make a jailbreak out of their pen on summer mornings, scurrying to find fallen apricots. They will strut over to our place, lock eyes with me through the window, and take a dump on our welcome mat. Chickens have no soul.

I couldn't fall asleep the night we moved from Santa Barbara to the Santa Ynez Valley, or I should say, I didn't want to. I lay there awake, grinning to myself, not ready for this moment of triumph to end. I had returned to my promised land, but for the first time, I wasn't alone. I knew, finally, I had come closer.

I am still working out what it means for a person to have a sense of place, though I suspect you can't discover it until you stay still for a while. You also can't find a foothold on this spinning rock without help. I am reminded that place is not only a point but a people. It is both soil and soul.

Perhaps you find home where a place gets inside you. You breathe in its air, graze at its farms, and drink its wine. After all the time I have spent here, the Santa Ynez Valley seems like a long, long table spread sideways from ocean to mountain, with a bottle of wine set at every place. That the contours of this land I love shape the contours of the wine in my glass is something I will never get over. Wine holds within it all the dimensions of a particular place—the life above, around, and under it. It gathers up the effects of the sun and the soil, the water and the air, and all the work and faith, celebration and struggle that brought each vintage to life. Each time I tip my glass, I drink this place. It tastes more and more like home.

I won't pretend that this place has answered all my questions. I doubt there is a place that ever could. Life in this valley is as slow as ever, and there still isn't much to do after work besides eat. Sometimes the idyll of this country landscape just seems idle. Four-way stops are standstills of infuriating politeness, and it takes a half hour to get through a checkout line because the clerk has to personally catch up with every single person ahead of you. I am trying to find that charming. I do think it takes a while for your heartbeat to slow to the rhythm of life here, but after it does, it's hard to imagine living at a faster pace again.

The village rumor mill still saws along as ever, but I am learning that maybe there are some days when the news of the outside world doesn't have to be *my* news. This valley where teetotalers and moonshiners lived together and where heat waves and cold fronts are next-door neighbors may be small, but it seems big enough to hold all my life's contradictions, successes and failures, starts and stops.

The Santa Ynez Valley has been my promised land for the better part of twenty years, but I don't know for sure that it will be my last. The pilgrim is still alive in me. We all have a settler and a pilgrim residing within us, a little stay and a little go. Wine is both the symbol of civilization and the drink of the pilgrim trail. I suspect the true center of my labyrinth path is not drinking pinot noir from the Santa Rita Hills in the McShire, as nice as that sounds. As Edward Abbey put it, "This is the most beautiful place in the world. There are many such places."

***

From my perch on New Year's Eve, I can see an old red barn and a vineyard of Bordeaux varieties at the base of the Mission bluffs. The vines are taking their final bows of the year in crinkling costumes of auburn leaf. My friend Vincent had his *Red Vineyard*, and now I have found mine. This valley is descending into the dormant season, which begins with leaf fall and will leave rows on rows of naked sticks. It is a beautiful death.

Winter is short in the valley, and it's easier to tell time here by the lifecycle of the vines rather than by the countdown of the traditional seasons. In the annual rhythm of the vines, I think of dormancy as the inhale, and bud break in the spring as the exhale. In just a few weeks, I will be at my friend Matt's vineyard, struggling through a row or two of winter pruning, preparing for the annual miracle of rebirth. Farming vines is a yearlong process of reduction, mercilessly casting off any growth that would keep a vine from producing the best possible fruit. We will cut off the old woody canes, and some of them will be piled up like old bones and cremated into ash.

As I look back on this life and wine odyssey of the last few years, I am both contented and keenly aware that I have lost a lot. I don't stand up in front of others as a Holy Man anymore, but my faith has survived through it all, though it is quieter now and humbled, like pruned winter vines. I am grateful I had so many opportunities to help others grieve because it has helped me grieve too. Wine has also been a comfort, since it makes both laughter and tears flow more freely, and I have needed both. Sometimes the old parts of your life, even when they were good and essential in a past season, can become a hindrance to new growth. They must be removed to give space for the new version of yourself to flourish. Pruning will make the fruit of the next season that much sweeter, the wines of the new vintage deeper and richer. Death makes a way for life.

# ACKNOWLEDGMENTS

I t takes a wine village to raise a wine book. I am the one who lashed myself to my desk and tamed this monster, but I am also fortunate to be a scribe to the collective wisdom of the wine masters of Santa Barbara County, past and present. Part of me wants this area and these wine dreamers to be discovered by more wine drinkers and beauty seekers, and a selfish part of me doesn't. So if you're thinking about visiting after reading this book, please join us, but be cool about it, okay?

You may assume I wrote this book with a glass of wine at the ready by my laptop, but the boring truth is that I wrote every word dead sober, so I cannot blame the wine or my equally sober (I assume) editors for all terrible humor and whimsy contained in these pages. I never would have finished this book if I were drinking wine while writing. As Brady says, "writing while drinking" is another term for procrastination.

I owe a barrel of gratitude to the winemakers and wine geeks who have been free with their knowledge, kindness, and pours over the years. There are so many, but a few in particular stand out:

Brady and Jess at Story of Soil, and Sunshine and Tater Magic at Future Perfect. All the vignerons in the Dragon's Lair. Ben and Matt at Coastal Concierge Wine Tours. Jim Adelman, Jim Clendenen (RIP), and the rest of the team at Au Bon Climat. Frank, Gray, Barbara, Lisa, Angel, and Brad's Bacon at the Hitching Post II. Chris and Gretchen at Fire & Wine Catering. The entire team at Rusack Vineyards, especially Steve Gerbac and Stephanie Varner. Antonio and Jeni at the Taste of Santa Rita Hills, Michael at Larner Vineyards, Ken at Ken Brown Wines, Karen Steinwachs at Buttonwood Farm, Krista Harris at Edible Santa Barbara, Matt at McKinney Family Vineyards, Kristin and Nick Luis at Cote of Paint. Geena Bouché Lober, Megan Bravo, Carlos Mascherin, Kylynne Barritt, Patton Penhallegon, Etta Murray, Liz Williams, Emily Bell, Max Gleason, Lisa & Derek Reynolds, Kat Neenan, Kristen Wood, David Fainberg, Matt and Leanne Pickett, Acacia Stowe, Alison Riede, and so many more. Kathy Burt and Julia Lander for offering me quiet and beautiful places to write. Marcy Gordon for organizing Writing Between the Vines retreats, and Moshin Vineyards for hosting me. Kevin Gleason for the glorious pirate treasure maps in the book.

Thanks to my editor, Cindy Bunch, for advocating for this quirky project, and for refusing to yield when I said this may not be the right fit for IVP. Are you still sure about that, Cindy? Thanks to Krista Clayton and the IVP marketing team for all their creative fermentations. Thanks to Scout and Boo Catley for sleeping on my desk while I wrote. And, thanks to my wife, Kate, for knowing this story and what it requires to write a book—and marrying me anyway. Life is good on the farm with you, lady.

# NOTES

## 1. Wine Happens

3   *Welch cooked up a few batches*: Paul Lukacs, *American Vintage: The Rise of an American Wine* (New York: Norton, 2005), 41-45.

## 2. The Way of Van Gogh

15   *The vessel carrying the wine*: Rod Phillips, *A Short History of Wine* (New York: HarperCollins, 2000), 16.

17   *In France we have nothing*: Stéphane Hénaut and Jeni Mitchell, *A Bite-Sized History of France: Gastronomic Tales of Revolution, War and Enlightenment* (New York: New Press, 2018), 58.

18   *Tronçais, among a select handful of French forests*: Hugh Johnson, *The Story of Wine* (London: Mitchell Beazley, 2004), 102.

21   *Vincent's recent defenders have proposed*: "Van Gogh Did Not Kill Himself, Authors Claim," *BBC News,* October 17, 2011, www.bbc.com/news /entertainment-arts-15328583.

22   *Red-headed fool*: These stories are taken from Irving Stone's biographical novel, *Lust for Life* (New York: Plume, 1984). Stone takes some imaginative liberties in constructing the narrative and dialogue.

*Pain did curious things to him*: Stone, *Lust for Life*, 17.

23    *However meaningless and vain*: Maria Popova, "Vincent van Gogh on Fear, Taking Risks, and How Making Inspired Mistakes Moves Us Forward," *The Marginalian*, Nov 2, 2015, www.themarginalian.org/2015/11/02/van-gogh-fear-risk/.

25    *What in the world have you done*: Stone, *Lust for Life*, 82, author's words.

      *Lost his mind*: "Borigines—Vincent van Gogh Borinage Belgium," Canalblog, Dec 16, 2020, http://vangoghborinage.canalblog.com/archives/2020/12/16/38706960.html.

## 3. Feast Day

34    *These are not solemn alcoholic dosages*: Robert Capon, *The Supper of the Lamb* (New York: Doubleday, 1969), 93.

37    *In 1309, after four years of wandering*: Williston Walker et al., *A History of the Christian Church* (New York: Scribner, 1985), 371-72.

## 4. The Train to Champagne

48    *Who cares?*: Don and Petie Kladstrup, *Wine & War: The French, the Nazis and the Battle for France's Greatest Treasure* (New York: Broadway, 2002), 84-85.

      *The French resistance notified British intelligence*: Kladstrup, *Wine & War*, 79-89.

50    *Clovis was a fifth-century ruler*: Stéphane Hénaut and Jeni Mitchell, *A Bite-Sized History of France: Gastronomic Tales of Revolution, War and Enlightenment* (New York: New Press, 2018), 16-17.

      *Queenie of Weenie*: Thank you to Erin Kiff, for once owning a hot dog stand in Los Olivos, and for calling herself "The Queenie of Weenie."

52    *This theme in medieval church art*: Gisela H. Kreglinger, *The Spirituality of Wine* (Grand Rapids, MI: Eerdmans, 2016), 51-52.

53    *The Champagne window*: "The Champagne Stained Glass Window," *Grandes Marques & Maisons de Champagne*, https://maisons-champagne.com/en/houses/heritage/rheims-and-surrounding-area/article/the-champagne-stained-glass-window.

## 5. A Sense of Place

55    *Planted in faith*: From Bernard's sermon "Mystical Vineyards and the Prudence of the Flesh," www.clerus.org/bibliaclerusonline/en/c0x.htm.

59   *the Gallic beverage of choice was* cervoise: Stéphane Hénaut and Jeni Mitchell, *A Bite-Sized History of France: Gastronomic Tales of Revolution, War and Enlightenment* (New York: New Press, 2018), 5.

61   *These are wines that correspond*: The Burgundy classification pyramid wasn't officially established until 1936, though it was recognized before then.

69   *Somewhereness*: Matt Kramer, "Why the Fundamentals Matter," *Wine Spectator*, October 4, 2016, www.winespectator.com/articles/matt-kramer-5-fundamental -rules-of-wine.

## 6. Blood from a Stone

73   *They danced for all the earth*: Hugh Johnson, *The Story of Wine* (London: Mitchell Beazley, 2004), 30-31.

74   *Wine was the catalyst for the dawn of agriculture*: Rod Phillips, *A Short History of Wine* (London: Penguin, 2000), 6-7.

75   *Keep the scroungers and sycophants at bay*: "Châteauneuf-du-Pape, the Heart of the Appellation," *Châteauneuf-du-Pape*, https://en.chateauneuf.com/history-of -chateauneuf-du-pape.

     *For only eating white food*: Stéphane Hénaut and Jeni Mitchell, *A Bite-Sized History of France: Gastronomic Tales of Revolution, War and Enlightenment* (New York: New Press, 2018), 69.

76   *Primal scream*: Karen MacNeil, *The Wine Bible* (New York: Workman, 2015), 235.

78   *Articles 1-2*: Joshua Malin, "The 1954 French UFO Craze That Led to the World's Weirdest Wine Law," July 7, 2015, https://vinepair.com/wine-blog/chateauneuf -du-pape-ufo-wine-law/.

## 7. The Dark Night of the Soul

89   *Local amateur historians believe*: Frances Dinkelspiel, *Tangled Vines* (New York: St. Martin's, 2015), 67-89.

## 8. The Sideways Effect

108   *Geologists have discovered pinkish rocks*: Thank you to Dr. Tanya Atwater at UCSB for all this sweet tectonic knowledge.

112   *No doubt the tales get taller every year*: All this comes from a conversation I had with Bob Ostini at the Hitching Post 2 on October 18, 2017.

113   *Because in the year after the movie was released*: William Etling, *Sideways in Neverland: Life in the Santa Ynez Valley, California* (Lincoln, NE: iUniverse, 2005), 25.

122   *Miles takes Jack into the Santa Rita Hills*: Officially, the AVA is spelled "Sta. Rita Hills" instead of "Santa" because a Chilean winery named Santa Rita Winery objected to the name of the appellation when it was certified in 2001. The compromise was "Sta.," which was an abbreviation used in the era of the California Missions.

## 9. The King's Highway

130   *It likely wasn't until 1778*: Thomas Pinney, *The City of Vines: A History of Wine in Los Angeles* (Berkeley, CA: Heyday, 2017), 5.

137   *Wine has always been high on the sacred traveler's list of needs*: I believe I read this in Hugh Johnson, *The Story of Wine* (London: Mitchell Beazley, 2004), which, if you care about the history of wine, you should read immediately.

138   *Clay jars would catch the juice*: Pinney, *City of Vines*, 18.

142   *Rancho Dos Pueblos*: Walker Tompkins, *Santa Barbara's Royal Rancho* (Santa Barbara, CA: Dos Pueblos, 1987), 3-15.

## 10. The Fairytale

147   *One of these historic land grants, called Rancho Tepusquet*: Otis L. Graham Jr. et al., *Aged in Oak: The Story of the Santa Barbara Wine Industry* (Santa Barbara, CA: Santa Barbara County Vintners' Association, 1998), 19-33.

150   *He ate four meals a day*: Judith Dale, "William Benjamin Foxen—A Santa Barbara County Pioneer," *Santa Maria Sun Times*, June 7, 2020, https://santamariatimes.com/lifestyles/columnist/judith-dale-william-benjamin-foxen----a-santa-barbara-county-pioneer/article_b78e7a57-4370-5a43-a267-7d038b022018.html.

      *Stars and stripes over Santa Barbara*: Walker Tompkins, *Santa Barbara's Royal Rancho* (Santa Barbara, CA: Dos Pueblos, 1987), 88-100.

157   *There were rumors of a ghost train*: William Etling, *Sideways in Neverland: Life in the Santa Ynez Valley, California* (Lincoln, NE: iUniverse, 2005), 8-13.

## 11. The Last Stop

162   *This is the guy who casually tasted a wine*: Rajat Parr and Jordan Mackay, *Secrets of the Sommeliers: How to Think and Drink Like the World's Top Wine Professionals* (Berkeley, CA: Ten Speed, 2010), 3.

165   *The track extension from Los Alamos*: Joanne Rife, *Where the Light Turns Gold: The Story of the Santa Ynez Valley* (Fresno, CA: Valley, 1977), 78.

166   *There, in 1914, the driver*: Walker Tompkins, *Mattei's Tavern: Where Road Met Rail in Stagecoach Days* (Santa Barbara, CA: self-published, 1974), 1-48.

167   *The new management was a team of first-round draft choices*: Winemaker Sashi Moorman is also a partner in Sandhi, who for years made killer syrahs with the Stolpman Winery and now partners with Raj at Domaine de la Cote.

170   *Cork dorks*: Bianca Bosker, *Cork Dork: A Wine-Fueled Adventure Among the Obsessive Sommeliers, Big Bottle Hunters, and Rogue Scientists Who Taught Me to Live for Taste* (New York: Penguin, 2017).

173   *I wanted a big life in a small town*: I think I got that phrase from the show *Friday Night Lights*.

## 12. THE BEAST OF BURDEN

188   *The ancient Egyptian hieroglyph*: Randall Heskett and Joel Butler, *Divine Vintage: Following the Wine Trail from Genesis to the Modern Age* (New York: Palgrave Macmillan, 2012), 35-55.

## 14. THE HEALING PLACE

200   *Everything seems low to the ground when you are newly single*: I first heard this phrase at one of Mike Birbiglia's comedy shows.

202   *They named it Solvang*: Joanne Rife, *Where the Light Turns Gold: The Story of the Santa Ynez Valley* (Fresno, CA: Valley, 1977), 121-52.

205   *Hans Andersen slept in this room*: Ann Philippas, "Hans Christian Andersen: The Eccentric Guest," Charles Dickens Museum, June 16, 2021, https://dickens-museum.com/blogs/charles-dickens-museum/hans-christian-andersen-the-eccentric-guest.

211   *I can see the vines cry sometimes*: Matt Dees, winemaker of the Hilt, who works for Stan Kroenke, who owns the LA Rams, Screaming Eagle, and Rancho Salsipuedes.

212   *Algae that live in a house of glass*: This description is from diatoms.org. Every time I despair about the state of the world, I remind myself there is a community wholly devoted to educating people about diatoms, and I feel better.

213   *It is a heartbreaking story*: Matt Kettmann, "The Miracles and Misery of Mt. Carmel: How the Failed Dreams of Cloistered Nuns Gave Birth to Santa Barbara Wine Country," *The Santa Barbara Independent*, December 8, 2014, www.independent.com/2014/12/18/miracles-and-misery-mt-carmel/.

214   *Mission San Gabriel's recipe for Angelica*: Laura Sanchez, "Gypsy Canyon's Angelica," *Edible Santa Barbara*, March 24, 2011, https://ediblesantabarbara.com /gypsy-canyons-angelica/.

## 15. THE PARADE

220   *California fever*: Richard Henry Dana, *Harvard Classics*, vol. 23: *Two Years Before the Mast and Twenty-Four Years After* (New York: Collier & Son, 1909), 199.

223   *Celebrated the spirit of Bacchus*: Elias Chiacos, *Mountain Drive: Santa Barbara's Pioneer Bohemian Community* (Santa Barbara, CA: Shoreline, 1994), 53-60.

231   *One writer says that the wine descriptions*: Michael Schuster, *Essential Winetasting* (London: Mitchell Beazley, 2009), 25.

232   *That vineyard is now Corton-Charlemagne*: This story is likely mythical, and in the myth, Charlemagne's fourth wife, Luitgarde, is credited with tearing up the pinot and replacing it with chardonnay or other white varieties. Also, apparently, Charlemagne did not have a beard.

## 16. THE STORY OF SOIL

245   *The compost pile is vital to his style of farming*: Britt and Per Karlsson, *Biodynamic, Organic, and Natural Winemaking* (Edinburgh: Floris, 2014), 111-32.